"Wayne Dyer takes us on a sacred journey where the spirit triumphs over the ego. This book will serve as an extremely valuable guide to all those who seek the exultation of the spiritual experience and who value total freedom as the ultimate goal of life."

—DEEPAK CHOPRA

"I was mesmerized by the beauty and wisdom in *Your Sacred Self*. Wayne Dyer has written a book that is as meaningful, spiritually on-target, and engrossing as any I've ever read in my life. This is sure to go on that very small shelf reserved for classic works."

—LOUISE L. HAY

"In Wayne Dyer's newest book he has given us the final 'to do,' and that is to get outside of ourselves and stop selfishness by getting into other people and making them worthwhile. The sacred quest to that final freedom is the most important thing we'll ever do in our lives."

—PAT RILEY

"Wayne Dyer's inspiring new book is a treasure of love and spiritual wisdom."

—BARBARA DE ANGELIS

Books by Dr. Wayne W. Dyer

Your Sacred Self
A Promise Is a Promise
Real Magic
You'll See It When You Believe It
What Do You Really Want for Your Children?
No More Holiday Blues
Gifts from Eykis
The Sky's the Limit
Pulling Your Own Strings
Your Erroneous Zones
Manifest Your Destiny
Wisdom of the Ages
There's a Spiritual Solution to Every Problem

HarperSpotlight

YOUR
SACRED
SELF

MAKING THE DECISION TO BE FREE

Dr. Wayne W. Dyer

HarperPaperbacks
A Division of HarperCollinsPublishers

This title is also available on cassette from HarperAudio.

Grateful acknowledgment is made to the following for permission to quote from copyrighted material:

From *The Quest*, by Tom Brown, Jr. Copyright © 1991 by Tom Brown, Jr. All rights reserved. Reprinted by permission of the Putnam Publishing Group.

From *Ordinary People as Monks and Mystics*, by Marsha Sinetar. Copyright © 1986 by Marsha Sinetar. All rights reserved. Reprinted by permission of the Paulist Press.

HarperPaperbacks   *A Division of* HarperCollins*Publishers*
              10 East 53rd Street, New York, N.Y. 10022

A hardcover edition of this book was published in 1995 by HarperCollins*Publishers*.

Cover photograph by Marybeth J. Hamberger

First HarperPaperbacks printing: March 1996

Printed in the United States of America

HarperPaperbacks, HarperSpotlight, and colophon are trademarks of HarperCollins*Publishers*

❖ 20 19 18 17 16 15

To my wife, Marcelene
As the earth thanks the sun

All my life I wanted to be somebody,
Now, I am finally somebody. . . .
But it isn't me.

Contents

Dear Reader,

Imagine this scene if you will. Two babies are in utero confined to the wall of their mother's womb, and they are having a conversation. For the sake of clarity we'll call these twins Ego and Spirit.

Spirit says to Ego, "I know you are going to find this difficult to accept, but I truly believe there is life after birth."

Ego responds, "Don't be ridiculous. Look around you. This is all there is. Why must you always be thinking about something beyond this reality? Accept your lot in life. Make yourself comfortable and forget about all of this life-after-birth nonsense."

Spirit quiets down for a while, but her inner voice won't allow her to remain silent any longer. "Ego, now don't get mad, but I have something else to say. I also believe that there is a Mother."

"A Mother!" Ego guffaws. "How can you be so absurd? You've never seen a Mother. Why can't you accept that this is all there is? The idea of a Mother is crazy. You are here alone with me. This is your reality. Now grab hold of that cord. Go into your corner and stop being so silly. Trust me, there is no Mother."

Spirit reluctantly stops her conversation with Ego, but her restlessness soon gets the better of her. "Ego," she implores, "please listen without rejecting my idea. Somehow I think that those constant pressures we both feel, those movements that make us so uncomfortable sometimes, that continual repositioning and all of that closing in that seems to be taking place as we keep growing, is getting us ready for a place of glowing light, and we will experience it very soon."

"Now I know you are absolutely insane," replies Ego.

"All you've ever known is darkness. You've never seen light. How can you even contemplate such an idea? Those movements and pressures you feel are your reality. You are a distinct separate being. This is your journey. Darkness and pressures and a closed-in feeling are what life is all about. You'll have to fight it as long as you live. Now grab your cord and please stay still."

Spirit relaxes for a while, but finally she can contain herself no longer. "Ego, I have only one more thing to say and then I'll never bother you again."

"Go ahead," Ego responds impatiently.

"I believe all of these pressures and all of this discomfort is not only going to bring us to a new celestial light, but when we experience it, we are going to meet Mother face-to-face and know an ecstasy that is beyond anything we have ever experienced up until now."

"You really are crazy, Spirit. Now I'm truly convinced of it."

This book you are holding in your hands is a literal interpretation of that metaphor, which I've adapted from a story told by Henri J. M. Nouwen. It is my attempt to introduce you to that glowing celestial light and to let you know the wonder of having your sacred self triumph over the demands of the ego self, which wants more than anything to hold you back.

I have organized this book around the following four understandings:

1. You are sacred, and in order to know it you must transcend the old belief system you've adopted.
2. You are a divine being called to know your sacred self by mastering the keys to higher awareness.
3. Your sacred self can triumph over your ego identities and be the dominant force in your life.
4. You can radiate this awareness beyond your own boundaries and affect everyone on our planet.

These understandings form the basis of the four parts of this book. Each chapter is written with the express purpose of helping you to specifically know these principles.

The ancient spiritual writings in the Cabbalah have a very pertinent teaching that I would like you to come to know. It is suggested in them that our purpose here is to move from lower levels of living to higher and higher planes. But in order to move to the next level we must actually fall down first—to acquire and generate the necessary energy to propel ourselves to the next level.

Thus every single fall that you experience is really an opportunity to acquire energy. The added energy provides the turbo boost to move up and fulfill your purpose on the next level. Your sacred self knows that your falls are necessary for the achievement of this goal.

A fall in my own life gave me the opportunity to generate the necessary energy to put my life at the spiritual level that I write about in these pages. I could not have allowed this book to be published unless I made this jump to that higher spiritual level.

The fall is always in divine order. Whether we choose to acquire the energy to move to a higher spiritual level is entirely up to each and every one of us. My message is clear. Use your falls to come to an awareness of the higher power and loving presence that is always with you. The energy that you acquire is similar to what the high jumper gets when he falls way back in order to propel himself over the bar at a higher level than before.

I *know* this spiritual consciousness, and I trust that this book will help you to know that sacred self that is always with you.

Love and Light,
Wayne W. Dyer

Part I
PREPARING FOR THE SACRED JOURNEY

BROKEN DREAMS
As children bring their broken toys
   With tears for us to mend,
I brought my broken dreams to God
   Because He was my Friend.

But instead of leaving Him
   In peace to work alone,
I hung around and tried to help
   With ways that were my own.

At last I snatched them back and cried,
   "How can You be so slow?"
"My child," He said, "what could I do?
   You never let them go."

—LAURETTA BURNS

1

YOUR LIFE'S GREATEST CHALLENGE

Making the Decision to Be Free

The greatest human quest is to know what one must do in order to become a human being.

—IMMANUEL KANT

I know in each moment
I am free to decide.

You have been facing the wrong way! The most important insight you can have is to realize that you have been facing the wrong way for the better part of your life.

Take a moment, right now, to experience what I mean. Picture yourself in any position that you like. Standing, sitting, lying down, whatever is easiest for you to imagine. Now look at that mental picture of yourself. What you see, in this exercise, is a you who is always looking away from yourself. Always looking outside of yourself. You are facing the wrong way!

Now imagine being able to shift around and face the opposite direction. If you could in some magical way do so, then you would be facing inward.

This is not some form of mental gymnastics in which you simply imagine yourself turning around and facing inward. I am suggesting a way of knowing your spiritual identity. I am suggesting you meet the challenge and take the path of your sacred quest.

We've all been taught to look outside ourselves for sustenance—to look beyond the self for power, love, prosperity, health, happiness and spiritual fulfillment. We've been conditioned to believe we get life's bounty from somewhere outside of ourselves. But it's possible to reverse our gaze from outward to inward. And when we do, we find an energy we've sensed but not previously identified.

DIVINE ENERGY

There dwells within all human beings a divine energy. The power of this energy permeates our entire being and permits us to perform every function in the vast repertoire of human thoughts and behaviors. There are two aspects to this divine energy.

The outer aspect causes the heart to beat, the lungs to inflate and the senses to function—it essentially keeps our physical bodies alive. The inner aspect of this energy is dormant, but it can be awakened.

This inner universe is vaster than the outer universe. Inner joy makes all joy that is experienced in the world of the senses seem meaningless. When the divine light within you is experienced directly, it adds a radiance to life unlike anything that can be described with words or pictures.

When you discover your sacred self, you awaken this dormant inner energy and let it guide your life. The word most commonly used to describe this inner force is "spiritual."

When I talk about spirituality and being spiritual, I am describing an attitude toward God and the inner journey of enlightenment. I am speaking of expanding the godlike qualities of love, forgiveness, kindness and bliss within ourselves. In my interpretation, spirituality is not dogma or rules. It is light and joy and focuses on the experience of love and inner bliss, radiating those qualities outward. I call the journey to discover your sacred self your "sacred quest."

DEFINING YOUR SACRED QUEST

The primary energy that you have been using all your life is the outer energy. This outer energy is life sustaining but does not provide the sense of fulfillment and bliss that we long for.

In his book *Mystery of the Mind* Swami Muktananda describes what the direct experience of divine energy is like:

> One day this light will explode, and you will see it everywhere. You will see the entire universe existing within it. The divine light of Consciousness will begin to fill your eyes, and then wherever you look you will see it. You will see its radiance in people, in trees, in rocks, and in buildings. You will see the same consciousness rising and falling in every wave of thought and feeling that passes through your mind; wherever your mind goes you will find your own inner Consciousness, the creator of the world. You will see that the entire universe is contained within your own Self. You will know that everything—all the infinite modifications of the world—is nothing but your own play. You will realize that it is you who are being reflected everywhere and that it is your own reflection that passes before you all the time.

You have within yourself this power of transcendence over the ego-dominated life. You can turn around and face inward, directly contacting your spiritual nature. You can then live each of your days, *regardless of what you may be doing,* with the sense of bliss that comes from being on the path of your sacred quest.

Making that light explode for yourself involves understanding who you are and what it is that you are doing here in this thing called your body, on this place called earth, at this point in your life.

A UNIQUE LOOK AT YOUR LIFE

The starting point to your sacred quest is understanding that the universe and our participation in it are not haphazard things.

Intelligence flows through everything in the universe, and has had many names. It causes the planets to orbit, the galaxies to stay in place, the seedlings to sprout, the flowers to open and you, yes you, to breathe and walk and think.

This invisible intelligence is in everything and it is everywhere. You cannot hold it or see it or smell it. But you know that it is there.

Outer energy, which controls matter and the physical world, is finite. This means that there is only so much oxygen, hydrogen and carbon. There is nowhere to go for more of these when we run out of them. All of the physical trace elements, identified by scientists and studied by schoolchildren everywhere on the planet, are finite.

Everything in our manifested world is made of these elements that exist in a finite amount. I like to think of all of our physical material as continually being recycled. Since we only have so much of this "stuff," it must constantly be put back into use when it changes from one "thing" to another "thing."

The drop of iron that is in your blood today is a part of the total iron supply. Obviously it was someplace else before you were conceived. Fifteen million years ago it might have been part of an iron ore deposit in Afghanistan. Today it is part of the outer energy that is you.

And so it is with all of the physical particles in the universe. A finite supply, continually being recycled. Material particles in one form, going back into the earth, and recycled as something else. Like one particle of magnesium from a sword showing up later in the femur of a panther.

Emily Dickinson wrote a stanza, "The Single Hound,"

describing this phenomenon. It is far more alluring than any prose I might use to make this point.

This quiet dust was gentlemen and ladies,
   And lads and girls;
Was laughter and ability and sighing,
   And frocks and curls.
This passive place a summer's nimble mansion,
   Where bloom and bees
Fulfill'd their oriental circuit,
   Then ceased, like these.

The physical you that we can see and touch is made up of the same stuff that everything else is made of. Yet you are different than the things outside of yourself. To comprehend this, consider the four categories describing the manifested world: mineral, vegetable, animal and human. If we were to take a sample from each of these categories, pulverize them and put the powder into separate containers for lab analysis, the report would show no discernible differences. The mineral, vegetable, animal and human samples all comprise the same raw materials. Yet all of these samples differ from one another in an invisible, beyond-the-physical manner.

The differences, however, are not in the physical makeup of things. The differences are in what we will call awareness. Each category has a different level of awareness:

Mineral. The mineral world includes all of the things that you see around you. To the unfocused eye they just lie around and do nothing. You can look at a rock and it will not do a thing, even if you stare at it forever. So we say that minerals, while made of the same physical matter as we are, have very little awareness. (I say "very little" because to a quantum scientist who studies things at the subatomic level and thinks in terms of billions of light-years, minerals are fascinating. When examined at the subatomic level they are alive, dancing and changing endlessly.)

Vegetable. The vegetable kingdom is made up of the same physical elements as the mineral would, but it has a much different level of awareness. The vegetable energy reproduces, bears fruit, stretches toward sunlight and protects itself from invaders. Somehow the organizing intelligence has taken the same elements and put them together to create a product that has more awareness than minerals.

Animal. Once again, all animals are made of the same elements as minerals and vegetables, yet their awareness level is greater than the vegetables and the minerals. Here we see mating, planning for the future, teaching the young, migrating and a wide variety of further examples of higher awareness. The organizing intelligence has taken the same trace elements and created creatures with higher levels of awareness.

Human. We too are made up of the same physical trace elements as the other categories, but we have even higher levels of awareness. We can do many of the things that the other categories can, and we can do more.

We have the power to make contact with the organizing intelligence and to create a life of bliss. We can know the divine organizing intelligence that is a part of us, even though it has been dormant for as long as we remember.

You know very well that there are major differences among these categories, and these differences have nothing to do with the physical world. Indeed, this is an intelligent system that you are a part of, and that means that your life on this planet is a part of that intelligence.

If the system is intelligent, and that intelligence is invisible, and our presence here is a part of that intelligence, we will never be able to discern what it is all about by using instruments that exist solely in the physical world. We need to look at that part of ourselves which is invisible. We will need to make direct contact with that part which I call awareness.

You need to begin looking inward at who you are and why you are here instead of outward at the physical world and things within it.

You Are Here for a Reason

There was an instant in time when you were no-where. The moment before your conception you were no-where. Then in one holy instant, you went from no-where to now-here.

There will be another holy instant when you will go from now-here to no-where. We call that moment death. Yet you—the divine, changeless, eternal, invisible you— will live on.

If it is true that we are a part of an intelligent system, we can assume that we go from no-where to now-here for some purpose. With this realization you can stop doubting that you are a divine creation with purpose and just accept that you are. You are a part of this intelligent system *and* you are here for some divine reason.

That reason, you can surely guess, is concerned with the spiritual inner energy I am writing about. Knowing your spiritual self is your sacred quest, and your life challenge.

So many of us have grown up believing that who we are is the body we carry around, the job we perform and the religion we practice. Our lives are involved with externals at the same time that we see they are always changing and shifting. Yet somewhere inside ourselves we feel the same.

You may not have given that self-aspect much of your awareness. But if you do, you will discover an inner self that never changes but is trapped in a changing world.

Someday your physical self will probably rest beneath a tombstone that records the date of your birth and the date of your death. But your inner soul knows you are eternal. You are formless in that part of yourself and have no boundaries. Without boundaries there is no birth, no death. What was born will die, what was never born, can never die. Your sacred self was never born! Your sacred self will never die!

Knowing this in a way that leaves no room for doubt will greatly enable your sacred quest. When you reach that state, knowing that who you are is the unchanging self, you will be "on purpose" in your life.

Sogyal Rinpoche, in *The Tibetan Book of Living and Dying*, puts this into words that are worth framing:

In the modern world, there are few examples of human beings who embody the qualities that come from realizing the nature of mind. So it is hard for us even to imagine enlightenment or the perception of an enlightened being, and even harder to begin to think that we ourselves could become enlightened.

. . . Even if we were to think of the possibility of enlightenment, one look at what composes our ordinary mind—anger, greed, jealousy, spite, cruelty, lust, fear, anxiety, and turmoil—would undermine forever any hope of achieving it.

. . . Enlightenment . . . is real; and each of us, whoever we are, can in the right circumstances and with the right training realize the nature of mind and so know in us what is deathless and eternally pure. This is the promise of all the mystical traditions of the world, and it has been fulfilled and is being fulfilled in countless thousands of human lives.

You can be one of those thousands of enlightened humans. This will happen as you discover the nature of your true self, and relegate the part of yourself that is centered on the physical to the background, where it belongs. From there it can cheer you on and support your higher self rather than act in ways that sabotage your true spiritual essence.

This whole business of a sacred quest is real, and you can know it, love it and cherish it. Once you do, you will never want to go back to any way of living that is inconsistent with your divine, though invisible, self.

You are not that name, that occupation, that social security number, that body. You are eternally light and divine regardless of what you have done or failed to do. Regardless of what family you lived in, or what you may have been labeled. In the God intelligence you are holy, and you have a purpose for being here.

That purpose will not be found in the physical world. When you discontinue searching for your bliss outside of yourself, your entirety, including your material world, will reflect your divinity.

The true definition of self-awareness is discovering your higher self and living joyously with that higher self in command. It is the awareness of your inner energy and the higher part of yourself. It is a connection to the divine and all that is changeless. Self-awareness is located in the ground of your self.

THE EXPERIENCE OF SELF-AWARENESS

How will you experience your physical life when you have met this challenge of facing inward and living by the directives of your spiritual self? You will still *chop wood and carry water,* as the ancient Zen proverb tells us. You will not suddenly develop totally new talents or interests.

However, you will have a level of awareness that lets you see things that have been hidden. These insights will give you a sense of peace and inner fulfillment.

The experience of self-awareness is not something that you can get from the physical world. But your interactions with the material world will be altered dramatically when you become self-aware. As a result of heightened awareness you will ultimately be able to manifest precisely what it is that you need in the physical world. You will participate in creating what your inner self knows is necessary for your sacred quest.

This participation with your inner self will lead to new experiences of heightened awareness. You can expect the following qualities of heightened awareness to become part of your daily life as you walk the inner path.

1. *You will experience and enhance the meaningfulness of coincidences.* You become aware that there are no accidents in this intelligent system. You realize that everything that shows up in your life has something to teach you. You appreciate everyone and everything in your life.

With increased awareness that there are no coincidences, you begin to rely on your sense that seemingly unconnected events have meaning. You even begin to create these situations as you need them. You start to know that you are a partner with fate rather than its victim. Ultimately you come to manage your coincidences and become fate's collaborator.

2. *You will become aware of a universal source of energy.* You have faith in the universal source of energy. You begin to exercise your ability to make contact with this source and make it part of your daily life. You develop a strong knowing about the God force and your ability to access this energy.

You are unable to entertain any doubts about the universal source of energy. You know that all beings are a part of it and receive sustenance from it. You are convinced that all weakness and falsehood come from a refusal to know this.

3. *You will feel loved.* You will call for and accept divine guidance. This vital spiritual nourishment is felt in both your inner and outer experiences. Immobilizing fear diminishes as you feel the presence of the divine energy with you. All seems as it should be, even though you may not understand it. You will feel peaceful about what you see and feel.

Your desires to right wrongs and fix the broken parts of your life are also part of this divine plan. You pursue your desires to serve God and humanity with clarity and peace.

4. *You will develop a sense of appreciation and awe.* You begin seeing beauty, and feeling awestruck at the magnificence of the universe. The feeling of appreciating beauty is actually the feeling of love when you are divinely connected. That love will fill you with a new sense of power.

By focusing your inner energy on the beauty that surrounds you, you will receive that energy from your surroundings. With practice, this kind of receptiveness will become a source of strength and sustenance in your daily life.

5. *You will feel connected to everyone.* As your higher self becomes the dominant force in your life you will become more and more conscious of your connectedness to others.

Just as you might observe thousands of flowers with different shades of color, originating from one source of light, so too you will observe many differing shades and shapes of people, with unique languages, customs and political persuasions, yet all originating from one essence. One light—many colors. One essence—many physical manifestations of humanity. This will not be a purely philosophical insight. It will be a way of life for you.

You will sense that anything that is destructive to one human is destructive to all. You will know that the essence or life force that flows through you flows through all. This higher awareness will lead you to the conclusion that Mahatma Gandhi came to: "God has no religion." That awareness will give you a loving energy that will help to bring all of us together.

6. *You will make a new agreement with reality.* When your soul becomes the guiding force in your life, you will break the ordinary agreement with reality, intellectually and physically. The limits of your perception will expand to include another world that coexists with ours. You will know that limits result when the social order defines our lives. You will transcend the social order and break the agreement that once defined your personal reality.

When you discover that you are limitless, your choices will begin to come from the limitless knowing within yourself. You will no longer believe in even the most solid-seeming assumption about yourself and your surroundings. You will know that all of the "powers" that have been ascribed to spiritual masters are within your capacity to manifest.

Your level of awareness will shift so dramatically that you will no longer feel bound by the agreement that defines reality for most others.

7. *You will experience surrender and acceptance.* You will finally stop fighting and simply let go, even when you fail to understand why so many things transpire that are inconsistent with how you would orchestrate the universe. You will accept that God knows what she is doing. This surrendering process will make you more effective in your sacred quest.

You will no longer judge God. Instead, you will know that this is an intelligent system. Hurricanes, tornadoes, "accidental" deaths, crime and poverty will be seen as parts of this divine plan in the same way as cloudless days, calm seas, compassion, prosperity and dying in one's sleep at the age of 105 are. Your desire to improve conditions is also a part of that plan. You will work on that, rather than being centered on why those conditions are "wrong."

8. *You will become a waking dreamer.* Your heightened awareness will permit you to be a waking dreamer. Everything that you are capable of achieving while dreaming will be possible while awake. The power of your mind to manifest what previously could only occur in sleeping dreams will begin to be your awakened reality.

In your dreams, when you want to closely examine an object, you don't have to get closer to the object—you bring the object to you with the power of your inner energy. You will begin to manifest objects in your awakened state of consciousness with the same energy.

As a waking dreamer, you will be able to move back and forth in time, to create the characters you need for your life drama, to communicate with the deceased, to be in more than one place at the same time, to make yourself invisible, to make yourself appear older or younger, and all of the other "tricks" that you enjoy in your dream state.

Some people take a lifetime to learn how to become a waking dreamer, to literally be in a dream state while awake. With your heightened awareness and the guidance of your higher self, you will become one of those waking dreamers.

9. *You will know the power and ecstasy of silence.* You will discover that when you "fall silent," you fall into the most sacred place of all. A moment of silence is the highest honor we can extend. You will find that it is the highest honor you can give yourself too. As Herman Melville wrote: "Silence is the only Voice of our God. . . . All profound things and emotions of things are preceded and attended by Silence."

You will shift away from the noisy life and seek

silence. Prayer and meditation will be integral to your life. The answers that you seek, the guidance that you need, the assistance that you require, will appear as you practice honoring your true self with moments of silence. You will be able to have these precious moments at will.

Noise and tumult will be unable to penetrate your silence. In traffic, in the midst of a rancorous meeting, during competitive exercise, at home with the children playing loudly—you will be able to access your own silence and know what Melville meant when he wrote: "Silence is the general consecration of the universe. Silence is the invisible laying on of the Divine Pontiff's hands upon the world." This will be your experience as you move into heightened awareness in your life.

10. *You will know that there is a spiritual solution to every problem.* In the realm of spirit you will find the answers to difficulties. Your higher self has the solution regardless of how grounded the problem may seem in the material world.

Problems such as addictions to drugs, food and alcohol have solutions in your higher self. By going within, you will see your excessive desires for something outside of yourself as an inadequate refuge from worldly pain. When you begin to achieve the highest levels of pleasure and euphoria by facing inward, the desire and the need for externals will disappear.

When you begin achieving perfect balance and centeredness by being peaceful and listening to your body, your choice to overeat and be indolent or lethargic will no longer rule your life.

Every problem—be it with relationships, finances, health or self-image—has a solution in the sacred self. When you are peaceful, experience silence, meditate and listen, really listen to God, you will be directed away from the worldly and toward the divinity that is within you. You will know what you need to do.

11. *You will shift from acquiring to sharing.* In this heightened state of awareness you will shift from personal desires to the question "How may I serve?" Rather than being focused on what is in it for you, you will be guided by the inner desire to help meet the needs of others. The irony of this is that you will begin to see abundance flowing into *your* life.

You will desire less and yet feel more fulfilled. You will shift your attention away from yourself and take pleasure in serving others. You will need less, want less and find yourself less attracted to acquiring and possessing. You will know what Albert Schweitzer meant when he wrote these words:

> Every man has to seek in his own way to make his own self more noble and to realize his own true worth. You must give some time to your fellow man. Even if it's a little thing, do something for those who have need of help, something for which you get no pay but the privilege of doing it. For remember, you don't live in a world all your own. Your brothers are here too.

12. *You will live authentically.* You will no longer have any difficulty just being yourself. You will know that a life lived authentically leads to universal truth and heightened awareness.

You will accept yourself knowing that whatever behaviors you exhibited in the past, even the ones that may have been destructive and immoral, were a part of who you were at the time and they had great lessons built into them for you to transcend. You will be able to say with conviction, "I am what I am." While some of the people who are close to you may find this difficult to accept, you will no longer be able to compromise yourself.

You will find it easier and easier to listen without being defensive because your inner knowing is strong and satisfying. You will live your life authentically—fulfilling your reason for being here, knowing that "life gives exams" and learning from those that you fail to pass. Your authenticity will be based on knowing that you cannot imitate others and still be true to yourself and to God.

13. *You will experience bliss as a natural state.* You will access an inner peaceful knowing that is like a warm shower running inside of you. You will discover that bliss is a natural state and can be accessed without the assistance of external substances.

Bliss is a state of grace, and a state of self-sufficiency. It is a connectedness to God, a connectedness to the universal truth. Your bliss provides you with the sense that you are "on purpose."

14. *You will be less judgmental and more forgiving.* Heightened awareness will erase your judgmental tendencies. You will begin seeing that judging others does not define them—it defines you. Consequently, you will be less inclined to judge anyone or anything.

You will accept that others are on their own paths. The things you previously found irritating about them will become a reflection of a part of yourself. As Carl Jung put it, "Everything that irritates us about others can lead us to an understanding of ourselves."

You will be able to view everything in this new nonjudgmental fashion. You will learn lessons for which you will be thankful. Thus, forgiveness will be quite easy for you to accommodate.

You will know that those misperceived "wrongs" that you experienced were somehow in divine order. The absence of judgment and the ability to forgive will bring a new serenity to your life.

You will also begin to forgive yourself. You will see mistakes as lessons for you to transcend. This will free you from the tyranny of self-recrimination. You have made the decision to be free.

MAKING THE DECISION TO BE FREE

The elements of heightened awareness described in the fourteen examples you've just read are all aspects of personal freedom. And they are yours to choose.

The difficulty is that human awareness is somewhat like a large house with many rooms. When we are born, it is as if we arrive in one of the rooms of awareness and live there until we die. At times we try to access the rest of the house by pushing against the door unsuccessfully.

To successfully open the door to heightened awareness, we must open it inward. When you realize that you do not have to be locked in one room of awareness, you have turned around to face in a new direction. And it is at this time that you make the decision to be free.

Freedom is the ability to leave the single room of awareness you were born in. In that room you learned the limits of your life. Outside of that room you learn that your life has unlimited possibilities. You needn't be one of the people Arthur Schopenhauer described when he wrote: "Everyone takes the limits of his own vision for the limits of the world."

A RADICAL DEFINITION OF FREEDOM

My vision of writing about freedom was expanded when my family and I had an "adventure on horseback" a few years ago on Maui. For me, the experience was a meaningful "coincidence." I have learned to recognize and honor such experiences. They greatly assist me in being on purpose in my life.

Adventure on Horseback is the name Frank Levinson, with his friend Amber, has given to the spiritual odysseys they lead through the backwoods of Maui. My family and I had the opportunity to spend a day on horseback with them at Frank's beautiful little home in the backwoods.

I told Amber and Frank that I was planning to write a book about taming the ego, getting in touch with the spiritual side of ourselves and allowing that element of our humanity to rule rather than vice versa. Amber said, "Well then, you'll be writing about freedom. Do read Florinda Donner's book."

She went into her bedroom and emerged with a copy of *Being-in-Dreaming* and insisted that I take it with me and keep it. "I'm through with it now," she said, "and I've been waiting for the right person to come along to read it. I want you to have it as a gift."

As we drove back to the other side of the island, I said to my wife, Marcelene, "I have a feeling that reading this novel is going to be a life-changing event for me." And sure enough, it put me exactly on the path that I was seeking.

Here is Florinda Donner's definition of freedom, in a sample of dialogue from her odyssey into the world of the spirit:

"What does freedom cost?"

"Freedom will cost you the mask you have on," she said, "the mask that feels so comfortable and is so hard to shed off, not because it fits so well but because you have been wearing it for so long." She stopped pacing about the room and came to stand in front of the card table.

"Do you know what freedom is?" she asked rhetorically. "Freedom is the total absence of concern about yourself," she said, sitting beside me on the bed. "And the best way to quit being concerned with yourself is to be concerned about others."

Can you imagine living one complete day without thinking about yourself? Nothing offending you, nothing disturbing you, nothing causing you to be angry? Is it possible to see the world the way it is? Is it possible to be unconcerned with yourself in this picture?

Would you then be able to reach out and help others, to live, work and provide, unconcerned about the returns? Just try to imagine not thinking about yourself even once all day. Not once questioning why you are not appreciated enough, not wealthy enough, not being treated fairly enough.

You notice only that others do what they do, without comparing yourself with them. You give of yourself and ask and expect nothing in return. You simply live. You are free!

Here are the final paragraphs in Donner's marvelous book:

> Florinda had told me that freedom is a total absence of concern about oneself, a lack of concern achieved when the imprisoned bulk of energy within ourselves is untied. She had said that this energy is released only when we can arrest the exalted conception we have of ourselves, of our importance, an importance we feel must not be violated or mocked. . . . The price of freedom is very high. Freedom can only be attained by dreaming without hope, by being willing to lose all, even the dream.
>
> For some of us, to dream without hope, to struggle with no goal in mind, is the only way to keep up with the bird of freedom.

Freedom, if defined as the absence of literal chains, exists for many. But if freedom means the ability to leave the room of constraints of daily awareness, if freedom means having limitless vision, if freedom means creating miracles and living in a radically new spiritual dimension—then freedom exists for very few.

If you can suspend your self-importance without

knocking out your self-esteem, you are choosing the kind of freedom Florinda Donner's book helped me envision. You also will know what Janis Joplin meant when she sang, "Freedom's just another word for nothing left to lose."

When you have nothing to lose, you are absolutely free, and when you are unconcerned about self-importance, you have freedom. You are on purpose, feel blissful and expect the world to be a divine place where you love others. You are actually cocreating *your* world with this newfound freedom. And you are not obsessed with getting the credit or looking good in the eyes of anyone.

YOUR ROLE IN THE CREATION PROCESS

Hundreds of books have been written in recent years on the mechanics of creation. My favorite is *Quantum Consciousness*, by Stephen Wolinsky. This book offers a readable, understandable approach to how things are created in the universe. I urge you to read Dr. Wolinsky's book and pay particular attention to the exercises he recommends for understanding the mechanics of creation.

What follows is an elementary description of how things are created, which will be helpful information for your sacred quest.

- The entire universe is made up of energy that can best be described as a wave.
- We call the tiniest particles we know about subatomic particles. They are not made up of matter, though; they are wave energy.
- These particles are so tiny that the only way we know they exist is by the trails they leave in particle accelerators.
- Particles appear to come into existence only when we observe them. Only when a conscious decision is

made to view a particle does the wave actually individ-ualize and become a separate identity.

• Our attention directed to the formless wave energy is what creates the reality that we call particle or solid, or the physical world.

Wolinsky writes: "The observer is the creator of the Part(icle)/mass aspect of the universe. . . . This means that how we subjectively experience events, interactions, and our inner self is observer-created . . . created by us."

Think about this as you consider your sacred quest. Whatever you have your attention centered on is what you will create in your physical world. I cannot fathom how these invisible particles function at the quantum level. But I do feel that this scientific evidence offers us strong clues about the effect and power of our con-sciously directed attention.

Consciously embracing the fullness of God in all that you see and do, and placing your attention on what it is that you want to manifest, is the secret of the mechanics of creation.

When you are operating from your highest self you are in charge of what you choose to create. You become a cocreator with God of everything in your life. It works at the tiniest level and is scientifically documented. This means it works at your human level as well.

In *The Tao of Physics*, Fritjof Capra writes: "If the preparation of the measurement is modified, the proper-ties of the particle will change." This means that when you place your attention on something and become the observer, the act of observing affects the creation. But, if you change your observation and remove your attention, the creation will also be affected.

Creation of anything in the physical universe is deter-mined by what kind of attention you place on it. Remove the observer (attention) and you alter the creation. The way that a wave becomes solid and independent is through the conscious attention of the observer.

This is the value of learning to face inward and focus your attention on what you want to create. The subatomic particles spring into existence and disappear depending on the observer.

The inner experience of keeping your higher self focused on the object of your desire is the creation process for your life. Or, as Gary Zukav described it in *The Dancing Wu Li Masters,* "What is *out there* apparently depends, in a rigorous mathematical sense, as well as a philosophical one, upon what we decide *in here.* The new physics tells us that an observer cannot observe without altering what he sees."

You can decide what is *in here* by facing in a new direction. Know that what you are observing and placing your attention upon inside will affect what goes on outside. You will cocreate a world of bliss and spiritual consciousness if that is where you choose to place your attention.

This is science talking now, letting you know that the mechanics of the universe and your sacred quest are the same process.

Up to now, I have described the sacred quest and how it will feel when you turn around your life. The following section offers suggestions for daily practice. These exercises will help you with the about-face process.

Suggestions for Meeting the Challenge of Freedom

- *Each day make an attempt to serve others in some small way and do not tell anyone.* Slowly, the questions about your own value and why you are here will evaporate. Just one small extension of help or love to another, with no thought of what is owed back to you, will put you on the path of higher awareness.

Copy this ancient truth and reread it daily: "When you seek happiness for yourself it will always elude you. When you seek happiness for others you will find it yourself."

- *Practice making meaningful coincidences.* Get a clear picture in your mind of something that you would like to see happen in your life. A job opportunity, meeting your perfect partner, quitting an addictive behavior. Keep your inner focus on this picture and extend love outwardly as frequently as possible, with this picture in mind.

  As you get proficient at keeping your inner energy on what it is that you would like to manifest, and you remain loving, you will attract the coincidences that fit your desire perfectly. This is called managing your coincidences, and it is something that I practice daily. It works.

- *Keep yourself appraised of the inner world where you do all of your living.* Begin to notice your thoughts and remind yourself that the simple act of thinking is evidence that there is an invisible energy that flows through you at all times.

  Become aware of the thinker of the thoughts—that is, the invisible you behind the actual thought. Practice knowing the knower, the invisible intelligence behind what we call knowledge. The known is always on the move; it changes and has no particular dwelling place. The knower is that which is changeless and eternal.

  With this awareness you will begin to know your divinity. Out of this awareness you will be able to cocreate the world that you desire.

- *Have conversations with God in private and important moments.* In these conversations, rather than ask for special favors, affirm your willingness to use all of your inner strength to create solutions. Ask for the strength and be willing to do what is necessary.

  To know that you are able to access divine guidance takes more than Sunday morning practice. Such experiences of knowing come from within and can never be doubted or shaken because these moments translate to how you lead your life.

- *Take time to appreciate beauty.* As you contemplate a bird, a flower, a sunset, a mother and her nursing infant, an aged man or a school bus full of children, open your heart to them. Allow the love to circulate from you to them and feel it being returned. The more you practice receiving love from your surroundings, the more energized you will become.

  There is energy in everything and everyone. The way that you receive this invisible energy is through the actual appreciation of the beauty and wonder of our universe.

  With practice, you will be able to send out the love that you are receiving through the simple act of beauty appreciation. Try it!

- *Attempt to remove all enemies from your thoughts.* The same intelligence that flows through you, flows through all other human beings. Forget about what nationalist interests want you to believe. We are all one, each of us a single cell in this body called humanity.

  When you have this global mentality you are freed from the disempowering hatred that divides humanity and you are unable to participate in violence. The act of hurting another, with words or weapons, is an act of separateness.

  When you know you are connected to all, you cannot fathom striking out at others, let alone feeling hatred for your assigned enemies. The answer to our problems of violence in the world is located in the spiritual realm.

- *Think of yourself as limitless as you make a new agreement with reality.* Picture yourself able to accomplish anything your mind can envision.

  Allow yourself the freedom to dream of flying, shape-shifting, practicing bilocation, disappearing and reappearing, and anything else that appeals to you that you are able to do each night in your dreams. Make your own agreement with reality that is dependent solely on what you want it to be.

  Let go of everything that you have been told is impossible or unrealistic and allow yourself the freedom to make your own contract with God about what is possible for you. Examine all of the doubts that you have about miracles and miracle workers and replace those doubts with openness.

  Your goal is to have your very own agreement with reality.

- *Surrender!* This involves an act of the heart. The act of surrendering takes place in a moment. Let go of your conflict with what is and what can be, and surrender. Stop asking, "Why me?"

  Accept the fact that your body will die and that you are eternal. Surrender to this fact when someone dies and stop telling yourself that their death shouldn't have happened the way it did. You can surrender and accept, and you can grieve.

  Notice any repetitious inner dialogue about the horrors and tragedies of the world. Surrender and let go(d). This doesn't mean you will rejoice in the suffering of others. It means you will not focus your inner divine energy on suffering. You will be freer to help eliminate suffering.

  Millions of people die every day, and millions more

show up here on our planet. It is a play of continuous entrances and exits. All of your opinions about how that should be taking place are nothing more than notions that you have of how God should be orchestrating this play.

But it is all perfect; even the part that you dislike or judge as bad. Surrender and know that you too are one of those characters who made an entrance and will experience an exit. But also know that your soul is eternal, and that is who you truly are.

Surrender now! It only takes an instant.

- *Dream awake!* That's right. Remind yourself that you do not have to go to sleep in order to dream. Give yourself free moments to dream without the luxury of sleeping.

  Allow your mind to create all that you can create in your sleeping dreams. By practicing this exercise you will someday be unable to distinguish between your waking dream and your sleeping dream. This is an exquisite place, because it gives you the opportunity to mentally create the backdrop for your total life experience.

  Dreaming awake can make you feel limitless. You did it as a child and were labeled as a day dreamer. But those were exquisite moments.

  When you free yourself from the self-imposed limits that you experience in waking consciousness, you are entering the world of spirit. It is here that you get to know your higher self, to directly experience God. It is here that you can have inner conversations with those important people in your life who have died. It is here that you can receive guidance and assurance of your immortality.

- *Give yourself time each day for silence.* It may be a form of meditation, but if that is not your choice, then simply allow yourself some silent moments. Experience your silence for at least thirty minutes each day.

When we are in love, we say we are speechless. You are searching for that divine quality of love within you as part of your sacred quest. So give yourself time to be speechless, to be quiet.

When we are in awe of something we say, "Words fail me." This is an indication of the value of silence. You will find God when you allow the spiritual part of your consciousness to dominate your life. Leave the noise and hustle and bustle of your life for just thirty minutes a day, and it will become a time that you treasure.

- *Imagine a spiritual solution to your problem.* Think of the most serious problem that you are facing today. Write it down so that it can stare back at you. Now go through all of the past attempts to resolve this difficulty. You will see that virtually all of your efforts to correct this problem were centered in the outer world.

  Now try a totally new approach:

  First notice the emotional part of the problem that is troubling you—the sadness, the anger, the pain, the fear. Then make a decision that this emotion is bad and unwanted in your life. Now notice how this inner experience feels.

  You are focusing your inner awareness on the badness of the emotion that surrounds your problem. Just notice. Now, remove the label of bad from the emotion and just accept it for what it is—neither bad nor good, just an emotion. Instead of labeling it, view it as energy and observe it.

  This is a spiritual approach to the resolution of your problem. You have become the observer. You are viewing the emotions concerning the problem simply as energy. Before long, you will see the emotions disappearing. Your feelings of sadness and anxiety and fear will dissipate, just through the act of observing.

  As you become less and less attached emotionally, the problem slowly disappears as the solution appears.

A spiritual solution is one in which you detach yourself personally from the outcome and see the energy as flowing through you. By observing that energy, you make yourself separate from the pain. The act of compassionate observation releases the problem.

- *Lighten your load beginning today.* Go through all of the possessions that you no longer use, and share them with others. You can do this with everything you own.

  The less you hold onto and store away, the freer you are. The act of sharing your possessions is an act of heightened awareness. Ultimately you will be able to give away the things that you are still using, and then you will be able to give your money away too. You will know that all that you give will be returned tenfold.

  Recall the maxim: "Plenty of people despise money, but few know how to give it away."

  As you lighten your material load, less energy is spent hoarding, insuring, moving, worrying, polishing and so on. The less attached you are to all of your possessions, and the more you are able to share them with others unconditionally, the more peaceful your life will be.

- *Work at being content with who you are rather than pleasing others by being inauthentic.* Say to yourself, "I am what I am and it is okay as long as I am not hurting anyone else in the process."

  This affirmation keeps you from having to shift from your authentic self to your false self. Who you are is divine, eternal and changeless. The rest is just the play of the body in the physical domain.

  Stay authentic with the invisible self. Do it quietly and without a lot of drama, but do it. Your behavior, more than your words, teaches people that you are unwilling to be something you aren't. No need to make an issue. A shrug, or removal of yourself from a compromising situation, or a firm statement is often enough.

  Be clear about your own inner value and you will not

be pushy when your inner inclination is to be serene, athletic when you *know* this is not your calling, or heterosexual when your inner guidance tells you otherwise.

This simply means being willing to trust your inner self and to stay with that inner guidance in the face of pressure by outsiders to turn into something else.

- *Direct your attention to what pleases you.* For example, if you are inclined to visualize disasters, shift this around. Remember that what you think about expands. Now, once you have played out the tragedy in your mind, replay it to have a pleasant outcome. This is important to do each time you find yourself slipping into internal catastrophizing, because if you don't you will bring about the results you dread.

  You have the power to make your inner world work for you or against you. Use it to create the images of contentment that you want to occur in your material world, and eventually that inner contentment will be the blueprint that you consult as the architect of your everyday life.

  You can live peacefully and blissfully. The choice is always yours to make.

- *Judge not.* If you see someone who is very different from you in physical appearance or in age or in economic status, use your mind to send them love rather than a judgmental thought. If you instantly, out of habit, have an inner judgment, recognize that you have just done that, and then send that person unconditional love for a microsecond.

  This will get you out of the judgmental habit and into the habit of using your mind to send out the kind of love that will reenergize your life with the elixir of heightened awareness.

These then are some suggestions that you can work on daily as you begin your quest for your sacred self.

You have the capacity to meet this challenge, but before you will be truly ready, you need to examine many of the habits that you have acquired over a lifetime of having your ego and the world of the material be the authoritative forces in your life.

2

RECOGNIZING THE LIMITATIONS OF YOUR PAST

We do our best to disprove the fact, but
a fact it remains; man is as divine as
nature, as infinite as the void.

—ALDOUS HUXLEY

No matter how much I protest,
I am totally responsible for everything
that happens to me in my life.

In the years following your arrival from no-where to now-here, you were taught many beliefs about what you were capable of doing and what was impossible for you to do. You also learned from others your beliefs about religion, education, love and who your enemies were. The influence of these early caretakers shaped your choice of friends and teachers. The person you are today is primarily the result of interactions with the important adults in your growing-up environment.

The scientific evidence presented in chapter 1 about how the particle takes on the energy of the observer applies here also. You absorbed energy from your early sponsors. The particle that became you was formed out of the quantum interaction of the observers of your growth. It is this energy, referred to as your past, that you must explore as you prepare to pursue your sacred quest.

I am not suggesting you look upon your past with disfavor or judgment. In fact, I encourage you to *not* recall it as good or bad. It simply was.

Keep in mind what you read in the first chapter and what I stressed throughout *Real Magic*. This is an intelligent system and a divine universe that we are sharing. Everything that happens is a part of the unfolding of that intelligence. A part of that unfolding now is your desire for heightened awareness.

So, it is time to let go of beliefs that have served you well but now keep you from moving along your sacred path. The process of letting go is easily understood if you can picture life as giving exams.

Just as we are required to pass exams throughout our school experience, so too are we required to pass exams in the larger school called life. If we pass them, we move on to the next level, and then take the exam for that level throughout our stay in now-here. If we don't pass, we repeat the course and continue at that level until we get the lesson.

Many years, even an entire lifetime, might be consumed repeating a lesson in order to pass a spiritual examination. We might find ourselves repeating the same behaviors tirelessly and depressingly, over and over, without getting the lesson that life is trying to teach us.

You may find yourself going from one bad relationship to another, even seeking the same person each time only in a different body. Repeatedly you might find yourself being dominated, unappreciated or taken for granted by an inconsiderate partner. Perhaps you continue in an occupation repeating the behaviors of previously unsatisfying job experiences. You could continually latch onto the same kinds of germs and repeat debilitating disease patterns.

People who successfully put themselves onto the spiritual path are living the life they love and feeling productive because they realize that life patterns are trying to tell them something. They understand that those situations are the exams!

The same responses—the same answers as they've given previously—will not get different results. The decision is made to pass this exam in this area, at this time, by responding differently. To move on to the next level in this curriculum called life, you have to pass the exams along the way.

MOVING ON TO THE NEXT LEVEL

First decide to draw up a new agreement with yourself concerning your reality. This new agreement will be anchored in the understanding that you are going to be the decision maker from now on. All of the input that you have received up until now will be viewed as examinations that you have passed.

Everything and everyone that came into your life had a reason for being there. They were there to teach you lessons. You took the courses; now you have passed the examinations.

You no longer are required to stay in the elementary classrooms redoing the same courses. Value those earlier experiences, but know you are ready to move on. Recall the increased sense of freedom that you experienced as a student moving from grammar school to junior high, to high school, to college. Remember that freedom is the experience you are now seeking.

Long after I had made the decision to be a writer I realized that I was going to have to come up with a new agreement concerning my own reality. I am always amazed how the teachers show up when we are ready. In this case my teacher was Jackson Browne, through whom I learned a lesson in the lyrics of a song written and composed by him.

I was driving my oldest daughter, Tracy, home from a shopping trip in southern Florida. *Late for the Sky* was playing in the car tape deck. I enjoyed explaining a song's lyrics to Tracy as a way to initiate long conversations as we drove. I began repeating a lyric out loud as the music played in the car.

Jackson Browne was then singing the song *For a Dancer*. I had heard this song hundreds of times, but this time the words felt so much a part of me that I was unable to continue my conversation with Tracy. Instead I just sat there driving along, thinking about how true the words were and what they meant to me. His lyrics refer to most people as dancers who are dancing away their lives doing steps dictated by others. He encourages listeners to examine their lives and become the choreographer rather than merely the dancer in their lives.

I knew that my purpose in life was to help others gain a sense of self-reliance by teaching them how to look within and trust in the inner wisdom they possess. In some way I always had been doing that, even as a little boy, demonstrating the value of self-reliance.

As I drove along I was experiencing a holy instant, sitting in my car, repeating the lyrics and vowing silently to make the meaning of the song come alive both in my own life and in the lives of all who wanted to listen.

After having listened to and loved *For a Dancer* hundreds of times, the lyrics moved me, when I was ready, to my next level. They became the impetus for the theme of this chapter and, in a larger sense, the theme of this book and, in the largest sense, the theme of my entire body of work up until now.

Most of us are doing the steps that we've been shown by everyone we've ever known, and often we don't realize that we are still dancing to that tune as adults. As Jackson Browne suggests, we must learn to toss some seeds of our own, and become the choreographer of our own lives, dancing to the tune that we compose.

The next level then, is the awareness that now is all there is. Today is the only day of your life. You do not have to be imprisoned or restricted by your personal history.

Renegotiate your agreement about what it is that is going to constitute your reality. No longer will you be just a dancer—you will also be a composer, choreographer and spiritual essence observing the new intricacies of that dance.

The ways you have lived until now have allowed you to function at the survival level and will be honored by you. You will not reject or judge your past. You simply are going to make the decision to move up a notch. At this new level you are the choreographer, doing the steps that you are creating, independent of your personal history.

LEAVING BEHIND YOUR PERSONAL HISTORY

Having a personal history keeps us from now. This is a radical idea perhaps, but I am asking you to consider the possibility of totally eradicating your personal history from your consciousness and simply living completely in the present moment.

The first thing that might pop into your mind, as it did into mine when I began to consider this possibility, is that it is impossible. I do have a memory, and it would be folly for me to pretend that I am not the product of my past. What I am asking you to develop is a "forgettery" to go with your memory.

The point is that as a result of being a product of your past, you are dancing to a tune thrown at you by others. In order to take the step up toward your sacred quest, you must toss out the idea that you are unable to take those steps in the first place.

In *Tales of Power*, Carlos Castaneda is indoctrinated in the ways of the Nagual, the spiritual master who lives in a world much different than that of average people. His teacher, don Juan, says to him, "One day, I discovered I didn't need personal history, so, like drinking, I dropped it." As Carlos contemplates this idea, he is told that if he can learn to erase his personal history he will be free of the encumbering thoughts of others.

When people know our personal histories they exert a certain amount of control over us. They expect us to be something that we have always been, or that we have been taught to be. If we don't live up to their expectations they become disillusioned about us. Then we take on the guilt of disappointing those who have been such loyal sponsors of our lives.

However, there is a simple alternative that can be put into practice in a moment of satori, or instant awakening. You can drop your personal history right now. Just drop it. To put it quite simply, if you don't have a story, you don't have to fit it.

Of all the enlightened beings I have met and have read about, the one similar quality they seem to possess is that they are not in any way tied to their past. They are free because they don't rely on the way things used to be to define their lives today.

They recognize that all of the people and events that transpired in their past were part of the intelligent system that has been their reality. But they know that this is a new, separate reality that begins and ends with now. They are free to have an open mind about all that is possible for them.

The *Course in Miracles* puts it this way:

To be born again is to let the past go, and look without condemnation upon the present. . . . You are but asked to let the future go, and place it in God's Hands. And you will see by your experience that you have laid the past and present in His Hands as well, because the past will punish you no more, and future dread will now be meaningless.

You do not need a teacher to teach you all of the elements of heightened awareness. You do not need a teacher to tell you how to erase your past and the limitations that you have come to believe in. What you need is a teacher to teach you that you have immeasurable power within you. This is what I wish to do. I hope to convince you of the reality of the existence of your limitless inner power.

In *Illusions,* Richard Bach explained that when you argue for your limitations, the only thing you get are your limitations. If you have been arguing for your limitations for a long time, you may be convinced of what is impossible for you to achieve. This is why it is such an important facet of your sacred quest to erase your personal history with a broad brush stroke and begin with now.

Let go of all the beliefs that convince you of your inadequacies and shortcomings. Clean out that closet of worn-out loyalties to what you can and cannot do. Just open yourself up right in this moment. Be like a clear, blank slate. Nothing is imprinted or projected onto this slate.

It begins with no. It ends with now. There is no guilt about erasing your personal history. There is great love and respect for all that you have learned up until now, but now is blank and, most important, open to all possibilities. No restrictions, no limitations, only the willingness to experience God and the entire divinity of the universe within yourself.

Your life is no longer to be constrained by what you've known as your personal history. Your individual soap opera has received its cancellation notice. In the instant that you drop that personal history you become eternal. You always have been. You always will be.

Finally, you are working on answering the question "Who am I?" Your answers no longer need be confined to the labels that defined your body and your life experience.

IF YOU'RE NOT YOUR PAST,
WHO ARE YOU?

The famed Lebanese poet Kahlil Gibran wrote that there was only one time in his life when he was rendered mute. That was when someone asked him, "Who are you?" It is a question that is literally impossible to answer with words, because who we are is formless, and words belong to the world of form. The answer to this question does not come from the physical domain.

Each of us is a soul with a body, rather than a body with a soul. Soul cannot be measured or observed with the tools that we use to observe the material world. Perhaps the best way to begin to answer the question is to look at what we are not.

I love the way Nisargadatta Maharaj answers this question in *I Am That.* He writes:

> Just as the colors in this carpet are brought out by light but light is not the color, so is the world caused by you but you are not the world. That which creates and sustains the world, you may call it God or providence, but ultimately you are the proof that God exists, not the other way round. For before any question about God can be put, you must be there to put it.

You are that invisible essence that proves the existence of God and the world. Further on in the same passage, Maharaj writes:

> The body is made of food, as the mind is made of thoughts. See them as they are. Non-identification, when natural and spontaneous, is liberation. You need not know what you are. Enough to know what you are not. *What you are you will never know* [italics added], for every discovery reveals new

dimensions to conquer. The unknown has no limits. . . . Set yourself tasks apparently impossible—that is the way.

Your personal history has attempted to convince you that you are one or several of the labels that you have been assigned. Ultimately, you adopted the labels as who and what you were. In the process of erasing your personal history, you need to remove all the artificial labels.

These are some of the things that you are not:

- *You are not your name.* The label that is your name originated in antiquity, usually based on the work of your ancestors.

  My name, Wayne, literally translates to "wagon-maker." The name Dyer refers to the occupation of a person who dyed hides. Native Americans used names like Dances With Wolves and Little White Dove to describe each other. In both examples, we know that the names, the labels, are not who the people are.

  Your name was given to you to help distinguish your body from the other bodies around you, and to give others a word to use when they want to refer to you. But don't for a moment think that that is who you are. Indeed, it is who you are not.

- *You are not your body.* Notice how the previous sentence uses the phrase "your body." This implies that the body is something that you possess. You are the possessor of the body and the invisible force behind the body, but not the body itself.

  The body is nothing more than a conglomeration of raw material, including bones, gristle, blood, iron, calcium, skin. As you consult your personal history you will find lots of trauma around the body's importance.

  Were you taught that your appearance said a lot about you? Most of us were taught to spend hours before mirrors worrying about posture, physique, skin, absence or presence of hair, weight, height and so on. But this is your false self at work.

You own the body. You are not the body.

- *You are not your mind.* Just as we say "your" body, we also say "your" mind. This implies the owner of the mind. You think thoughts with your mind— therefore, there are the thoughts and then there is the thinker of the thoughts.

  When Maharaj was asked if the mind is the true person, he replied:

  > Examine closely and you will see that the mind is seething with thoughts. It may go blank occasion- ally, but it does it for a time and reverts to its usual restlessness. A becalmed mind is not a peaceful mind. You say you want to pacify your mind. Is he, who wants to pacify the mind, himself peaceful?

  What a wonderfully provocative question to ask yourself. Who is the owner of the mind? Is the owner, who seeks peace, himself at peace? Who you really are is not the mind but the you behind the mind. And that owner cannot be found in the physical world.

  For most of your life you have been taught that you are your mind. You have been training your intellect, attending classes ad infinitum and identify- ing yourself somehow with what you know.

  As you leave your personal history behind, you will leave behind the notion that you are your mind. (This is such an important concept in attainment of the sacred self that I have included a chapter called "Cultivate the Witness" later in this book.)

- *You are not your occupation.* You are not engineer nor teacher nor secretary nor shopkeeper. These are choices that the invisible divine you has made as your way of fulfilling your heroic mission while visiting now-here.

The more your position becomes defined as who you are, the more difficult it is for you to know truth and freedom. It is easier for an anonymous wanderer who has had many occupational titles to be blissfully alive and aware of his divinity than it is for a celebrity trapped in the role of maintaining a public image.

The role identification itself can keep you away from your own true higher self. It can inhibit you from knowing your higher self, since the role of occupation is the dominant force in your life.

Dropping your personal history involves shedding the notion that you are what you do. Remember this exercise in logic: If you are what you do, then when you don't, you aren't.

When you believe that who you are is your work, you find yourself performing your routine in order to feel important. You work even though it no longer makes sense. You perform those tasks as if somehow the divine you was involved in this drama.

As you drop your personal history, you drop this idea. You become what Stuart Wilde in his refreshingly honest and brilliant book *The Whispering Winds of Change* calls "becoming a minimalist." This excerpt will whet your appetite for reading this important book:

> Never go forward in a hurry. Walk slowly, speak deliberately. Never get emotional and never let people manipulate you. . . . There's always another deal, always another time, and there's five billion other people. . . . Tell them you have all the time in the world—because you do, you're infinite. Remember the greatest wisdom you can develop is the wisdom of *not doing*. It's the deals and situations that you avoid that help you conserve energy and remain independent and strong. . . . Everything you commit to will have weight.

Make every effort to remove these labels from yourself, and know that you are not what you do, nor are you the doer. You are the one who watches the you who is doing.

- *You are not your relationships.* Certainly the love energy between you and all of those in your immediate circle is very significant, but it is not who you are.

    You are an individual soul that is connected to the whole, but you are not the relationship to that whole. Your identification with your relationship provides you with great frustration because every time there is a glitch in it, as there always will be, you find yourself feeling worthless.

    Remember that you are eternal, that which is changeless. You are in a great number of relationships, all of which have validity, but they come and go just like your life here in form comes from no-where and goes to now-here and then back to no-where. It is a relationship of coming and going, and thus it changes.

    Dropping your personal history means dropping the belief that a failed relationship makes you a failure. There are no failed relationships. Every person who enters and exits your life does so in a mutual sharing of life's divine lessons. Some have longer roles to play than others, but ultimately, you will return to your relationship to the absolute.

    You do not have to ever judge yourself in negative ways because of the nature of your relationships. You can learn from them all, knowing from your observer's position that you are the one observing it all.

- *You are not your country, race or religion.* You are an eternal spirit, not an American or a Chinese or an African. It matters not what sort of a body you showed up in, where you arrived geographically or what religion you place after your name. There are no Buddhists or Catholics or Presbyterians in the no-where. Those are classifications made to distinguish us from one another in our present form.

Identities are found in a temporary phase in the parenthesis in eternity that we call life. Discard these names and you will identify with the realm of the spirit rather than the world of the ego. Then you are no longer willing to fight the fights of your ancestors who have tried to convince you whom to hate and whom to love. You will no longer participate in the tribal consciousness in which you perceive yourself to be better than another by virtue of your birthplace or skin color.

Your personal history has trained you in the ways of your tribe. These are limitations that you do not need to have. Let go of that identification with the labels and choose a new perspective of unity consciousness. You are united with all souls. Their packaging or location is irrelevant.

Those who are still stuck will call you a traitor and an ingrate. You will be able to send them love and not take on their guilt.

The cries of nationalism, tribalism and theism have been the source of wars and of the slaughter of billions of human beings. You know in your heart, as do all who play out this game, that this is a violation of God's laws, that it is inconsistent with the teachings of all the spiritual masters who have ever walked among us.

Yet the pattern persists. Why? Because we hang on to our personal histories as if they were our true identities. Refuse to identify yourself with tribal labels.

Seeing yourself as a spiritual being without labels is a way to transform the world and reach a sacred place for all of humanity. Begin by making your decision to be free by letting go of your personal history.

When you let go of your personal history, you know that you are not your name, your body, your mind, your occupation, your relationships or your ethnic or cultural identity. So who are you? What is left is the invisible, intangible you, which is the heart of the message in this book.

What we have now is similar to what a seeker asked Nisargadatta Maharaj to clarify. He states to his teacher, "When I look within, I find sensations and perceptions, thoughts and feelings, desires and fears, memories and expectations. I am immersed in this cloud and see nothing else."

Nisargadatta Maharaj, who sat on the outskirts of Bombay in his humble abode, shunning all possessions and only seeking to help those who wanted spiritual awareness, replied:

> That which sees all this, and the nothing too, is the inner teacher. He alone is, all else only appears to be. He is your own self, your hope and assurance of freedom; find him and cling to him and you will be saved and safe.

What a great message for you. That inner witness is your entire being. It is the answer. It cannot be described in words, but it will become better known to you as you drop your personal history.

3

RELEASING
OLD BELIEFS

✳

One of the most striking differences
between a cat and a lie is that a cat has
only nine lives.

—MARK TWAIN

My past is nothing more than the
trail that I have left behind.
What drives my life today is the
energy that I generate in my
present moments.

✳

It is now time to begin the task of recognizing and releasing beliefs and opinions that do not fit into your new agreement with reality. Take a look at some of those ingrained beliefs and shift them out of your consciousness.

Your personal history is replete with beliefs. These beliefs are at the core of your understanding of what it is that constitutes your reality. You have used them to explain why your life has taken the course it has. Resolve to remove those that are inconsistent with the new agreement with reality that you are creating.

Throughout this chapter you will be asked to identify and then change core beliefs that you no longer want. You might wonder why one would hold on to unwanted belief systems. In *Be As You Are,* Ramana Maharshi, one of India's twentieth-century sages, has this to say in response to why human beings continue to repeat self-negating ways:

> Pleasure or pain are aspects of the mind only. Our essential nature is happiness. But we have forgotten the Self and imagine that the body or the mind is the Self. It is that wrong identity that gives rise to misery. What is to be done? This mental tendency is very ancient and has continued for innumerable past births. Hence it has grown strong. That must go before the essential nature, happiness, asserts itself.

This chapter may help you answer the rhetorical question that is being posed by Ramana Maharshi, "What is to be done?"

Here are ten of the most common and difficult-to-undo beliefs that are taught in Western civilization. Examine each of these core beliefs in terms of how it operates in your life. Then consider some of the suggestions that I have offered. In the process, you will be rewriting your new agreement with reality and perhaps creating *your* answers to the question "What is to be done?"

Remember that your entire life is concerned with the accumulation of energy. The more beliefs that you remove from your inner space, the more room there is for new energy. Ask yourself if these ten beliefs are ones that you want to maintain or let go of. And keep in mind that if these beliefs do not serve you, they are lies that live endlessly, as Mark Twain suggests in the epigraph to this chapter.

BELIEF #1: MORE-IS-BETTER

More-is-better is a twentieth-century disease that can obscure the path of the sacred quest. Has this belief become a part of your daily life? Where is the peace in more-is-better?

The pursuit of more confines one to a life of striving. It is impossible to arrive and enjoy life. Have you been conditioned to accept this belief? If you've spent a lot of life energy on more-is-better it can be difficult to halt the momentum. You need to know if it is a cornerstone of your life.

Some of the signs that more-is-better is the foundation of your life are the following: you must be busy to be fulfilled; you must make more money than you currently are making; you must get a promotion to prove your worth; you need to have more of everything. To change this, you will want to declare a halt to your constant pursuit of more by knowing that you don't need anything else in order to be free.

More-is-better keeps us exclusively in the physical domain. The spiritual self is not allowed in our daily life. Inner energy is concentrated on accumulations, acquisitions, rewards, trophies, approval and money.

Some people experience guilt, shame and self-reproach thinking they are being lazy and worthless, and feeling irresponsible when they are not pursuing more.

We are taught the game early. Starting in school we learn to pursue higher grades, additional diplomas and external titles. There is no peace in this pursuit.

The feeling of peace is there when you are facing away from more-is-better. It indicates that your spiritual self is calling you. "The good and the wise lead quiet lives," Euripides said centuries ago.

It is not because the pursuit of more is inherently bad that I include it at the top of this list. It is because it denies you the peace and harmony that are intrinsic to your sacred quest. You do not have to become inert to be at peace. You can abandon the idea of more-is-better and replace it with an inner serenity that does not need more in order to be acceptable.

You have received beliefs from an endless chain of

people who have been willing victims for generations. When you let go of these beliefs, you will open an inner reservoir of space that allows you to accumulate a different kind of energy, which will direct you toward peace rather than toward tumult and a bypass operation.

SUGGESTIONS FOR RELEASING MORE-IS-BETTER

- *Simplify, simplify, simplify.* I can't repeat it enough. Examine carefully how much of your life energy is used in pursuit of what you don't want or need. Practice one day at a time, the idea of saying no to more. A very emphatic "No, I will not pursue that item."

  In place of pursuing more-is-better, spend time playing with your son or granddaughter. Read the New Testament instead of chasing after another object. Go for a long walk along the riverfront rather than spend time trying to get ahead.

  As you release the energy you previously applied to pursuing more, you free yourself up inside to experience the joy of being rather than the drudgery of always doing. This is freedom, the ability to choose to be rather than to accumulate.

  You will discover, as you practice simplifying, that many items that you previously chased after, including money, will begin to show up in your life without pursuing them. This is one of the great ironies of life. Less is more!

- *Give yourself regular moments of silent contemplation.* Treat these moments as absolutely essential in your daily routine. The practice of meditation or silent prayer will get you back in touch with God. As Mikhael Aivanhov put it in *The Mystery of Light,* "Wherever there are no limits, where Infinity and Eternity and Immortality exist, that is where God is."

These moments of contemplation remove you from the idea that you have to have more. You will come to know that everything that you need for a peaceful, blissful, loving life, you already possess, and this awareness will pervade all of your daily life practice.

- *Practice saying, "I pass."* When you start to feel the pressure to go after more, just say the words "I pass." It is freeing to let the pressure for more subside with these simple words. After saying this a few times you will feel an inner freedom. This inner space is available for your higher spiritual self.

- *Get back to nature.* Wilderness is therapy. Give yourself time in the woods, trekking in the mountains, walking in fields or along the beach. Just being in nature is a way of letting go of the disease of wanting more.

  Spend a night sleeping outdoors with your children or a loved one, or solo. Look at the galaxies and sense your place in the endless magnificence of a night sky. I guarantee you will gain a new perspective on life. You will see the beauty of the natural world and let go of your belief that things and accumulations are needed for you to feel complete.

  Add to these suggestions the words of Peace Pilgrim: "A simplified life is a sanctified life." You can be a CEO of a large corporation, the head of a bustling household, a sales representative constantly traveling, a head physician in a large hospital, a shopkeeper in a busy mall—and still live a sanctified life. It is an inner awareness that you need to have, one that stops singing the tune "More-is-better" and replaces it with "Peace-is-better."

BELIEF #2: EXTERNALS ARE TO BLAME FOR THE CONDITIONS OF MY LIFE

If you were raised on blame, it is a habit for you to reach for this excuse whenever you wish to explain why something is not working in your life.

You can, for instance, blame lack of prosperity on a lot of externals: your culture, the stock market, politicians, your parents, lady luck, the greed of others. You can blame illness on heredity, the flu season, bad luck, the environment. Your sour relationships can be blamed on your partners, their inability to love you, your upbringing, your parents. Your personality can be blamed on your parents, your genes, your childhood, your siblings, your birth order. Your physical appearance can be the fault of genetics, the food manufacturers, advertisers, the polluted environment. This is potentially an endless list.

The alternative to blame is self-responsibility—becoming an inner-directed person. You may not have been taught to consider taking responsibility for the events in your life. But if you are unwilling to discontinue the blame game, you will be unable to initiate your sacred quest.

When you blame something outside of yourself for the circumstances you are experiencing, you give control of your life to that outer phenomenon. Relying on externals means abandoning your sacred self. The sacred quest is realized in an inner environment of peaceful knowing. It invites you to turn around and make contact with your inner loving presence, where you will find your solutions.

The key to you is always within. It is impossible to lose the key to yourself outside of yourself when you are on the path of the sacred quest. When you let go of blaming others and search within for your key, you will always find what you need.

Instead of blame, you can choose to know that all of the events and people who have shown up in your life have had a divine role.

In our dream state, we create all of the characters we need. From an awakened perspective, we don't blame the characters and events in our dreams. So too we can know that the things that we do not understand or approve of are still in our life to teach us something.

Shed the fault-finding tendency. Know that you are the creator of your life and that a loving presence is with you. Your ability to be self-reliant will overtake your habit of assigning blame.

Suggestions for Releasing Blame

• *When you are inclined to think that someone else is responsible for your circumstances, take an instant to say a prayer of thanks for the lesson.* The lesson is to become aware that you are the one experiencing the feeling.

When I am about to blame gun enthusiasts for the violence in our society, I stop myself and appreciate the reminder that it is *me* experiencing this anguish. I then look within myself for a way to end the violence, rather than blame an entity called gun lovers.

You can do this the instant that you recognize yourself playing the blame game.

• *Feel thankful toward those you've let anger you.* Give inner thanks for the reminder that the feeling you are experiencing is inside you, not outside you.

Now you can turn your attention inside, toward the way of the sacred quest. From this focus you can comfort the angry feeling, make a choice about your connection to the person outside you, seek whatever is in this situation for you to learn and respond from your centeredness rather than angered outerness.

Most important, turn your attention away from blame to a loving presence within. Here you will find centeredness, love, solace, learning and solution—just by sitting with your attention on the inner emotion rather than blaming the other.

The love you activate for yourself within will begin to radiate out as you continue your journey of the sacred quest. Soon, there will be love where blame once was.

- *Remember that blaming is futile.* Paste this reminder from Emerson's *Self-Reliance* somewhere so you can read it daily:

    At home I dream that at Naples, at Rome I can be intoxicated with beauty and lose my sadness. I pack my trunk, embrace my friends, embark on the sea, and at last wake up in Naples, and there beside me is the stern fact, the sad self, unrelenting, identical, that I fled from.

    You see, blaming your surroundings is a futile exercise because wherever you go, you are still there. You must cultivate the inner knowing that everything in your life has been divinely designed by your collaboration with your highest self.

- *Be a learner instead of a blamer.* When silently meditating, ask, "What do I have to learn from this lesson?" rather than, "Why did he [or she] do this thing to me?" Reexamine the troublesome and traumatic events of your life. These are what you had to go through to arrive at this place on your path. See if you can view current happenings from the perspective of a few years hence.

    You will see that blame or fault-finding is a waste of your energy. All of these things had something beneficial for your development. With this perspective, you will begin sailing through traumas rather than being beached by them.

- *When you are inclined to get into the blaming habit, remind yourself that you are abandoning your loving inner presence.* If you've chosen the way of the sacred quest, you will no longer wish to ignore this part of your humanity.

Say to yourself, "I do not want to be right, I want to know the truth. I want my higher self to rule. No one is to blame for how I am feeling. It is my feeling and I respect that." These affirmations will lead you to self-reliance and to the way of the sacred quest.

Your spiritual soul will then become the guiding light for the remainder of your time in the nowhere.

Belief #3: Idealism Can't Coexist with Realism

"Don't be such a dreamer—be realistic." "Forget about your inner vision, look around you at what is happening. That is what is real."

Have you heard similar pronouncements often in your life? If so, you probably developed an attitude about what was possible and what was impossible. If the ideals that attracted you were labeled impossible, you probably sacrificed them for a way of viewing your world that was based on what others determined was "realistic."

Discarding that old belief about reality can be a major task on the path of the sacred quest. Are you ready to reconsider your view of reality? Perhaps William Blake's statement will inspire you:

If the doors of perception were cleansed,
Everything would appear as it is . . . infinite.

Can you imagine your reality in that way? Everything infinite? When your perception is expanded, nothing is real and nothing is imagined. All there is, is perception. When you cultivate this awareness, your reality is no longer defined by the physical world.

At the tiniest quantum level, time is not a reality. Particles can be in more than one place at the same time, and they appear and disappear according to how we observe them and what measuring devices we use. All of this constitutes a new reality. Always remember, *we are made of the same energy.*

Given this perspective, it is very important to hang on to your dreams and ideals. Quietly but determinedly, know that anything that you can conceive of you can manifest in the material world of physical reality.

If you want a richer experience of your life, abandon the idea that your reality is only what your senses report. Your inner world and all the energy of your higher awareness create a reality different from that which you have been taught.

In this reality, your higher spirit, the loving presence within you, is dominant and very real. In this world you rely on something quite different than ordinary reality. Choosing the way of the sacred quest means you will learn to rely on this new reality.

Shift back to being the idealist who had inner inklings about the world of spirit. That idealist within you will happily do the following according to Buddha:

Rely on the message of the teacher, not on his personality.
Rely on the meaning, not just on the words.
Rely on the real meaning, not on the provisional one.
Rely on your wisdom mind, not on your ordinary, judgmental mind.

SUGGESTIONS FOR RELEASING REALISM
AND WELCOMING IDEALISM

- *Trust your intuition.* Quietly affirm that you will define your own reality from now on and that your definition will be based on your inner wisdom.

  Your affirmation does not require you to judge what others define as their reality. Instead, you will see it as the path that they are on. This will help you nurture your idealistic energy, because you are giving yourself and others permission to trust the loving presence within all of us.

  There are no limits within, and within is where you are going from now on for your direction.

- *Make a list of all the things you believed in before you were told they were impossible.* Writing and drawing about those early beliefs will help to reenergize them.

  My early training convinced me that coincidences had nothing to do with "real" life. However, I now know that when I concentrate on manifesting something, coincidences happen to facilitate that vision. A recent example illustrates what I mean.

  I had gone to the western coast of Florida to work on this book and forgot to bring a portable tape player with me. When I unpacked, I thought of it and mentioned it to my wife in our nightly phone conversation. Before I went to sleep I could see the tape player in my mind and considered calling the front desk to see if one was available. But I didn't and went to sleep with a vision of the tape recorder.

  In the morning, I was preparing to start writing and I wished I had the tape deck to listen to some taped notes I'd made to myself. I turned on the lamp by the desk, and poof, it blew out. For a moment I felt frustrated, then I reminded myself that I was preparing to write about the divine design in our lives. I called Housekeeping and asked for a new light bulb.

Within minutes a man named Cliff arrived to replace the bulb. Cliff noticed my books, papers, typewriter and manuscripts strewn around the room and said, "I've always wanted to read your later books, especially *Real Magic,* but I just haven't gotten around to it. Now, I come to your room and meet you in person. What a coincidence!"

We chatted and I gave him a copy of *Real Magic,* telling him that I saw it not as coincidence but as evidence of the power of his inner thoughts. Then I thought to ask him if he knew where I might get a portable tape recorder for a few hours.

His response was immediate. "I have one in my car. You're welcome to use it while you're here. It would be my pleasure. In fact, I was noticing it in the car this morning and wondering why I have it there, since I never use the thing."

A coincidence? Perhaps. A conversation with my wife about wanting a tape recorder; a vision of it as I fell asleep; a light bulb burning out; Cliff wanting to read *Real Magic;* his decision to leave the tape recorder in his car, though he didn't know why. All of these events collaborating with fate?

In my reality, these events occur synchronistically when I am centered on my inner purpose. Call me an idealist if you want. *I* know that my reality is not exclusively defined by my five senses.

- *Practice experimenting with your new reality.* Keep a vision of what you want to occur or someone you want to call you. Anything that is important to you. Meditate on it manifesting into your life. Keep track of all the little things that lead up to bringing it about. After a while, you will notice that your reality has become one in which you play a role as cocreator.

Belief #4: There Is Only One Existence and It Is Physical

As a child, you were aware of a second aspect of your being. Here, I am calling that your double, or your ethereal body.

As you grew older you learned to discard this second self and to believe only in your physical self. The second body, your double, is an energy body that coexists with your physical body. This body of energy is not visible or discernible with the ordinary senses. Nevertheless, it coexists with your physical body at all times.

You have lost touch with this ethereal energy body. That does not mean that it is unavailable to you. Your physical body is what you've come to believe is who you are. Yet this body in and of itself is neutral. Your body can bring you neither peace nor turmoil.

By itself, your body has no purpose. It derives its purpose from the invisible self that is you. Thinking of your body as your reality is a mistaken perception of the ego. Your body is, more accurately, your chosen home for this tour of earth.

It is almost impossible to make contact with your higher self when you only believe in your false self and the material world. Somewhere within you, you are aware that all of the material world is energy. This energy appears solid from the perspective of your eyes, your perceptual equipment.

A closer look at the physical world reveals a dance of particles in endless voids of empty space. A closer look at those particles reveals that they are involved in another, tinier dance of more particles in a field of emptiness, ad infinitum until there is only energy and no particles. *This* is our reality. But we've been persuaded that what we see with the limitations of our eyes is the only reality there is. Your body is a part of that perceptual system you have been conditioned to accept.

.

Your task is to dissolve the barrier that separates these two aspects of your being. When you do this, you leap into the unimaginable.

Helen Keller, who lived without the use of almost all her five senses, made a profound observation concerning the ethereal body: "It gives me a deep comforting sense," she said, "that things seen are temporal and things unseen are eternal."

In childhood you probably could feel things without seeing them, as Helen Keller described. If you were not supported and encouraged to be this way by family or teachers, you abandoned those special feelings.

In *The Art of Dreaming,* Carlos Castaneda describes this phenomenon in a conversation with his spiritual teacher. They are discussing these currents of energy that are available to all of us. When asking who experiences them, he is told:

> "Every human being does for that matter, but average human beings are too busy with their own pursuits to pay any attention to feelings like that."
>
> "What do these currents feel like?"
>
> "Like a mild discomfort, a vague sensation of sadness followed immediately by euphoria. Since neither the sadness nor the euphoria has an explainable cause, we never regard them as veritable onslaughts of the unknown but as unexplainable, ill-founded moodiness."

On the path of the sacred quest you discover that the world you observe with your senses is not the only world there is. You become aware that you have a band of energy with you at all times, coexisting in every encounter of your life. This energy can help you make that leap into the world of spiritual consciousness.

Stop paying so much attention to the superficial pursuits of your life. Learn to turn within and know higher levels of awareness. You need to become acquainted with this part of yourself and believe in the energy of the loving presence that is a part of you. You will be able to use it to fulfill your divine purpose.

SUGGESTIONS FOR RELEASING YOUR BELIEF IN PHYSICAL EXCLUSIVITY

- *Open yourself to the possibility of other dimensions of reality being available to you.* Affirm to yourself that this is a possibility.

  Very few people believed in the existence of microscopic life before the invention of the microscope. There were zillions of tiny creatures swimming around in their own pool of reality, independent of anyone's opinion about them. They exist now in your skin, your eyes, fingernails and hair.

  All of those things that you sense to be solid are alive with invisible activity. Apply the same awareness to this notion. You can't see it, but you are an energy body and a physical body. Your double would like to introduce itself to you.

- *Begin to pay attention to rushes of energy, feelings that you cannot explain, currents that you experience but cannot relate to outer experience.* Start to notice the inner reality that you call feelings and try to focus on the invisible currents.

  Everything that you do, everyone that you meet, has an associated exchange of invisible energy. You can learn to store this energy. But first you must let go of judgment and notice the beauty in those people and events. Ultimately this will translate into love.

- *Slow yourself down with moments of contemplative silence.* Do nothing. In these moments, appreciate your body and all of your physical universe. Just be appreciative and notice the inner waves of pleasure that you are beginning to experience.

It is like someone tickling you very lightly with a feather. A sense of pleasure. As a child you loved this kind of experience. Try it with one of your children or grandchildren.

My children often ask me or their mother to tickle them this way. They become ecstatic as they enjoy the waves of energy up and down their backs.

Relive those experiences in your mind. Create your own inner goose bumps. Soon you will make contact with the energy body that coexists with you at all times.

BELIEF #5: WE ARE SEPARATE AND DISTINCT FROM EVERYONE ELSE

Our education emphasizes believing in sensory experiences. Such experiences seem to tell us that we are separate, unique, special and disconnected from each other. Very few of us learned that there is some kind of unity. The truth is that everything is linked, including you to all other beings.

While on a speaking tour with my friend and colleague Stuart Wilde in Australia, I had the opportunity to have long discussions with him concerning this matter of our interconnectedness. In *The Whispering Winds of Change*, Stuart gives an easy-to-understand explanation of our connectedness. Read his words and let them dissolve some of your old beliefs concerning our separateness:

We are all in a dialogue deep within the collective subconscious mind. That doesn't mean you can't be an independent particle out from the wave, it just means that we can communicate with each other. . . . Everything is linked. . . . If you come up with an idea that no man or woman has ever considered, the very fact you have had that thought will allow others instantaneously to think the same thing. We are interconnected because we come from the same place. Your body exists in the modern day, but its components are very ancient. . . . Every human came from that first compressed place as did every galaxy and all of the stars. We are one. We straddle time from its inception to this day.

Stuart also describes in depth how our bodies radiate heat like solar flares out to about an inch and electromagnetic flares out about three feet. He calls this the etheric energy and believes we can train ourselves to see it in each other.

The naked eye can be trained to observe this etheric energy by engaging the peripheral vision, which has been weakened over thousands of years of disuse. By tapping this etheric energy and training ourselves to use it, we can see the energy patterns of others.

Stuart showed me how to do this by tapping into the etheric energy of those who were unaware that he was making this demonstration. Here is an example from his book (I can attest to the veracity of this; I witnessed him doing the same thing in Australia):

Recently, I was sitting at a hotel in Hawaii. Between the hotel's restaurant and the sea is a foot path that holiday-makers wander along, going from one end of the beach to the other. Sitting there at dusk with friends discussing the etheric phenomena, I started to lock on to the passersby—what I call "tapping." I'd point out a passerby to my friends and then I'd tap that individual and make them turn toward me. I counted as I ran through about forty people. Only four failed to turn.

In *The Whispering Winds of Change,* Stuart describes how to create this awareness in yourself.

The notion of being a unified oneness defies our senses and most everything we've observed. We look at others and see a distance. We conclude that because there is space, there is no connection.

I spend a lot of time walking on the beach. I always marvel at the shore birds as they fly along the ocean surface in large groups. The entire group will turn left and then swerve simultaneously to the right, then swoop up. They appear connected, as if sharing one mind. I know that there is a connection, even though each bird appears to be disconnected. Some invisible energy permits them to move together as one.

This invisible energy also connects you to everyone else. When you recognize this, you will let go of your sense of separateness. Once you are inwardly convinced of your connectedness to all, you will become aware of your ability to communicate with others through your etheric energy.

Your knowing will reveal to you that your thoughts can be projected to the rest of the world. Your knowing will also reveal your connectedness to higher awareness.

While reading the Rig-Veda (Hindu Scriptures) I came across a passage that clarified this better than anything I'd read before:

Truth is one; sages call it by various names,
    it is one sun which reflects in all ponds.
It is the one water which slakes the thirst of all;
    It is the one air which sustains all life.
    It is the one fire which shines in all houses.
Colors of the cows may be different, but milk is white.
Flowers and bees may be different, but honey is the
    same.
    Systems of faith may be different, but God is one.
As the rain dropping from the sky wends its way
    toward the ocean,

So the prayers offered in all faiths reach the one God, who is supreme.

One light, many colors; one water, many thirsts; one essence, many shapes of human. But still we are all connected. Failing to see the connector with our eyes does not mean that it is not there.

Discard the belief that you are separate from everyone else. You will acquire a reverence for everyone that will turn into love.

SUGGESTIONS FOR RELEASING THE BELIEF IN YOUR SEPARATENESS

- *As you consider this idea of oneness, remind yourself that every ugly thought that you have toward another is something you are thinking about yourself.* Every attempt at revenge or harming another is a dig at yourself. If you can begin to think this way, you will understand Jesus Christ's statement: "For they know not what they do." It means they know not that they harm themselves and everyone else when they harm anyone.

- *Practice tapping into your etheric energy by using the technique offered by Stuart Wilde.* Train your peripheral vision and practice connecting to others with this energy. This ability to tap into the energy field of others can be used to demonstrate to you that there is a connection that exists even though you cannot observe it with your senses. This inward documentation will help you to treat everyone you encounter with reverence.

- *Know you have the ability to communicate telepathically.* I encourage you to read *Mutant Message Down Under,* by Marlo Morgan. Marlo was in her fifties, a white woman who found herself on a spiritual journey with a tribe of aborigines in the desert of Australia.

She trekked for over one thousand kilometers during a period of several months. One of her many keen observations was how these people, who had no radios or telegraph systems, had not lost their *natural* abilities to communicate over long distances. She observed communication patterns between people as much as twenty miles apart.

If you rely on the available technology for all of your long-distance communication, you have lost your telepathic abilities. But the ability is still there. Banish the doubt and use this amazing capacity to further your sacred quest.

- *Follow the most important guideline ever passed on to us from the spiritual world: "Love thy neighbor as thyself."* Make this a daily affirmation.

    Sometimes we forget that we love each other. We fight needlessly. Remind yourself of this. You will be acknowledging your connection by loving others as you love yourself.

BELIEF #6: THERE'S AN "US" VERSUS A "THEM"

This opinion is related to the previous one. When you know that you are connected to others there is no Them. However, you've been influenced by a Them-versus-Us civilization. Some of the signposts of this style of civilization are the following:

- *Us is family.* Everyone outside of the family is Them.

Identify with the clan and you know where you belong. When this doesn't work, then:

- *Us is some of the family.* Some family members are ostracized from the Us group. They are then a part of Them. Or:

- *Sometimes Us is only your immediately family:* yourself, your spouse and your children. But when the children develop different values and ideas, then:

- *Us is you and your spouse.* Everyone else is Them. But now you start to notice that your spouse is different, so:

- *Us is you and your new spouse* and maybe the new children. The ex-spouse is Them. But now you notice that your new family is difficult so:

- *Us is coworkers.* Everyone in another company is Them. But soon you start to notice that there are many on the job who want your job and are competing for your position, so you shift to . . .

It sounds silly, but you know there is truth in this silliness. The way of the ego is to define who is with you and who is not.

I have been told many times that I could charge a higher speaking fee, based on what others with similar professional credentials charge. When I'm told this, it feels like an Us-versus-Them situation, which is unacceptable for me in my life. The point seems to be that *They* will pay more if I request it. But I see myself connected to the all and can't charge more if it seems to me to be exorbitant.

My purpose is to get the message out into the world and help people to be self-reliant and collaborate with their higher awareness. The more people who hear this message, the more my purpose is fulfilled. Consequently, I now encourage the sponsors of my talks to tape my presentations and keep the money they make from selling the tapes to their audiences.

The people who hire me to speak are no longer a part of a category labeled Them. We're an Us teaching global self-reliance and helping change the consciousness of the world. Those who hear the tapes want to hear more. They go to bookstores and purchase books, tell others about them and talk about the message. Allowing others to be entrepreneurs recording my presentation and selling tapes has created a network of people who are promoting the ideas I talk about.

When we lose our sense of Us versus Them, and know that we are all Us, then we have a win-win relationship with life.

SUGGESTIONS FOR RELEASING US-VERSUS-THEM THINKING

- *Practice letting go of your ego's needs to be separate from others*. Begin viewing yourself as a member of the human family called Us.

    Share your "toys" with others, especially neighbors and even strangers, as if they were a part of your family. As the English proverb says, "The hand that gives, gathers."

- *Treat everyone as if they are part of the tribe you love belonging to*. Don't mentally note their difference. Carry an inner determination to see others just as much a part of you on a spiritual level as is your child or your spouse.

    Create an affirmation expressing the idea that you are my brother, my sister. You are a part of my Us. There are no more Thems in my life.

• *Note how many times you use the pronoun "I" in an hour.* Eliminate some of them! Instead of talking about yourself and your immediate Us group, inquire about others.

When you don't focus on yourself as distinct from others, you have more energy to extend your awareness outward. The constant use of "I" indicates a strong attachment to an Us life attitude.

• *Think globally rather than locally.* People who look different, who speak a different language, who have different beliefs—are a part of Us. We are all in nowhere together. In the eyes of the loving presence there are no favorites.

Begin to practice this inner awareness. Seek the divinity and connectedness. Focus on the similarities among us rather than the superficial things that make us appear to be different.

BELIEF #7: PETTY TYRANTS SHOULD BE IGNORED

You have been taught to believe that there are some bad people in the world who are best ignored. I am suggesting the contrary.

Everyone who comes into your life in any capacity is valuable. The petty tyrants in your life are just as divine as those who provide you with encouragement and support. Emerson put this important lesson like this: "The whole course of things goes to teach us faith." The *whole course.* This means everything that comes your way.

Perhaps the single most significant person in my life, the one person who made the greatest difference for me and my own spiritual development, is a person who by all accounts was a petty tyrant. This man was my father.

He abandoned his family, spent time in prison as a petty criminal and was abusive toward his wife. At the age of forty-nine he died from excessive use of alcohol. I have no memory of him. My knowledge of him is based on what I heard and later discovered to be true when I investigated his life.

Yet this petty tyrannical con man was the main character leading to my transformation. I wrote about forgiving my father in *You'll See It When You Believe It.* I discarded the hatred and bitterness that I had carried with me for a lifetime. A single act of forgiveness and letting go opened the way to my sacred quest and the writing, speaking and living of the miracles I write about.

I learned what I had to transcend. When I now occasionally slip into some of the behaviors that I know destroyed his life, I remind myself that this is not my path. This is not the kind of father I wish to be. This is not the kind of man I wish to be. It is his example that helps me get myself back to the path that I know is my spiritual destiny.

God indeed works in mysterious ways. That which we judge to be unfortunate and evil can teach us our greatest lessons.

The bully in your life, pushing your fear and panic buttons, might just be God in disguise, teaching you how to rely on your own wits and transcend this petty tyrant's behavior. The thief who cons you out of your money could represent a divine lesson teaching you to let go and not be attached to your things. The drug pusher may be teaching you how to experience addiction and down-in-the-gutter depression so that you will transcend this reliance on external substances for your highs in life.

All people, and I do mean *all,* are in your life to teach you valuable lessons. Don't ignore those lessons. Get the message and bless them, and move on. When you ignore them, or simply dismiss them as evil, you fail to understand the truth Emerson knew: Truly, the "whole course of things goes to teach us faith."

So don't ignore parts of the course by judging them worthless.

SUGGESTIONS FOR RELEASING DISDAIN FOR PETTY TYRANTS

- *Be thankful for those petty tyrants.* They are there for a very important reason. Ignoring them guarantees that more of them will appear in different bodies later on in your life. Prayers of thankfulness are wonderful affirmations of this truth.

  The experience of being deserted by a spouse might teach you to be independent. This type of situation may introduce you to the loving presence within. Perhaps you will learn the difference between aloneness and loneliness and decide to love the person you are alone with.

  The alcoholic years can teach us that we are greater than any substance. We might learn to be thankful for those drunken teachers and consider them instructors from God. Even physical abuse may have a powerful lesson in it. We may discover that we are more than a body. It's possible for us to know that no one can reach our inner self with their blows.

- *Make a list of all the people you have written out of your life as evil or scumbags.* Write down everything that their presence taught you. Have you learned to not repeat victim behaviors?

  Reconsider that so-called scumbag's value to your life. You could not have learned the lesson without the person. The evidence for this is that you obviously needed to bring that person into your life—because you did.

- *Look for the fullness of God in everyone.* Realize that in some unfathomable way the fullness is operating even if you cannot see or feel it. Remind yourself that the other is not his or her body.

Belief #8: Goals Are Essential

for Success

So many aphorisms guide our lives. One of the most erroneous is that we have to know where we are going in order to get there. Nothing could be further from the truth of success. I am pretty much convinced that there is a formula for failure (trying to please everyone and ignoring our inner impulses), but I do not believe there is a formula for success.

Living the spiritual life does not mean setting goals and following them assiduously. The way of the sacred quest is different than that. The difference is sensed in this little stanza by Rumi, a Sufi poet who lived a thousand years ago:

Do you think I know what I am doing?
That for one breath or half-breath I belong to myself?
As much as a pen knows what it's writing,
or the ball can guess where it's going next.

As an instrument of God you are ever in the presence of a loving guidance. With this inner awareness you will not lose sight of yourself and become a homeless bum begging for your next meal if that is not the way of *your* sacred quest. You will know your purpose, pursue it with vigor and trust the universe to handle the details.

It is this kind of awareness that has led me to work

even harder and produce more effectively and feel more purposeful. Not a set of goals that I strove toward. I can truly identify with Rumi in this regard. I have never known where I am going. I quiet myself, listen and then allow myself to be guided.

Having goals is a way of abandoning now in favor of a plan for some future now. The absence of a lot of specific goals helps cultivate your awareness that you are not alone on this journey. You begin to trust in the divine guidance to assist you in your present moment. You come to know the universe will handle the details if you surrender and let go somewhat. This is probably inconsistent with all that you have been taught. But that is the purpose of this chapter—to help you erase the personal history that you no longer believe or want, to help you begin in the now with your new awareness.

Have you been told that you must attend certain schools for a specific curriculum? I want you to know that it doesn't matter what school you attend.

If you have the inner drive to know something or excel in a given area, nothing will dissuade you. There are books in all kinds of libraries—at small community colleges, in your home town. You will find them! If you are at a prestigious Ivy League school and you don't have that inner drive, your presence in that location will not make a bit of difference.

Whatever it is that you want to know or accomplish in your life, if you are truly ready and trust in your divine powers to manifest it, the teachers will be there. You will be guided. Money will not make a difference. If you want the education (or anything else), you will find a way to create it.

Only you are responsible for what you think. It is at this level that you exercise choice. I encourage you to change your thinking about the importance of goals. Instead, have a divine idea of how you would like to serve and help and how to improve the quality of life for others. You will find the way.

Far more important than goals in your life is your willingness to allow things to happen and your willingness to know. Willingness is the key. As it says in the *Course in Miracles,* "Miracles are merely the sign of your willingness to follow the Holy Spirit's plan."

I had no idea as a teenager that I would become a writer and lecturer. Nevertheless, I was writing a great deal as a teenager, and I was practicing public speaking— first as a student in speech class to help me overcome my fears, then as a schoolteacher, later as a professor and then as an after-dinner speaker at charity events.

I had only an inner understanding that I was being propelled in this direction and a willingness to go with that inner pull. I have always loved writing, but I had no goal to write books or articles. I only had an unfolding experience of being willing to write and exercising the discipline to accomplish it.

Goals seem to be etched-in-stone plans that one must follow. I recommend that you relax about your future and simply allow yourself to be propelled in the direction that God has in mind with you.

SUGGESTIONS FOR RELEASING THE IMPORTANCE OF GOALS FOR SUCCESS

• *Be willing!* This is the most important suggestion I can offer. Be willing to do whatever it takes to turn that inner knowing and future pull into your reality.

  Take a look at a simple tulip bulb and you will see what looks like a grungy mass of brown biological matter. But you know that somewhere within the confines of that bulb, in the invisible world that defies measurement, there exists a future pull. If it is planted and nourished it will become exactly what it is destined to become, and nothing else, because it has a built-in picture of its future. It will not become a better tulip by being tugged at and coaxed as it emerges from the ground. It will be all that it is going to be according to its inner picture. Creation will reveal its secrets regardless of your goals.

The same is true for you. With your higher awareness you can choose your inner pictures. Keep the picture and refuse to allow anyone to smudge it. Be willing to do what it takes to make the picture your reality by listening to the loving presence, by facing inward. This is a different way than setting outer goals.

- *Keep in mind that your job is simply not to interfere.* You will enjoy a fuller life and more happiness if you stop interfering with the plans and goals. Instead, be willing to receive God's plan.

  The absence of interference translates to a conscious surrendering of worrying about and organizing everything in your life. When you know that it is all in divine order, and that you are a part of an intelligent system, you can follow your inner pleas without the need for a detailed map. This is the way of the sacred quest.

- *Relax about the future and let it go.* Instead, make an active commitment to enjoy this day a little more. The more peaceful you are with yourself and your role here, the more productive and efficient you become. It is very difficult to accomplish anything when you are stressed over the outcome. When you relax and get peaceful, you become inspired and efficient.

  Toss out the goals and live your life knowing that you are cocreating it.

BELIEF #9: YOU MUST ALWAYS DO YOUR BEST

Throughout our lives we hear: "I don't really care how well you do, as long as you do your best." Examine this idea and you may come up with a different conclusion.

You don't really have to do your best. In fact, your best is something that you can never measure or even know. You can drive yourself to neurotic extremes with this idea of having to always do your best.

Your best leaves no room for improvement. It means that you have to go all-out, 100 percent every single time you do anything.

When you remove the stigma of having to perform at a given level, you remove the ego's need to be judged better than others. You are better off to simply do and enjoy and be willing to learn.

Doing your best involves enormous stress and pressure. You are measuring yourself against a standard imposed on you by your well-meaning caretakers and sponsors of the past. There is no peace in doing your best, there is only constant striving to acquire a "best" badge.

Having to constantly measure yourself against externally imposed achievement levels that come under the rubric of "your best" puts you in the position of having your life controlled by those externals. You cannot be self-directed when the demands of the ego are your constant companions.

Your higher self simply wants you to be at peace, to feel blissful and purposeful. When you have to measure this against "your best" you give the control of your life to your ego.

The way of the sacred quest is to become a sensible person, which is different than striving to do your best. The ancient book of wisdom the Tao-te Ching comments on what it is that constitutes a sensible person:

The five colors can blind,
The five tones deafen,
The five tastes cloy,
The race, the hunt, can drive men mad
And their booty leaves them no peace.
Therefore the sensible man
Prefers the inner to the outer eye.

The inner self has no "best" to perform, it simply listens and knows, and goes about its business in a purposeful manner, with no concern for how everything turns out. When you get to purpose in your life, you are in the process of being spiritual, and you cannot measure this with worldly formulas such as "your best" or "the best."

SUGGESTIONS FOR RELEASING THE BELIEF THAT YOU HAVE TO DO YOUR BEST

- *Stop imposing on yourself and your children the belief that you must do your best.* Experiment with performing tasks that seem to flow from your inner promptings. But detach yourself from the need to measure to see whether your efforts have been worthwhile.

- *While meditating, get a picture of yourself being able to do anything.* Give yourself permission to be with this image and to forget about the outcome. See how peaceful you feel when you are not being tested, when you are allowed to just be. Give yourself this same permission in all of your daily undertakings.

  You will find, ironically, that your performance will improve and that you feel more energized. This is because you are enjoying the moment rather than thinking about how well you're doing.

- *Make an effort to compliment others without focusing on the outcome.* They will be grateful for your interest and for your not telling them that they always have to do their best.

You will find that there are a few things you want to excel at. In these areas of interest you will be more diligent. But in all other areas of your life, you simply want to do. You don't have to take the best walk of your life or the best bicycle ride or play the best softball game.

I have run seven marathons and not once did I do my very best. If I had, I would have had faster and faster times. This kind of pressure would have kept me from running at all, since I run to relieve pressure rather than to take more on.

Had I insisted that I had to do my best, I would not be able to say I ran seven marathons. That kind of pressure eliminates so many of life's pleasures and puts the ego at the controls of daily life.

BELIEF #10: DREAMS ARE NOT REALITY

Most of us were taught to believe in two separate realities. One is our waking reality, the other is our dream reality.

In this formula, when we are in a dream state, we are in a world that is unreal. We disregard dreams as a mental exercise that happens while we sleep. All of the things that we create during those dreaming hours are considered not real. Waking consciousness is considered reality, and dreaming consciousness is treated as an unreality. I suggest you reconsider this belief.

Imagine that your dreams are simply different aspects of the same reality, and that they contain teachers for you on your sacred path. Begin with understanding that this is primarily a world of energy and only secondarily a world of material objects.

To know your sacred self you need to perceive energy directly. This is what you are capable of doing in your dream state. The entire basis of your perception shifts from concrete objects to energy shapes. When this is part of your reality, your dream state becomes something that you share with other spiritually attuned beings.

Eventually you can be aware that you are dreaming while you are dreaming. This is called lucid dreaming. In lucid dreaming you can control your dreams and be able to dream awake. Through the process of dreaming you perceive other dimensions of reality, which are shut out by your conditioning.

I am not writing about dream interpretation. I am talking about knowing your dream life and being aware of experiencing dimensions of a reality while you are sleeping, which will also become available in your waking moments.

Your dreams are created with the same body and the same brain as is the rest of your perceptual world. It is all yours—you do not leave every night and take on a new brain to experience your nighttime reality.

Everything that you are capable of knowing and being convinced of in your dream has a potential for being experienced at all moments of your daily life. Everything! Yes, this is a radical notion, but it leads you to know the power of your energy body.

You enter your dreaming world with a complete absence of doubt about what you can experience. With that absence of doubt there are absolutely no limits. When you awaken to what you call your waking consciousness, you still have the same body, brain and perceptual equipment, but you introduce doubt.

I believe that your dreams do not reveal things about you but that they are you. They are real and they can become highly effective in helping you to experience your highest spiritual self.

Suggestions for Releasing a Disbelief in Dreams

- *When you go to sleep, encourage yourself to be aware that you are entering your dream state.* Just this awareness is the first step toward higher awareness through dreaming. As you drift off, make a mental note to yourself that you are about to enter the dream state and that you are pleased to be aware of it.

- *Make an effort, before you drift off, to consciously see elements of your upcoming dream.* Tell yourself you will make a note of an object, a room or a specific location while you are in the dream. Experience as much detail as you can concerning the object while dreaming.

  If it is a lamp, for instance, bring it closer to you with the power of your mind. Examine the color, shape and intensity of the light.

  You want to make direct contact with your energy body, that special body of energy that coexists at all times with your physical body. By examining the content of your dreams you will give yourself access to this higher energy. You will prove to yourself that your mental energy is a phenomenon that you can manipulate with practice and effort. Eventually you will be able to access this energy in all moments of your life.

  Your energy body has appearance but no mass. Get familiar with this appearance of your energy and know that it can transport you anywhere in the universe with your command. Sounds strange, but it is within you to make this happen. First in your sleeping dreams and then in your waking dreams.

- *See if you can make yourself go from one dream back to another, and then return to the same dream.* As you drift off, first become aware of your upcoming dreaming state; then, while in the dream, become aware that you are dreaming, and shift to another dream. After years of experience I have been able to do this only on an occasional basis. But give it a try. It will give you practice for the ultimate key to higher awareness: cultivating the witness. (This is discussed in detail in chapter 5.)

- *Make an attempt to observe yourself dreaming.* Carlos Castaneda calls this the third gate of dreaming. In *The Art of Dreaming,* he writes, "The third gate of dreaming is reached when you find yourself in a dream, staring at someone else who is asleep. And that someone else turns out to be you."

  This is a state of heightened awareness wherein your physical self is being witnessed by your energy self, and you are conscious of it taking place. You are conscious of simultaneously dreaming and watching yourself dream.

  This is a shift—from what you've been told about dreaming, into a new world, a world that allows you to become a sleeping dreamer and a waking dreamer and to begin to punctuate your waking life with the magic of dreaming consciousness.

- *Become aware of your dreams and see if you can shift to lucid dreaming each night.* When you awaken in the middle of the night, note the content and objects of your dreams, and then reenter them while staying conscious of your dream state.

  It is in this realm of dreaming and waking consciousness that you are going to get to know the existence of the highest energy in the universe.

This concludes my list of ten of the most erroneous beliefs you have been taught. Shedding the past is simply a matter of changing your mind without any accompanying anger or guilt about what you were taught to believe. All that you were exposed to was in divine order. All of the exams that life has presented to you were a part of the curriculum you signed up for when you elected to travel from no-where to now-here.

Be thankful for it all, and be thankful that you are ready to transcend those beliefs. This book is in your hands with the same divine providence that guides your sacred guest. And keep in mind that any beliefs that you hold on to that no longer serve you are impertinent intruders into your life. Let them go.

Now is the time to begin recognizing the four keys to higher awareness. They are the subject of the next four chapters.

Part II

THE FOUR KEYS TO HIGHER AWARENESS

When the five senses are stilled, when the mind is stilled, when the intellect is stilled, that is called the highest state by the wise.

—KATHA UPANISHAD

4

BANISH THE DOUBT

Our doubts are our traitors.
—SHAKESPEARE

I rid myself of my doubts by
remembering that there
is a valid reason for
everything that happens.

※

In the first part of this book I described the ideas and opinions you've been exposed to that have probably influenced your life. Many of those ideas, given to you by others, may now be your daily reality, defining for you what is possible and impossible in your life.

I've encouraged you to abandon many of those beliefs and make a new agreement with reality that is based instead on what you *know* is your truth. Once you know your personal truth, your reality will be free of doubt.

You might not think that doubt could have much of an effect on your life. But part of the damage that it creates is that it is so thoroughly etched on to your belief system that it becomes impossible to think any other way. Doubting our potential achievements, we proclaim with certainty just what is and what is not possible. But when doubt is banished, we come to a knowing that leads to creative and inspired solutions far beyond what we *believed* was possible.

With the attitude of doubt you are unable to successfully

tread the path of your sacred quest and realize your sacred self. Be steadfast in recognizing this obstacle to higher awareness. You will need to deliberately and actively work at banishing doubt from your inner world. When it is removed from your thoughts it will disappear from your outer world, and you will find yourself on a most satisfying inner and outer journey.

Andrew Cohen, in his blissfully simple book *Enlightenment Is a Secret: Teachings of Liberation,* explains one way to get rid of doubt:

Q: I'm not clear on how to get rid of doubt.

A: By throwing it out. If you saw your child playing in the kitchen, noticed she had found a bottle of rat poison and could see she was about to drink it, what would you do?

Q: I would slap it out of her hand.

A: Yes. Because you know how dangerous it is. When you know how dangerous doubt is, you will do the same thing. An ignorant person doesn't realize how dangerous doubt is, so they allow themselves to indulge in doubt and by doing so they destroy the possibility of truly waking up in this birth.

As you begin banishing doubt from your life with this first key to higher awareness, recall this dialogue and how simple it is.

The presence of doubt can prevent you from awakening. Seven simple words describe why that is true: *As you think, so shall you be.* We do become what we think about all day long. Don't allow your thoughts and actions to be dictated by doubt.

Permitting doubt is the same as having a traitor at the helm of your life. Doubt is a traitor because it uses limitations and shortcomings to influence the course of your life. To travel the path of the sacred quest, guided by your higher self, means you must banish doubt.

Can you imagine your reality if you were brought up in an environment free of doubt? How would your life be different if you had never heard, "It can't be done," "That's not possible," "Accept your limitations"? What if you had been encouraged to exercise the energy of your mind? You might have used that energy to explore your power to influence other beings, things, the weather, your creativity.

That may sound a bit weird to you. But remember, you are assessing the possible and the impossible with doubts that automatically creep in when anyone suggests something you believe to be outlandish or absurd. If you had been fortunate enough to be raised without doubt you would possess an incredible inner sense of your magnificence.

Never would you utter sentences that reflect doubt, such as: "I'm not talented enough," "It can't be done, get real," and "Don't you know there are limits to everything?" With doubt-free processes you would have had a handle on your divinity much earlier in your life. You would have known your inner capacity to create the world and tackle social evils and ills with no doubts about your ability to create Utopia.

You would know that mankind is fundamentally good. Human shortcomings would not be blamed on inherent inferiority or the devil. Satisfaction of the ego's demands would be known as the activity that created those shortcomings.

The sacred self knows no doubt. It has no limits and no boundaries. What would our world be like if we had learned this in childhood? It is time to know that we have a personal responsibility to incorporate the sacred quest in our lives and to introduce our children to this aspect of human life.

I offer my own children opportunities to learn about their inner limitlessness in a variety of ways. For example, I invite them outside with me to make clouds. After dinner, we often take a blanket outside to lie down on, and we engage in what has come to be called cloud making.

The children start by creating an inner picture of a form they want to see in the clouds. Then they concentrate their energy on a particular cloud, attempting to influence it to design their inner picture. The neighborhood has gotten used to hearing my kids shout, "I'm making a house, Daddy. Watch my cloud move. I'm moving it with my mind!"

Many of the children in the neighborhood may be thinking, "Those Dyer kids are crazy, actually believing they can make clouds into designs." But why shouldn't children learn that they have the same divine intelligence flowing through them that moves the clouds? If it is in everything, which we know is true, then it is in both my children and the clouds. Why not feel so connected to it that they use it to make their own cloud shapes? Our children have very few doubts, and this inner knowing allows them to create the world that they want for themselves.

You do the very same thing every night when you go to sleep. You enter your dreaming experience with a complete absence of doubt. In fact, you are unable to bring doubt into this nightly divine kingdom. It is as if God has a "No Doubts Allowed" sign at the entrance to your dreams.

In your dream state you are able to do anything that your mind can create. You can fly, visit the past, project into the future, converse with the long departed, see those who have died and know that they are there with you, jump over tall trees, breathe underwater, create dozens of characters and perform an endless list of other activities and scenes. For this one-third of your life when you are asleep, you have no doubt—and hence no limitations.

Then, when you wake up, you instantly introduce your constant companion, doubt, back into your waking consciousness. Awake, you believe that those things are not possible for you in your waking moments. The difference is that in your sleep you *know* what you can do and you do it; in your waking moments, you *believe* that you can't, and you don't.

Take time to really examine carefully the difference between these two opposing attitudes.

WHAT YOU KNOW—WHAT YOU BELIEVE

If you are able to make a clear distinction between that which you know and that which you believe, you will recognize the crucial role doubt plays in your life. The ultimate goal of putting this into practice is to shift all beliefs into knowings.

Here are the main distinctions between that which you believe to be true and that which you know to be true.

- *Beliefs are handed to you. Knowings come from within.* Your entire inventory of beliefs was handed to you by people who have come into your life for this purpose. In chapter 2 I outlined ten of these most common beliefs and gave suggestions for turning them around. Now I ask you to examine *all* of your beliefs. As you do this, think of yourself as a sponge that absorbed the beliefs of others and then called them your own.

  Throughout your life you've been subjected to thousands of beliefs, ranging from what the moon is made of, to how people should react to each other, to whether sports were of any value, to the edict that poetry is for sissies, to how fast human beings can run, to what your neighbors are really like, to what you are capable of achieving, to the fact that you are just like your father and his father. There is a long list of things that you believe about yourself, the world, God, your potential, the fate of capitalism and so much more. These beliefs, which came to you from outside of yourself, became your very own dance.

Your knowings, however, all came to you as a result of your own experience of having decided to transcend a belief. No one can hand you a knowing. You must have the direct experience of the decision-making function to make it a known.

I could talk to you forever about how to ride a bicycle, or even why it is impossible given the laws of balance and air/speed/wind ratios. You could have a belief about bicycle riding, but you will know that it is possible only when you get on, wobble about a few times and then experience it. Once you have experienced bicycle riding, then no one, ever, can convince you that you should believe that it is impossible.

All of your knowings are like this. They come from the direct experience of your own life, and therefore they exist within you free of doubt.

- *Beliefs will let you down in a crisis. Knowings never let you down.* When you believe in something without knowing it, there is doubt attached to the belief. The doubt resides somewhere deep in the recesses of your mind. Nevertheless, it exists as a thought that you will ultimately call upon when you want to put that belief into practice.

I remember believing that I couldn't do a backward dive into the swimming pool. Every time I said to myself, This time I can do it, that nagging little doubt would surface at precisely the moment I would attempt the back dive. I'd find my body turning around at the very last second. The tiny doubt attached to the belief about my ability was what I relied upon at the moment of execution.

If you believe something based only on what others have told you is true, when a big test shows up, that belief will often let you down. Suppose that you believe that you are capable of riding a motorcycle. If you try to escape a dangerous situation by taking advantage of a motorcycle that happens to be there, the chances are high that the doubt attached to your belief will keep you from escaping on that nearby motorcycle.

That which you *know* can never let you down. Ever! If you had absolute certainty about your ability to jump on that motorcycle and zoom away, that knowing would propel you away safely. Because a knowing is not laced with internal doubt, you have absolute certainty about your position. This becomes true in everything that you experience, both physically and metaphysically.

If you have a belief that God will be there for you in a moment of trauma, and that any suffering that you are experiencing is just as divine as any joy that you have experienced, *but you do not know this,* you will find the pain of your disappointment will become an affirmation that God doesn't really exist for you. Your belief will be shattered in a moment of trauma. This is because you are attempting to have a vision of God that has come to you from outside of yourself and it is weakened with doubt.

Knowing God and suffering in the way William Blake wrote about in the following poem would pull you through your trauma "safely," as the poet suggests:

Man was made for Joy & Woe
And when this we rightly know
Thro the World we safely go
Joy & Woe are woven fine
A clothing for the soul divine.

Knowings can never let you down because they are woven into the fabric of your being. If you cannot doubt that which you are, and you know that you are, then you will never be disappointed. Again, beliefs have that insidious doubt attached to them, while knowings are free of such contamination.

- *Your beliefs are mental exercises. Your knowings are physical exercises.* Your beliefs are located in the mental realm as thoughts that you constantly reinforce. Your behaviors in the world are strongly affected by the limitations of those beliefs. These are strictly mental exercises that you constantly practice until they become your reality—that is, a reality based upon the doubt that is attached to these beliefs.

You may believe that people shouldn't wear jewelry in their noses, or that people who don't attend church are evil. These kinds of beliefs will influence your conduct and cause you to judge others (until you change your belief and perhaps search out a nose piercer!).

Your knowings are located in the physical domain, even though they originated in the mental. When you know something, it is a part of your total being, originating in the mental and residing in your complete being.

That which you absolutely know with certainty—such as how to dance the mambo, or ice skate, or swim, or make love or ride a bicycle—is a part of your cellular being. It resides so deeply within you that it is in the cells of your humanity. That which you once only believed, because it was given to you by some external person, has now been transferred into a knowing. All of your physical knowings began as beliefs and ended up with this certainty.

You may also have some beliefs within you that you actually treat as knowings. These include beliefs that are so strongly ingrained that they act like knowings within you. Some of these entrenched beliefs may be judged by you to be knowings, but they really are not.

For example, you may believe that you have no talent for art, but somewhere deep within your consciousness there exists a tiny smidgen of doubt about whether it would prove really true were you to actually apply yourself in a new way. Similarly, you may believe that you cannot master a foreign language, but you also have some doubt about this proving true were you in a situation where your life was at stake.

When you know something, it becomes your physical reality and you act on this knowing at all times. When you merely believe something, whether it be negative or positive, you have a tiny tiny bit of doubt connected to it, and that doubt becomes your reality. Beliefs are mental. Knowings are physical, though they originate as mental beliefs.

- *Beliefs restrict you. Knowings empower you.* Since your beliefs are imposed upon you, they are literally the inner workings of other beings within you. Therefore, your beliefs do not resonate with authenticity in your daily life.

  That ever-present shadow of doubt about whether these beliefs are true for you, even if they were true for your ancestors, tends to place restrictions upon you. Your thoughts create your reality. Any thought that you doubt is like a restriction upon yourself.

  That which you know empowers you to higher and higher levels of awareness. When your heart knows something is right and you follow your heart, you experience progress and growth. The inner knowing permits you to take the step that you would have avoided had you listened to your mind.

  Louise Hay is a perfect example of what I am writing about. She is a beautiful and sensitive woman who has written many powerful books on healing and is the publisher of a collection of my personal affirmations and daily reminders titled *Everyday Wisdom*. We were on a national television hook-up together when a caller asked whether Louise had ever considered any traditional approaches to treating her cancer eight years earlier. Louise gave the kind of answer that I hope you will be able to cultivate as you see how knowing can empower you to higher levels than you might have considered. She responded, "I knew in my heart that I could not allow them to radiate me or put chemicals into me or cut me. . . . I just knew that this could not be my method for dealing with this cancer. My knowing led me to other alternatives, which I have written about, and ultimately to the eradication of the cancer from my body. I am not disparaging any other form of treatment, I just knew inwardly that I couldn't go in that direction."

The key here is her use of the word "knew." She didn't *believe* in an alternative therapy, she *knew* that those traditional methods were inconsistent with who she was. She consulted her knowing. That knowing empowered her.

When you learn not only to abandon beliefs but to convert them into knowings, you will have only that inner knowing to consult when traumas surface in your life. A mere belief is simply a mental note attached to your lapel by your mommy. A knowing is etched into the cells of your being and therefore lives within you with an absence of doubt.

- *Your beliefs are transitory. Your knowings are eternal.* Think about many of the beliefs that you have today and how they have shifted over the years. In fact, many of the beliefs that you now hold were met with revulsion and disgust when you first experienced them.

  Can you remember how many people were shocked to see men wearing long hair and earrings when this style of dress was first introduced? Many tried to get these young men banned from schools. They labeled them sissies and weirdos. Today those same people sport shoulder-length hair themselves and watch football played by mastodons of masculinity with earrings and long hair protruding from their helmets.

Beliefs change. Many of the beliefs that you hold today will be rejected by you in the coming years.

For example, I receive letters almost daily from people who tell me that when they first heard me talking about some of these ideas two decades ago they thought I was promoting selfishness, and today they find those same ideas comforting. As for me, I find my ideas on God and spirituality have changed drastically since my earlier agnostic days as a teenager and very young adult.

My ideas on welfare, capital punishment, politics and evil have altered. As a young man I only *believed* with a strong conviction. I didn't *know,* and I always had some doubt about my position on these issues, particularly because I studied spiritual masters who had ideas that conflicted with mine.

Those things that you have had a knowing about are still with you today, even though you have undergone a complete physical transformation. Imagine this! Today you are in a body that did not exist on the physical plane only a decade ago. Every cell of your being has been replaced by new cells.

You have new legs, arms, arteries and even a new brain. The actual molecules of your physical being are constantly changing. You are being replaced even as you read these words. Millions of atoms come and go, forming new physical parts for you, even though those new parts look identical to the old ones.

This is the phenomenal part: although you are not the same body that you were a few years ago, your knowings have somehow been transferred from the old body to the new one—not physically but *meta* (beyond) *physically.*

I knew how to ice skate as a young boy and I still know how, even though I stayed away from this activity for thirty years. The knowing is still with me, even though I have new legs and feet and a totally new brain.

So you can see that when you know something in the cells of your being, it stays with you even though your physical being is constantly undergoing inevitable change. You are changeless in that inner world, and so are your knowings.

These then are the five characteristic differences between that which you believe and that which you know. It is obvious that most of our knowings are in the physical domain and they remain with us as long as we are in our physical bodies. The one characteristic that separates knowings from beliefs is the presence of doubt. Beliefs and doubts go together, while knowings have no doubt whatsoever attached to them.

It is my intention to help you shift many of your old beliefs out of your consciousness. But even more helpful for your quest for your sacred self, I hope you will learn to shift those that remain from mere beliefs to knowings.

Your knowings do not have to be restricted to the physical domain. You can have knowings in the metaphysical domain as well. For instance, you can *know* your guides—your angels and the loving presence—rather than just *believe* in their existence. Similarly, all of the qualities of the higher self, which are included in part 3 of this book, are available for you to know rather than merely to believe in.

Nisargadatta Maharaj, in *I Am That,* describes the process this way: "Mere knowledge is not enough; the knower must be known. . . . Without the knowledge of the knower there can be no peace." This is a radical idea—getting to know the knower. It is the subject of the next chapter, but it is helpful for you to be acquainted with this idea now.

There is the physical you who has knowledge, and there is the known. But most significant, there is the knower of the known. This is your true identity.

The peace that Maharaj mentions and the way of the sacred quest become available when you are guided by that true identity, which is the highest part of yourself. To attain that peace and to find the way of the quest involve letting go of old beliefs and shifting to a new dimension— where knowing supplants believing and where faith replaces fear.

FEAR AND DOUBT

There is an old saying (the origins of which I am ignorant), "Fear knocked at the door, and faith answered, and no one was there." Fear stems from doubts we have about our divinity. The antidote to fear is faith.

I know within that I am not alone, ever. I know that I have divine guidance available to me at all times. This inner knowing makes fear impossible. You too are not alone, and you also have omnipresent guidance accessible at will.

When you truly know that the loving presence is always with you, the possibility of living with both doubt and fear evaporates. It has to have the quality of being a knowing. Then the notion of fear vanishes.

As you begin to rid yourself of fears, you will develop a kind of confidence that reflects your inner awareness of your divine mission. Gabriel Saul Helig, writing in *Tenderness Is Strength,* describes how fear dissipates when doubt is banished:

> We still tremble before the Self like children before the falling dark. Yet once we have dared to make our passage inside the heart, we will find that we have entered into a world in which depth leads on to light, and there is no end to entrance.

Fear is our prison. We must eradicate it by knowing the absurdity of being afraid of anything in this intelligent system we are a part of that has infinite intelligence flowing through everything. Bringing this one simple awareness into consciousness when you are experiencing any fear will help banish both the fear and the doubt.

The things we most commonly fear can be explained away by lengthy research and investigation. Or, fear can be eradicated with one short and simple statement. I have chosen the second way, hoping to stun you with the simplicity of eliminating fear.

- Fear of failing. *Get rid of it!* You cannot fail at anything. Everything you do produces a result. It is what you do with the results that counts. Labeling yourself a failure is meaningless.
- Fear of disapproval. *Get rid of it!* You do not need external validation. You are a divine creation of God. Your path is unique and special. The opinions of others will invariably be judgmental. When you know that you are on a spiritual mission, you become independent of the good opinion of others. Get on with your purpose.
- Fear of suffering. *Get rid of it!* You cannot suffer when you know your sacred self. Only the person you imagine yourself to be suffers. Your joy is divine and so is your suffering. All of the woe is a part of God's plan, bringing transcendent wisdom when you stop judging it.
- Fear of isolation. *Get rid of it!* You can never be alone. When you know this, you will never fear loneliness. There is a gigantic support network of loving souls with you on a similar path. Know that to be true. Stay focused on your purpose and forget about feeling isolated. When you do this, all of the guidance and love that you need will begin to be known by you.
- Fear of looking foolish. *Get rid of it!* When you are doing the work of the higher self, you are always on purpose. Whether others judge you as foolish or not is irrelevant.

- Fear of success. *Get rid of it!* Replace the fear with knowing that you deserve any prosperity or abundance that comes your way. Know that when you are on the way of your sacred quest, external measures of success will appear. Your success, however, is an inner matter. It is your personal feeling about yourself, and certainly you do not want to be afraid of yourself.

These are the six fears that interfere the most with the way of our divine purpose. Know that you possess the inner tools to transform your life, and the fear will be gone before you can utter, *"Get rid of it!"*

One of those inner tools is to acknowledge to yourself when fear enters your personal picture. When you do notice yourself experiencing fear, please be sure to gently allow it into your awareness. Feel it. Refuse to judge it.

I have a friend who takes the time to have a silent conversation with her fear-thought. She tells me that this alone often causes the fear to dissipate because it is welcomed as an old belief that once was a loved part of herself. Other times, she and the fear-thought agree on a new "job description" for it. Feel the fear and do not let its historical effect continue.

The first time I walked out on stage to speak before several thousand people and had forgotten my notes, I experienced severe feelings of fear. Not acknowledging my fear would have kept it right there on stage with me. But I surrendered to the fear while I reminded myself that I was not alone. I went out on that stage with my fear as my companion. Before even a few minutes had passed, I was absorbed in my mission and my fear was gone.

By acknowledging the fear and then doing whatever you were afraid of anyway, you serve notice on those kinds of self-defeating thoughts. You also take a giant step toward banishing doubt from your life.

Fear and doubt are partners. That which you doubt will cause you to be afraid. That which you fear creates doubts about your ability to deal with it. As I mentioned a few pages earlier, the real antidote to doubt and fear is faith.

Developing faith as a means to eliminate fear from your life is a supremely spiritual lesson. *A Course in Miracles* beautifully elucidates this point, with the emphasis on knowing:

> If you knew Who walks beside you on the way that you have chosen, fear would be impossible.

FAITH AS AN ANTIDOTE TO FEAR AND DOUBT

In most cases, the use of the word "faith" is associated with developing a religious framework for our lives. Faith and worship, in this context, go together. I am not writing about faith that way. I honor whatever your religious persuasion is, but I do not want you to confuse religious beliefs with the actual presence of faith.

Faith is akin to knowing God, which is different than believing in God. Knowing, as I am writing about it, is an experience on a cellular level of personal experience, which has not one iota of doubt attached to it. To me, faith is an inner knowing and capacity to see God in *everything*, including myself. This kind of faith does not come from books.

The kind of faith I am describing does not need a religious service or a holy book. It comes from having the direct inner experience of God as a part of your higher self. It is demonstrated in countless ways in daily life. You do not necessarily have to see this inner light with your senses, yet the experience is known. You know that what you do not see is there for you.

I've seen my wife, Marcelene, demonstrate this inner faith on seven different occasions when she has given birth to our children. Throughout her pregnancies, she talks to me about her faith in God being with her. She *knows* that bringing a child into the world is more than a physical experience. She knows that it is a holy opportunity that she has been entrusted with.

She has absolutely no doubt about her ability to proceed through all stages of her labor and childbirth without complications, pain or any suffering. This faith literally puts her into a higher state of awareness, and her physical appearance changes. She has left the confines of her body. Through the power of her miraculous concentration on what she is to do, she proceeds unaware of surrounding distractions.

Her inner faith has literally served to banish the doubt about her ability to deliver a baby in a spiritual and pain-free environment. She doesn't *believe* that God is there for her, she absolutely *knows* it. The idea of any doubt being present is ludicrous for her.

I have been in the labor room with my wife while women all around her were out of control with fear and doubt. Marcelene, relying on her faith, is participating in the act of creation as an observer and a faithful participant. In fact, she has taken that same inner knowing, based on faith, to assist other women in having their babies. She accompanies them through the entire process—from the first months of pregnancy through delivery—helping them access their inner selves and reassuring them that if they banish doubt they will have a spiritual childbirth experience. I have yet to see it fail.

She instructs women to ignore all of the negative and doubt-filled sentences they hear from other "experienced" mothers. She helps them learn to go within, become peaceful, meet God and use faith to guide them through their experience. She is now in the process of writing a book about this spiritual approach to childbirth and infant care.

Understand that faith is a decision that you make internally. As your decision becomes a knowing, you will begin to sense the sacred energy that flows through every-thing in the form of divine intelligence in the universe. It is a mental decision to know that everything is on pur-pose. Faith then becomes an energy that resides within you at all times.

One evening, as I sat and watched a spectacular sunset on the Gulf of Mexico, I had a stunning realization. This entire planet, with everything on it, must weigh a zillion zillion trillion tons and more, and there is some energy propelling it around the sun giving the illusion that the sun is actually setting. What was really happening as I sat there was that I was setting and moving in orbit around the sun.

I contemplated the enormous amount of energy that is ceaselessly working to move this enormous planet and keep it spinning and staying on course in its yearly excur-sion. The same energy is moving the sun in a larger orbit and moving the zillions of other celestial bodies in tril-lions of orbits.

This energy gives the illusion that the earth is standing still, yet we know there is enormous movement. We have faith in that energy. We trust that there will be a sunrise tomorrow morning in the east. We don't believe in it—we know it and have faith in it.

That same energy is propelling you through your life and is within you at all moments. That same energy allows your lungs to fill with air, your heart to beat and your body to stay together rather than disintegrate. You know it, you have faith in it.

That is the same kind of faith that you must develop about your entire life. You are being guided by that heav-enly energy. Start to know it. You don't have to see it to believe in it, any more than you have to see the wind to know it is there.

This invisible energy that is doing so much is what you want to know. The inner faith becomes a power that was previously hidden from you.

I have seen people walk barefoot as much as forty feet

on red-hot glowing coals without blistering. Before they undertake this adventure, they are trained in nothing more than faith. Their faith gives them the ability to concentrate with an intensity that can prevent their feet from blistering.

I have used this kind of faith to swim across a lake in 45-degree water without experiencing any sensation of cold. I type for hours and see poems and chapters emerge, without writer's block, because I know that I am not alone. The cosmic energy is there within me for my use in fulfilling my personal destiny.

I have witnessed precisely the right people showing up in my life to assist me with whatever I needed when I went to this inner faith and banished all thoughts of doubt. On one occasion, while sitting in a phone booth in New York City, looking up the phone number of someone I hadn't seen in years, I looked up to see him standing there—an amazing coincidence or a connection to the universal energy that flows through both of us.

I have often had precisely the right book or article show up in the mail when I was stuck at a particular place in my writing. Frequently I have visualized the appearance of a particular writer in my life by concentrating on his or her words, and then "magically" had them appear in my life. Inner faith can produce the people and events that you need; it will work. (However, this is not to imply that obstacles will not surface as well.)

FAITH AND FRUSTRATION

Even after you develop this faith in God and yourself, you will find that there still are obstacles in life. The act of doubt-free thinking and knowing does not mean that riches and abundance automatically flourish. However, as obstacles and struggles appear, you will begin to process them in a totally new way—a way based on faith rather than frustration.

When you are tempted to view obstacles as hindrances, remember that life gives exams. Create a saying to remind yourself of the potential value in the obstacle. Your saying might be, "This restriction has shown up in my life to teach me something. When I get the lesson, I will then see my inner faith manifesting itself in positive ways again. I will bless this occurrence rather than curse it, knowing always that the ways of God will sometimes be mysterious to me."

Recently my wife and I spent some time in Santa Fe, New Mexico, on a retreat to renew ourselves and our marriage. On the first night there, we saw a menu in the hotel lobby from a health food restaurant and decided to have dinner there. However, there seemed to be a hundred obstacles that kept cropping up as we set out to find the restaurant.

I kept getting lost and ending up back where we started. I'd make a turn that seemed to be the right way and end up back at the hotel. Santa Fe is a city that was laid out in concentric circles, and the street names change arbitrarily from one block to another.

The frustration was mounting after we'd spent over an hour and still hadn't found the restaurant. I had asked at least ten different people for directions and finally made a phone call to the restaurant for help. All the while, I was also determined to discover what this exam was about.

When we finally arrived, the restaurant was completely filled. As we walked in, a woman from Naples, Florida, named Mary Reinhart entered ahead of us. She was being escorted to the only vacant table, and she turned and said, "Would you like to share this table rather than wait?"

We ate together, and in the course of our conversation she told us about a beautiful spiritual woman named Gangaji who was scheduled to conduct *Satsang* (a meeting for truth) in Santa Fe beginning the next morning and continuing for the length of our planned visit.

For the next five days, my wife and I attended *Satsang* along with hundreds of other people. We thought we had come to Santa Fe to be alone.

We came to know Gangaji. She is an enlightened soul who had been on her own course of self-discovery in India and was now traveling the world conducting *Satsang,* bringing the message of love, peace and personal empowerment. She did not take any money for her work, and she provided us with so much spiritual food.

In a private audience with Gangaji, she told me that her sister had read one of my books and that its message had contributed to bringing them back together. Her sister had chosen to leave when Gangaji had undertaken her own unique spiritual path. In our conversation, I received from Gangaji the missing link I needed to organize and write this book. She talked to me about the idea of freedom as a decision to be made each day and gave me the subtitle of this book. It was her focus on freedom as an absence of self-absorption that guided me to write on this subject.

Our trip to Santa Fe had been planned many months in advance but had been postponed three times because a woman who was due to deliver her baby with Marcelene as her coach was overdue. Now, put this together with all of the information contained in the previous paragraphs and you see a multitude of obstacles and "coincidences."

The postponement of the trip, getting lost trying to find the restaurant (which turned out to be within walking distance of our hotel), incorrect directions, wrong turns, Mary Reinhart walking in at the precise moment that we did and inviting us to eat with her, Mary asking us if we were in Santa Fe to meet with Gangaji (whom I'd never heard of before), being invited to meet privately with Gangaji because an audience participant recognized me and the story of her reunion with her sister. And then the exact missing piece of organization for this book was handed to me by one of the most spiritual, lovely, kind, on-purpose human beings I have ever encountered. All of

these so-called obstacles and coincidences conspired with
fate to collaborate in producing the book that you are
now reading.

You too have stories like mine that you may not have
paid much attention to. I'm encouraging you to try on a
new perspective when you are caught up in difficult
times.

Detach from exclusive emphasis on your physical surroundings and your own body, and be on the lookout for
what fate is conspiring to hand you. With this attitude
you will have faith even when those obstacles seem insur-
mountable or overwhelming.

All the deaths or "accidents" in your life, including
your transition back to no-where from now-here, are a
part of the divine order. They may not be understood,
particularly considering how we are conditioned to view
these matters. With faith and without doubt you know
what Edna St. Vincent Millay meant when she wrote:

Man has not invented God;
He has developed faith,
To meet a God already there.

Your faith can remain strong in the presence of obstacles. Your frustration that God is not working at the pace
you think she should can be replaced with the inner
knowing that everything in your life is there to teach you
something. Your sacred quest will lead you to the knowing that the enormous energy that moves planets and
galaxies, keeping them always on course, is flowing in
divine order through you too, and keeping you on course,
though your limited vision prevents you from seeing it.

Your faith cleanses your vision. What you then see are
perfectly placed obstacles instead of frustrating impedi-
ments. The irony is that as you develop this faith and get
the lessons, fewer and fewer of these blockades appear in
your life.

How to Banish Doubt

Below are some specific suggestions for removing doubt from your inner inventory. Keep in mind that doubt not only inhibits your sacred quest but can also be a destructive force in your daily existence.

• *Make a decision that you are going to meet the invisible God within, the loving presence, so that you will know her.* This means being willing to spend time in the inner silence of your being. Create the time and space for quieting and listening. Do nothing else, but do this daily. (Chapter 6 gives some specific ways to shut down inner dialogue.)

As you push out your thoughts and revel in the silence, you will feel the energy of the loving presence flowing through you. Give yourself a holy instant to make a silent affirmation that you are with God.

Do not feel that you must share your experience or convince others that you've felt God within. Simply notice for yourself how you shift from a belief to a knowing when the smidgin of doubt you'd harbored is gone.

• *Allow the moment of revelation to be free from any inner criticism or doubt.* Andrew Cohen puts it this way, in his book *Enlightenment Is a Secret*:

When there is a profound revelation, in the very recognition that "this is revelation," you have to become serious about your own life. The instant you recognize that you are seeing the truth as it is, you must realize the implications of what is being revealed to you. If not betrayed even once then your confidence in that revelation can only grow. The stronger the confidence, the deeper will be your wisdom. But if in the face of that revelation you needlessly allow yourself to indulge in doubt, you begin to walk down a precarious road, because by doing so your confidence will be undermined.

- *Keep in mind always that doubt is produced by your ego.* Doubt is not a part of your higher spiritual self. With this awareness you can learn to observe your doubt rather than choose to own it.

  You are working at knowing the knower, and the knower is your higher invisible self. Use your capacity to detach yourself from doubt and watch how it enters your inner world. Then observe how doubt literally forces you to act in predetermined and limited ways. This act of observation will in itself cause doubt to dissipate.

- *When doubt surfaces within you and you recognize it, you now have to be willing to say no, I no longer allow these thoughts in my life.* Many people and thoughts will attempt to sway you from your quest. You must be willing to see them as your tests and take the advice we give to our children about drugs: Just say no!

- *Do you doubt your ability to know God?* You may have no doubt about the existence of an absolute reality called God, but you may doubt your ability to know that higher part of yourself fully. If so, I suggest you reexamine your logic.

  The self-doubt may be an excuse you use to keep yourself from changing. If you have no doubt about God's existence, then you are in the field of knowing. By acknowledging that you absolutely know the existence of a higher power, you've banished the doubt within. If you then realize that this higher power is in everything, you cannot doubt that it is in you.

  If you are alive, then you have the life force of God

within you. It is as simple as that—your aliveness confirms the existence of the highest awareness within yourself.

• *Begin to change the vocabulary you use to describe yourself and your expectations.* Rather than using words that reflect your doubt, shift to words that indicate your knowing and your faith.

Catch yourself when you use words and phrases such as maybe, possibly, God willing, if I'm lucky, perhaps, one never knows. Start using words and phrases such as certainly, absolutely, God is always willing and so am I, I'll work until it does happen, I know I can do it.

When you use words and phrases that reflect an absence of doubt, you will conduct your life the same way. Your actions will follow what you say, and what you say follows from what your inner world is. Change the words even if you don't mean them yet, because eventually they will become your reality.

Friends and family members suggested that I wouldn't be able to sit and write for two months to complete a draft of this book because I had not written for several years. I simply responded with sentences like, "I trust that I will be able to do it. I am not alone and I will be given the guidance and assistance I need in order to create this book."

Never did I use a word or phrase that indicated any doubt, even if there existed some inner questioning. I said those words outwardly, began writing and, sure enough, the magic was there in the form of divine assistance.

Your words and phrases suggest to your physical self exactly what course that physical self is going to take. Be careful of what you say, and when you speak, do so with conviction and faith.

• *When you find things cropping up in your life that tend to substantiate your doubts, shift away from your old thinking habits.* Here are examples of old expressions you can try to change: See, I knew that this was a lot of bunk. God doesn't really care about me. It's a cruel world and one has to accept it. Examine the following list of statements for new ways of expressing yourself:

- If my joy is divine and I trust in a higher power when things are going well, then my suffering must also be divine.
- I will refuse to judge this and instead will know that in some way that I do not understand at this moment, I will know why this happened as it did.
- I will trust in God and the energy that is in everything and know that this too is in divine order, even though I do not like it in this moment.
- I know that the soul is eternal and that all form will pass along, so why should I question when this occurs?
- I will grieve the person who has died, but I will not question why he [or she] has returned to God at this time.
- Now, or thirty years from now, is a speck in this thing called eternity.

These kinds of inner sentiments will help you banish doubt and stop judging the ways of the universe. Keep in mind that *your joy is divine—your suffering is divine.*

- *Make a list of the beliefs that you still hang on to which no longer serve you.* Seeing them in writing will help you identify how absurd it is to stay rooted in the beliefs of others.

   As you examine your beliefs, see how many start with "should" and "shouldn't." These kinds of sentences were your earliest training and may still occupy such a large space inside you that you have no room for new knowings.

Look for sentences like: You should pay attention to what your neighbors think. You should be angry when people mistreat you. You should hate your enemies. You shouldn't disagree with me. You shouldn't be happy when others around you are suffering. You should feel guilty about your success when others have so little. You shouldn't forget about what your father always believed.

There is a long list of should-beliefs that inhibit your entrance to the bliss of a spiritual life. Those beliefs must be replaced with knowings that come from your personal experience.

• *Practice retraining your mind.* Your inner world, your mind, is like a recording stuck on replay. The play of the mind can become so intense that you create vast images of disaster that become confused with your reality.

In *The Mystery of the Mind,* Swami Muktananda relates how absurd our inner beliefs can become and how they can actually rule our world, with absolutely no basis in reality other than that we believe them to be so. Here is one of his examples:

Once there was a poor laborer named Sheikh Mahmoud. One day his employer gave him a clay pot full of ghee (clarified butter) and told him to carry it to the next town. "If you do this," the employer said, "I will give you two rupees. If you drop the pot, you will have to pay for the ghee."

Sheikh Mahmoud put the pot on his head and set out along the road. As he was walking, he started to think, "I'm going to get two rupees. What shall I do with them?" In those days, everything was very cheap. For one rupee, you could buy twenty-five chickens. Sheikh Mahmoud said, "That's it, I'll buy chickens.

They will multiply, and soon I'll have one hundred chickens, five hundred chickens, one thousand chickens, ten thousand chickens. Then I'll sell all the chickens and buy goats. I'll have goats and sheep and a big farm. The goats and sheep will multiply, and when I sell them I'll buy goods. I'll become a big merchant. Then I'll get married and have a house. I'll go to an office, and I'll return home for lunch. I'll have a very good cook to make delicious dishes. But if the cook doesn't bring the food on time, I'll get angry and slap his face. After all, I'll be a big merchant." As he thought about slapping the cook's face, he raised his arm. As soon as he did so, the pot of ghee went flying to the ground.

So the ghee did not reach the next town. Mahmoud did not get his two rupees. He did not buy chickens. He did not buy goats and sheep. He did not get married. He did not have a house. He did not go to an office. Nor did he slap anyone. He sat down and put his head in his hands. After a while he returned to his employer and confessed, "Master, I spilled the ghee."

The employer replied, "How could you do such a stupid thing? You've lost my week's profit!"

"O master," said Mahmoud, "you lost a week's profit, but I lost my chickens, my goats, my house, my wife, my office, and my cook!"

Don't lose what you don't have simply because you have not learned how to discipline your mind and banish those incessant doubts that you create in your fantasies.

- *Go back to the feelings that are present in you that are supporting the pictures you create in your mind.* For example, if you would really love to manifest prosperity and abundance, but you have doubts about your ability to do so, then first get the visualization of yourself having abundance.

Then go beyond the picture or image and ask yourself, "How would I feel if I were to experience this prosperity I visualize?" You would probably think you'd be something like content, fulfilled, grateful, happy or euphoric. These are expressions of feelings that you can generate completely with your inner thoughts.

Once you can get to the feelings behind your desires and know that you have the capacity to create these feelings by your faith and the discipline of your thoughts, you will realize that needing anything else to feel prosperous is only a belief and is inauthentic. Do this exercise with anything you wish to create in your life. Go first to the visualization, then to the resultant feeling. Then work at generating that feeling and you will feel your doubts dissipating.

- *Keep in mind always that doubt is a mental experience.* If you want a thought to disappear, you can very simply send it away in this moment. Just as you can refuse to think an unpleasant thought in any moment, because you are in charge of those thoughts, so can doubt be eradicated when it shows up.

  Say to yourself as if you are two people (the one talking and the one listening), "I have this doubt because I have allowed the persuasions of others to become my own beliefs. Now I will think for myself and know that I do not have to live with doubt."

- *Love is the truest antidote to fear and doubt.* When you feel unconditional love for yourself as a divine creation who is here with a purpose, you release all doubt and fear concerning yourself and your place in the world. Therefore, when you experience a moment of fear and doubt, give yourself a portion of mental love and remind yourself that you are a holy creation.

As you practice sending yourself love, that becomes what you have to give away. And it is also true that the more love you contain, the less room you have for the energy of fear and doubt.

The banishment of doubt from your life forever will put you in touch with a mysterious power that previously had been obscured. I encourage you to let go of the doubt that you were so carefully nurtured on, and let in a new knowing. The famous Native American Sitting Bull described this power in the following words.

Behold, my brothers, the spring has come;
The Earth has received the embraces of the sun
And we shall soon see the results of that love!

Every seed is awakened and so has all animal life.
It is through this mysterious power
that we too have our being.

Notice that Sitting Bull refers to this power as love. That love within all things is also within you. Send doubt out of your consciousness and welcome the knowing that has been the subject of this chapter.

This first key to higher awareness is also spoken of in the Bible (Deut. 30:14):

It is something very near to you, already in your mouths and in your hearts; you have only to carry it out.

I leave the rest up to you. You have only to banish the doubt and *carry it out.*

5

CULTIVATE THE WITNESS

In truth it is life that gives unto life—
while you, who deem yourself a giver,
are but a witness.

—KAHLIL GIBRAN

> I realize that I am always free to
> let go and observe my life.

Cultivating the witness is the second of the four keys to higher awareness leading you further along the way of the sacred quest. There are many benefits from assuming this witness stance.

In this chapter I ask you to shift your self-perception and cultivate a higher aspect of yourself known as the compassionate witness. Rather than think of yourself as a human being who has thoughts, feelings and behaviors, begin practicing stepping outside of yourself. I am showing you the way to a new kind of freedom where you witness your life and no longer are a dancer choreographed and directed by others.

WHAT DOES IT MEAN TO BE THE WITNESS?

Take a moment to reflect on how you view yourself. As you do this, think of what you might mean if you said, "I was thinking to myself . . . " You'll find that the phrase implies there are two people rather than one.

One person is the I doing the thinking. The other person is the self receiving the thinker's thoughts. The I is talking to the self, which, when you examine your inner dialogue, you know you do hundreds of times each day. When you cultivate the witness you remove yourself from both the I and the self position.

Here, from an invisible space outside of your physical body, the witness is detached from your emotions, feelings and behaviors. Here the witness lovingly watches your entire life transpire.

Several years ago I had a client who was suffering from what she called terminal sadness. She was always depressed. She described her feelings with statements like: "Every part of me is depressed. I am depressed all day every day. I wake up depressed and I go to sleep depressed. I can't seem to shake this awful feeling of depression."

One day I asked her a question that became the turning point in her experience of this blanket of sadness that characterized her daily life. "Tell me," I asked, "have you been noticing this depression more frequently in recent weeks?"

She responded, "Yes, I have noticed it creeping in more and more in everything I do."

"Now think about this carefully before you answer," I went on. "Is the noticer depressed?" She asked me to repeat the question. "Is the noticer depressed?" I repeated.

She was stumped for an answer. But for the first time she was able to contemplate that there existed another aspect of herself than her depression.

That aspect was the part of herself which was noticing her depression. This noticer was the witness, the observer who was unable to be caught up in the depression. This invisible, formless, boundaryless entity was her higher self, the loving presence. Prior to that session she had never met that part of herself.

I spent several months teaching this woman to stop identifying with the depressing thoughts and feelings. She learned to detach from them and observe them from the position of compassionate witness, outside her thoughts and outside her physical body.

Becoming the witness is an act of love. It removes you from the world of boundaries and forms, allowing you to enter the place of pure love.

So, begin now to notice things about your life. Notice how peaceful you feel, or how much anxiety you have. Notice your physical appearance. How much you weigh, how fit you feel and the level of fatigue. Notice how much time you want to spend with your family, your job, traveling, playing and praying. Notice anything and everything. Your fingernails, your driving habits, your lawn!

Now examine the number of times I've used the word "notice." Remind yourself that there is definitely an activity called noticing, and it includes the noticer and that which is being noticed. At this point, concentrate on being the noticer and getting accustomed to going to this place in your consciousness more frequently in your daily life.

WHY BECOME THE WITNESS?

"In my world, nothing ever goes wrong." This was spoken by Nisargadatta Maharaj in response to an interviewer who, in exasperation, asked Maharaj to talk about the problems in his life. It is for me the single most powerful affirmation I have ever heard. I use it every day of my life and I have it posted strategically in my office as a daily reminder of its supreme value in my life.

The female interviewer insisted that Nisargadatta must have problems like every other human being. Nisargadatta said, "You do not have any problems, only your body has problems. . . . In your world, nothing stays, in mine—nothing changes." Why would this enlightened master say that in his world nothing ever goes wrong? I believe it is because he was speaking from the position of compassionate witness.

Within all of us is the eternal changeless dimension of our higher spiritual selves. This is the invisible I that talks to the physical self. This is the thinker of the thoughts. This compassionate observer is not revealed with scientific instruments and doesn't appear on autopsy reports.

When you are genuinely able to live in that spiritual domain of the witness, then nothing goes wrong because wrong is not possible for the witness. It is all in order. Nothing is questioned from that perspective. It is like being able to live in heaven where eternity and the soul are, at the same time that you are within the physical body. But in this space, the body is not the focal point of existence.

I am not suggesting that you need to sit in an ashram and discard all of your physical possessions in order to find this key to higher awareness, although that certainly is a possibility. Instead, I want you to consider how these words of *nothing ever going wrong,* of *having no problems* and of *living in a world of the changeless* apply to your spiritual awakening.

There is so much to learn from these ideas. Cultivating the witness will put you on the path where your higher, sacred self begins to influence your physical, ego self instead of the other way around.

As Maharaj puts it: "Give it your full attention, examine it with loving care and you will discover heights and depths of being which you did not dream of, engrossed as you are in your puny image of yourself." These are startling words describing the power and value of cultivating the witness.

The ordinary way of attachment and suffering can be changed when you learn to access and cultivate the witness attitude of detachment and observation. Here are the principal advantages that will accrue to you as your compassionate witness becomes known:

1. *When you cultivate your compassionate witness, you become aware that you are more than your daily thoughts, feelings and sensations.* You learn that you are much more than a captive of a learned set of beliefs and behaviors that you have practiced over a lifetime. You will achieve an expanded view of who you are, and this new awareness will lead you to higher levels of living.

It puts you in direct contact with your eternal soul. By creating that knowing of your divine self you are able to soar to personal heights that your previous beliefs restricted from your view.

In relationships, you will begin to go beyond your ego self and let go of the need to be right. Simply observing yourself will reveal how your old conditioned ways of being with others are limiting. The compassionate witness will open the door to spiritual partnerships with your loved ones.

Learning to cultivate the witness adds a new dimension to life, leading to a more spiritual and blissful existence.

2. *When you cultivate the compassionate witness, you become aware that you are more than what bothers you.* As you cultivate the witness, the truth of "Nothing in my world ever goes wrong" becomes apparent.

You develop a knowing that transcends what you call your problems. The witness does not identify with the problems. You see those problems as the concerns of your body, which can be resolved without inner despair. Detached in this way, problems cannot get a lock on your inner world.

You will become almost indifferent because you possess the knowing that in this world of the body everything changes, nothing remains the same. Problems will change too. They too will come and go. The saying "This too shall pass" takes on a more personal and relevant meaning.

If you learn to view difficulties not as something that you must own internally but as the natural comings and goings of the physical world, you will cultivate the witness on the path of your sacred quest.

3. *When you cultivate your compassionate witness, you take an action that can dissipate problems.* Earlier in this book I wrote briefly about the mechanics of creation. That same explanation applies to cultivating the witness.

To briefly recap, here are two sentences summarizing Nick Herbert's *Quantum Reality: There is no reality in the absence of observation. Observation creates reality.* Therefore, the act of witnessing—all by itself, without any other infringing activity—will create your reality.

When you compassionately witness the troubling event in your life, keeping your attention on it in a way that *knows* that it is going in the direction of resolution, that is what occurs. Sitting with a problem in the nonjudgmental way of the witness creates the observer energy for it to move on. I find it very satisfying to make problems vanish from my life through this process of witnessing.

For example, in the past I allowed myself to become very anxious under the pressure of a deadline to complete a writing project. The anxiety manifested in the form of an upset stomach, fatigue, jittery feelings and a general level of physical discomfort.

When I learned to witness I found that I could close my eyes and refuse to identify with "the problem." It remained part of my body but separate from me, the witness. As I observed myself in the state of discomfort, compassionately detached from my body in the act of observation, I could notice the symptoms of anxiety dissipate. I actually found myself feeling calm and confident.

As thoughts of deadline urgency would reenter my mind, the discomfort returned, but it was different. Now I was not the thought but the observer of the thought. Gradually, the thought would disappear and be replaced by a calm feeling, and then it would reenter.

After thirty minutes of being witness, watching the thoughts come and go and allowing my body to shift from comfort and calm to discomfort and then back again, the entire scene dissolved. It literally left my being. I found I was then able to sit down and write rather than be caught up in my body's and my mind's interpretation of the deadline.

The act of witnessing from a detached perspective created a new energy within me. That energy dissolved the problem and allowed me to function at a healthier and more productive level.

4. *When you cultivate your compassionate witness, you bring peace into your life.* It not only puts you in touch with the sacred part of your being, it also allows the peace and harmony of that loving presence to be a basic experience of your daily life.

Stephen Wolinsky describes it this way in his book: *Quantum Consciousness*: "If I can begin to observe and witness my reactions, then I will feel freer and more at peace. It is only by the identification and fusion with a thought or feeling that I limit myself from being the observer to becoming the experience itself."

The ability to assume the witness viewpoint means allowing our higher self to observe in its nonjudgmental and compassionate way. When you can witness your ego self, you are not your ego self.

Your ego self subsides as your sacred self is more intimately integrated into your being. You will find that this new peace will take you through the tasks of your material world with greater efficiency and productivity.

5. *When you cultivate your compassionate witness, you take the first step to liberation.* When you begin to step away and watch, you are no longer controlled by the physical events of your life.

For instance, when you experience anger, step back and observe it for a few moments. You will notice that you are liberated almost immediately from the pain associated with the anger. Events will continue to happen, but you will no longer be the one who identifies with those events.

Being able to witness events, including your own body events, frees you from having to experience the pain that you once thought was the only available option. My wife and I have raised eight children; if we had not had the attitude of witnessing available to us, many times we might have been distraught and miserable.

With an attitude of witnessing, we can step back and observe our thoughts and feelings, as well as those of our children. We know that we will be liberated if we can detach from the sometimes chaotic physical world of our large family. From the compassionate witness space of nonidentification with the problem, the problem disappears.

The solution comes from our ability and willingness to trust that we can nonjudgmentally offer advice and guidance, without identifying ourselves as parental failures or parental successes in the process.

We are liberated by the act of witnessing. And so are you when you cultivate your witness.

6. *When you cultivate your compassionate witness, you put yourself in contact with God.* It is in the act of cultivating the witness that I have come to know God more clearly in my life. The act of observation is the closest I have ever been able to come to actually experiencing another dimension of reality unfettered by the constraints of the material world.

It is very much an out-of-body experience, in

which you actually see your body and its thoughts without identifying with them. A regular practice of observing gives you an appreciation of Carl Sandburg's comment: "Something began me and it had no beginning; something will end me, and it has no end."

From the position of witnessing, you know that you are not only that which you are seeing. A spiritual reality is available when you leave your material self. The connection to the higher part of yourself is felt from this position.

The godforce within you wraps you with love and peace as you witness the thoughts, feelings and sensations of your body and its physical journey. This process of cultivating the witness is the process of knowing the truth of St. Matthew: ". . . with God all things are possible" (Matt. 19:26). Now, you tell me if that leaves anything out. We know that all things are not possible in the physical domain, therefore God is being referred to as that part of you that is beyond the physical. It is through cultivating the witness that you can know this as your reality.

So these are the six major benefits for you as you move into the way of the witness on the path of your sacred quest. You will slowly emerge as a being who knows that you exist outside of your thoughts, emotions and physical sensations, and therefore they will not play the major role that they have.

FOUR CATEGORIES OF OBSERVATION

In order to cultivate your witness, you need to develop your powers of observation about yourself and the world. You need to learn to observe your reactions in order to go beyond them. It is the "going beyond" that is the crux of the sacred quest. I have divided the different kinds of observation into four categories.

OBSERVING YOUR BODY

This is one of the areas of being the witness that most of us have practiced somewhat. In general we allow our body to function without interference. We are aware that there is the body and that there is a "ghost in the machine."

Ever since you first looked into a mirror and saw your face staring back at you, you have been observing your body. The owner, or occupant, of your body is a you that remains a mystery.

Even as the occupant though, you have frequently identified yourself as your body. Sometimes you forget and assume that you are this body. But, essentially, you have been watching your body go through its motions, aware that an invisible formless you is somewhere inside, observing.

Over your lifetime you have seen your body go through many changes. Still, there has always been within you the changeless self. There is still a young child within there, viewing itself in terms that defy time and limits. It knows that it is not this body, while at the same time it worries that it is indisputably connected in a way that will cause its death when the body dies.

When you look into a mirror and see a new wrinkle, the formless part of you who sees the wrinkle has not changed, even though the skin sags. I see hairs growing in my ears and my nose and wonder why they are there now and where the ones are that used to grow on my head! But I am the same inside. When you see silver where brunette used to be, you know the real you is not silver, and if you think about it, you know the real you wasn't the brunette either. You see liver spots and you know some part of you is spotless.

For as long as you can remember, you have been observing this phenomenon of a body. It is also true that you know that the entity that is doing the observing is removed in some dramatic way from that which it is witnessing.

As you are reading this sentence, you are allowing your body to act out its destiny without your meddling. You are not busy beating your heart, or filling your lungs, or oxygenating your blood supply or circulating your vital fluids. You allow your body to operate itself and you allow another part of you to know the way of being the divine, quiet, noninterfering observer. This way has served you well.

By just observing your body and detaching yourself from its functioning, it works as perfectly as it was ordained to. If you were constantly monitoring and attempting to control your bodily functions you would be unduly attached to its outcome, and you would inhibit its natural functions. The times in your life when you worry or interfere with the natural functions of your body are the times when you find it breaking down.

When you fail to respond to your body's inherently perfect instincts, you find that it will go out of balance and break down in some way. By being a meddlesome intruder, rather than a compassionate observer, you create toxic reactions that will ultimately break the foundation of the divine building that houses your soul.

Feed your body the wrong foods and it will respond with lethargy and disease. Fail to exercise it and it will become overweight and groggy. Ignore its need for fresh air and healthy environments and it will fall into disrepair. Feed it narcotic substances or artificial drugs and it will react with violent symptoms.

When your body is in any state of disrepair, from being overweight to having back pains, nervousness, influenza, cancer or anything that is not the way of perfect health that your body knows at the cellular and genetic levels, then you are being called back to the position of loving witness.

True awareness is a state of pure witnessing, without any attempt to fix or change that which is being witnessed. It is a kind of nonjudgmental love that, by itself, is healing. Even if what you observe is "sickness" or "infirmity," the compassionate witness notes the trouble spots and observes them with unconditional love. The absence of judgment in the act of observation contributes the appropriate energy of love that the situation needs.

The more you can practice witnessing in this way, the more you will find that the mere act of nonjudgmental witnessing will keep your life moving on its sacred quest. The mechanics of creation are such that where you place your loving attention and maintain it is where the wave begins making the shift from no-where to now-here.

OBSERVING YOUR MIND

You may have become accustomed to witnessing your body. It doesn't seem difficult because you imagine that you are doing the observing of your body with your mind. So what do you use to observe your mind? Here is where you will suspend your old set of beliefs and enter a new world of the witness.

Try to view your thoughts as a component of your body/mind. Think of thoughts as things. Things that you have the capacity to get outside of and observe.

Your mind is filled with thousands of thoughts each day. They come and go like trains in a terminal—one enters, another takes it place; one exits, and along comes another. This goes on all day.

You've been led to believe that these thoughts are not always within your control. Your belief may be that the thinking process just goes on and on even when you would like it to stop. I am not asking you to stop your thoughts (the subject of chapter 6), but merely to know that you have the ability to be the witness to your thoughts. Just observing the flow of thoughts will slow the mind down to the still point where you can experience God.

First you want to watch your thoughts. Then you want to watch yourself watching your thoughts. Here is the door to the inner space where, free from all thoughts, you experience the bliss and the freedom that transport you directly to your higher self.

The simple exercise of watching your mind manufacturing its thoughts will eventually cause unwanted, unnecessary, erroneous thoughts to dissolve. In the process of cultivating the witness, you learn to quiet your mind, take inventory and dispose of or reassign thoughts that generate self-defeating or ego-centered responses. In this simple process, you also come to know your spiritual self.

A while ago, the Congress of the United States was debating the provisions of a deficit reduction act. One of the key proposals was a provision to raise the taxes of people who were in my income bracket. At the very same time that I was studying *I Am That* and learning to put this witnessing technique into my life, I was also following with intense personal interest how this new law was proceeding through Congress. If it passed, my tax bill would go up considerably.

Nisargadatta Maharaj's writings were encouraging me to learn how to witness my thoughts from a detached, nonjudgmental and unconditionally loving perspective. So I sat and watched my thoughts about increased taxes. What I saw was pure, in-the-world, ego thinking.

Ego-generated thoughts play a huge role in creating the world that the ego wishes to create. Each of my thoughts seemed to demand it be considered the most important. As I became better at witnessing my thoughts, I noticed one in particular that reappeared often. Its words expressed this thought: "How dare they say that I am not paying my fair share of taxes. Don't they realize that I have only one vote, yet I send in more money to that government bureaucracy than 99 percent of all the other people. How dare they accuse me of not being a fair-minded citizen." I noticed this thought from the position of the noticer.

Then, within moments, another contrasting thought would stream into consciousness: "There is a huge deficit, and I have been very blessed with an abundant income and many financial niceties. Many people will benefit from my paying more tax dollars, and I can afford it. So what's the big deal?"

This thought was followed with: "Wait a minute, they have no right to make me pay a higher percentage of my income in taxes. I don't mind sending in more money, but why should any one citizen be required to send in a greater percentage of their income and thus be penalized for being successful? More money, yes. A higher percentage, no!" My witness remained loving but neutral from its higher viewpoint.

Back and forth these thoughts flew in my mind while I observed my thoughts rather than owned them. As I practiced being the witness and just observed the thoughts coming and going, I noticed an interesting phenomenon. The anxiety over this issue began to dissipate. I no longer cared one way or the other, and I realized that I was not the participant in this drama any longer. The events would take place independent of my thoughts about them, and the more I just watched my thoughts, the more they tended to evaporate.

I realized that I knew now what Nisargadatta meant when he wrote that "self-knowledge is detachment. . . . When you know that you lack nothing, that all there is, is you and yours, desire ceases. . . . Don't disturb your mind with seeking. . . . Mind is interested in what happens, while awareness is interested in the mind itself." Once I witnessed my thoughts, I was no longer attached to them or their outcome in the physical plane. I was free.

This position of witnessing your thoughts is unrelated to the level of your income. Your thoughts will not influence Congress either way. So become the witness and learn how to keep your thoughts from running your life.

It truly did not matter to me whether they passed the bill or not, since I had very convincing arguments from my mind on both sides of the issue. What I was left with was freedom of choice to choose how I wished to feel about the issue and/or to leave it in the hands of God. In this exercise I learned that they can't tax me, they can only tax my body.

The ability to figuratively stand in back of yourself and watch your thoughts is the same as the ability to look within and participate in the divine act of cocreating your spiritual life.

Troubles begin with a thought that you put into your mind and allow to fester to the point of anxiety. The anxiety begins to manifest in your life in physically destructive ways, which we call things like arthritis, high blood pressure and career cardiacs.

The loving, nonjudgmental energy received from the observer, the witness, will allow those thoughts to flow in and out as naturally as the ocean tides. Tide's in, tide's out. Thoughts in, thoughts out. You will learn to be a witness to your thoughts in the same way that you observe the tide. And the process will cleanse and redistribute and remove thoughts in much the same way as the driftwood on the beach. What remains is generally quite pleasing.

Witnessing your thoughts will take some practice. With proficiency comes wonder and delight. Trauma is dissolved in the thinking stage and prevented from manifesting into your everyday world. I've given several suggestions for this practice in the final section of this chapter.

OBSERVING YOUR LIFE ENERGY

Everything in life is energy. Understanding the energy principle is vitally important to the process of learning to cultivate the witness. Your emotions are energy. The typewriter I'm using is energy. When you meet another person, there is an exchange of energy. Every single event in your life involves an exchange of energy. Your lifetime of events and exchanges between all of the people you have encountered has involved an enormous amount of energy.

When you choose to witness your entire life, you begin to see your life from an energy perspective. All of the conflicts that you have participated in throughout your life have in some way drained you of spiritual energy and left you with lethargic energy.

These encounters, ever since childhood, represent a stored energy that has caused you to focus the emphasis of your life on ego, on your self-importance. You have identified yourself with the events and the people who have influenced you. This has created the lethargic energy level of awareness that inhibits you from knowing your higher self.

You contain a lot of negative, invisible energy that your senses do not report in a language that you have been taught to understand. The Naguals (Meso-American spiritual masters) have a ritual training process called the recapitulation, which can decrease the negative, lethargic energy and increase your witnessing capacity.

Taisha Abelar, in *The Sorcerers' Crossing,* describes the recapitulation process as one of "calling back the energy we have already spent in past actions. . . . To recapitulate entails recalling all the people we have met, all the places we have seen and all the feelings we have had in our entire lives—starting from the present, going back to the earliest memories—then sweeping them clean, one by one."

When I first made an effort to recapitulate my life and to sweep the negative energy that I had collected, I thought it would be an impossible task. But it wasn't. It merely meant using my internal attention in such a way that I witnessed a specific event, and then with a sweep of my internal attention, I left it behind.

The process sounds strange, but when you practice doing it there is a strong sense of leaving behind all of the old conditions and reenergizing the present. What I found most astonishing was my ability to recall seemingly long-forgotten people and events.

One day I decided to recapitulate my fourth-grade classroom. Simply by being the willing witness to that room at Arthur Elementary School in Detroit, I was able to see every single classmate, the teachers, the places where everyone sat, the book Mrs. Engel read (*The Secret Garden*), the lessons in fractions, the world globe in the corner and the names of everyone in the class.

As I witnessed myself in that room, I realized that I had spent an enormous amount of energy being fearful of not being accepted. It was my first year in that school because we'd moved from another neighborhood. I was able to recall that misspent energy to my energy body. I was flabbergasted at the ability of my mind to recall all of those seemingly insignificant events and long-forgotten classmates.

The recapitulation process is an energy process. All memories, like everything else in the universe, are in the form of energy. Recalling lost energy and removing draining energy sounds unfeasible, but I can assure you that cultivating the witness in this way will have the dramatic effect of raising your level of awareness and introducing you to the higher part of your being.

As you go within and begin the witnessing process of your entire life, you will begin to be filled with an overwhelming sense of awe at how it all fits together. What you struggled with as a teenager—when you can see it from the perspective of the detached witness—led to a higher plane of existence as a young adult, or as a mature senior citizen. The energy you spent fighting your parents, or conforming to silly rules, can now be recalled and used in a more propitious manner.

From the witness perspective, you are detached from any rightness or wrongness of the events, your behaviors and the reactions of others. As the witness to your life, you are removing the energy caught in the prejudices, anger and inner futility that you might have experienced at the time and are still storing within your body today. Through witnessing, you will discover that you possess the ability to return to every single moment of your life and act as if you were once again in the same situation.

Witnessing your life and changing the existing energy pattern is accomplished with enormous discipline. You may not choose to put yourself through this kind of an ordeal. However, convincing yourself that you have the power to do so, and knowing that you can go into the witness stance at will and relive those events from a detached perspective, will help you to clear out all of the blockages that inhibit you.

Any energy that you give to past events that is not based in love (the unconditional variety) is energy that is keeping you from knowing your spiritual self.

OBSERVING THE WORLD AROUND YOU

You have the choice to take on the witness posture in terms of how you view everything going on around you. This includes events in your neighborhood as well as globally significant events. As the witness, you are refusing to identify with what you see taking place. You are instead being a detached, passive but noticing observer. You are not the event, you are that which is noticing it.

When you become the witness to events in the world around you, you remove your self-importance from what you are observing. You do not see it in terms of how it affects you. You simply notice. You are not attached to the rightness or wrongness of it. You have an inner knowing that, in some mysterious way, it is all in order. You are not questioning God in any of it. You simply notice.

The advantage to assuming this non-self-important position is that you begin to see how this event affects everyone. If it constitutes a problem, you see the solution clearly. You know that you feel that it shouldn't be happening, but you don't ask why and you don't judge or get angry about it. You are the silent witness. If the event is a hurricane or an earthquake, for instance, you do not become internally torn apart. You know what has happened, you know what needs to be done and you are able to get on with doing it.

Learning to observe the world from the perspective of the detached witness does not, however, mean being emotionless. It simply means being free of immobilizing emotions. Abraham Maslow described the highest functioning human beings in his studies as "self-actualized," stating that the highest quality they possessed was that they were "independent of the good opinion of others."

When you no longer need to view the events of your life from your self-centered perspective, or from the point of view of how you should react based on how you will look to others, then you have achieved a measure of freedom.

Freedom is what the witness alignment offers. It gives you the freedom to be in an airport, for example, watching others upset over a flight cancellation while you silently witness their behavior along with your own internal and external behavior.

During the time I was learning to practice witnessing, I was on a flight that got into some unbelievable turbulence. As the oxygen masks dropped and the plane tossed violently and passengers screamed in panic, I found myself witnessing the event, including my behavior. I let my body sit there and be tossed around and watched from a position above my head. I experienced no fear whatsoever. I was detached, and consequently it wasn't me that was in danger but that which I was watching. I knew in my heart that I could not die, that I was eternal, and that is the place I went to as the witness.

That calming witness kept me from panicking, and it seemed to ease the fear in the person sitting next to me too. For all I know, that silent witnessing may have brought the plane out of its gyrations!

You can extend this witness position toward all of the things that you find so upsetting in the world. The wars will go on and on, independent of your inner turmoil. Being the global witness might actually help to create a collective energy of peace. Certainly your anger isn't going to eradicate wars.

The same is true of violence, hunger, disease and all of the "troubles" we experience in our world. By becoming the witness, you do not become passive or uncaring. You become the observer who sees what is happening for what it is, and who sees the solutions too.

By taking on the anger of the warriors, you become one more warrior who is creating additional disharmony in the world. As the witness, you radiate the calm energy of observation and detachment. This is what our world will ultimately grasp as we who notice and witness participate in the spiritual revolution.

These then are the four categories of observation available to you. They may sound a bit strange if you believe that we affect the world only with our physical or intellectual selves. I admit this is a new and perhaps radical notion, but give it a try. Who knows, it may end up transforming your life and helping you to tap into the power and wisdom of your sacred self.

SUGGESTIONS FOR PUTTING THE WITNESS INTO YOUR LIFE

What follows are some specific suggestions and ideas for putting the witness to work in your life.

- *Notice the noticer!* As you take note of your worlds, both inner and outer, begin to familiarize yourself with the noticer who is behind that which is being noticed.

  If you do this several times each day, you will begin to see that you are much more than just a body and mind going through the programmed motions of your life. Your realization of your true self as the witness behind that which is being witnessed will bring you a new dimension of creativity and bliss.

- *As you become familiar with the noticer, remind yourself that you cannot hurt or suffer in any way.* Your compassionate witness reveals for you your corner of freedom where you are immune from embodied anguish.

  I suggested to a waitress who was feeling harassed by some inconsiderate customers to witness their behavior rather than be the victim. She didn't understand and asked me to explain.

  "You have three protective coverings between the real you and the outer world," I told her. "First you have the waitress uniform. That certainly isn't the real you, so don't identify yourself with waitress.

  "Second, you have your body, but you don't want to make the mistake of believing that you are your body. If you do, anyone can violate you with an unflattering comment about your body. You own the body, but you are not the body.

  "Third, you have your mind, but notice that it is your mind. Now who is the owner of your mind?

That's the witness and that's who you are. Not your mind, which you are using to discuss being harassed; not your body, which is feeling anxiety and pressure; and certainly not your waitress uniform, which is a costume.

"Let no one enter your inner kingdom unless they come with love. All others, you simply stand back and witness them and yourself in this little drama that is unfolding. Once you stop the false identification of yourself, you are free. Being the witness is your ticket to freedom. Go for it."

She loved the idea and took the new sense of relief and pride in herself to ward off unpleasant energy from other inconsiderate customers.

You can do this any time in your life by becoming the witness.

- *Post this affirmation in as many places as possible:* *"In my world, nothing ever goes wrong."* Look at it each day, and let it remind you that everything that is happening to you is in divine order and comes with a lesson. Also, it will help you to live in the spiritual realm—the realm of the changeless and eternal.

  You will begin to identify yourself not with the problems that bombard your body but with the silent witness. You will see solutions pouring forth when you take this approach. If you know that your problems are not yours, but only your body's to own, then the act of witnessing will keep you from becoming inwardly immobilized. That serenity will present the solution for resolving your body's problem.

- *When you find yourself troubled by anything, say out loud: "I am more than what bothers me."* Just this simple statement affirming yourself as something more than a receptacle for troubles will keep you from allowing those troubles to run rampant in your daily life.

You are not those troubles, you are that which is aware of them. Your higher awareness can provide a sanctuary when you start believing the old messages that you are your troubles and that until you resolve them you will be in pain.

• *Try this exercise: Think of something that has been bothering you for a long period of time.* Now go to a quiet place and close your eyes. Just see the problem surfacing on the blank screen in your consciousness. Notice all aspects of the problem. What it looks like, when it shows up, what you feel when it is on your mind, the pain and fear that you have when it is present, how you have dealt with it unsuccessfully in the past. Think of everything that you can which is related to the problem.

Then detach yourself in your mind from the problem. Just allow it to sit there on the screen of your mind. Look at it from the viewpoint of the compassionate witness, who just nonjudgmentally notices the screen. Watch it like a movie, allowing it to change in whatever way it does; just observe it with loving permission for it to do what it wants to do.

You will see it change and fade in and out of awareness. With each change or movement on the screen, remain in the caring witness mode of knowing the energy will do what it will and will also be accompanied by the loving energy from the witness. Often, this act of observation will result in a feeling of the problem having dissipated. If that happens, observe that also from the position of caring observer.

I practiced this act of observation when I was injured and unable to play tennis. I reacted at first to the pain in my foot with statements like: "This injury is keeping me from doing what I want to do and I'm really upset about it." I found that no matter what I tried, the pain persisted and I was unable to pivot and consequently had to discontinue an activity that I loved.

I then took the witness stance. I no longer saw myself as having an injury. I attributed the pain only to my body, and not to me. I witnessed the entire thing and merely watched it. I lovingly witnessed the pain, the way it showed up, my feelings of frustration about it, the color of the swelling, everything. But I refused to think of it as mine. It was only my body's problem. The very same day that I did this, the entire discomfort disappeared. I mean it was gone from my body!

I had put my attention on what was occurring, and detached myself from it, and in what seemed like a few hours, I no longer had the pain and was playing tennis as if I never had experienced any injury at all.

- *In order to know the benefit of witnessing, you will have to banish the doubt about this as something that will work for you.* Remember, you have been conditioned to believe that your body is the essence of your humanity. You've been taught to tackle problems with your physical and intellectual apparatus, not your higher self.

   This radical awareness is reinforced by the words of Carlos Castaneda in *The Power of Silence*: "What we need to do to allow magic to get hold of us is to banish doubt from our minds. . . . Once doubts are banished, anything is possible."

   If you do not put banishing doubt into practice as you work at cultivating the witness, then you will only find yourself experiencing frustration, which will lead to doubt, and then you will see the fruits of your doubt manifesting in your life.

- *Do not get involved with the idea of succeeding or failing at knowing the witness.* Take on this venture with complete detachment from the results. Just know that there is a knower of the known within you. A noticer of that which is noticed. A silent divine spirit that is omnipresent in your life. Ask nothing more.

Don't take on the temptation of evaluating your progress. Merely give yourself permission to welcome this new witnessing phenomenon into your life as a gift to your physical self from your higher self. Eventually you will notice the results.

- *Practice new self-talk sentences to replace your old identification with your physical body.* "I am that which owns this body. I am not the body itself. I can't be reached if you come with hatred or anger. I cannot worry when I refuse to be the worrier and simply observe that worrier and those worries."

  Self-talk sentences will keep you centered on your spiritual domain. You will find that many things that you worried about or experienced in a negative fashion are slowly diminishing from your life.

- *Rather than engaging in confrontations with others, try being the witness.* Rise above the temptation to make someone else wrong, and instead watch yourself and your "opponent" from the witness perspective.

  You will soon see the folly of engaging in this anxiety-producing confrontation, and you will shift to a more spiritual response. Keep in mind the one sentence that does more to defuse confrontations and improve relationships than anything I've ever heard: "When you have the choice between being right and being kind, always choose kind."

  I heard that sentence while I was witnessing myself being in turmoil over something that my wife wasn't understanding. I had been so busy attempting to make her wrong and convince her of the rightness of my position, that I became increasingly anguished. When I was witnessing this event, that sentence came to me. I've found it to be very useful in defusing situations.

- *In a quiet place, practice observing your thoughts for thirty minutes.* Just shut your mind down and watch as thoughts come and go. While you are doing this, keep reminding yourself that those thoughts are not you.

You will find one thought popping into your head, and in a few moments, a completely opposite thought will surface. Notice the thoughts that come and then watch them go. This is particularly useful when you are troubled by some external happening in your life, like what job offer to accept or whether you should sell your home.

Your attention will shift to those thoughts that provide you with a solution. What you should do will often become crystal clear. You will have banished all doubt and created a knowing within you, all through the act of witnessing from a detached point of view.

It is inevitable that you will have tasks to perform that are unpleasant or that have absolutely no interest to you whatsoever. Rather than grumbling to yourself about how unfair it is, or how boring you find these jobs, remind yourself that you are not this body, you are that which is eternal and changeless and you have the option of not feeling victimized.

You can detach from your body, observe it going through the motions of tedium and refuse to identify with it. You are then in the position of watching yourself without identifying with the body that is laboring away. This process of observation immediately takes the judgment out of the activity and puts you in a state of bliss.

I used to apply this technique when I was a young man working for a large supermarket chain. One of my tasks was to unload a huge semitrailer full of heavy boxes. Often I had to do the job alone. It was boring, hot, back-breaking work. I didn't know that what I was doing was called witnessing, but as I look back now, that's what I was doing.

I would watch myself going through all of the unloading motions, and the boxes were no longer heavy. I wasn't lifting them. I was watching my body do that job. The time would fly by and before I even had time to think boring thoughts or to feel exhausted, the job would be completed. I was able to transform myself and do this job from the perspective of the observer, thus removing the stress and judgment from the undertaking.

I have talked to prisoners who have used this technique to get through their sentence, particularly when they were in solitary confinement. Some are able to observe the entire experience rather than hang onto it, and they find their feelings of isolation disappear. In fact, those who have survived torture in POW camps often report that they refused to think of themselves as being tortured. They managed to leave their bodies and watch the torture being inflicted, thereby removing the pain from their awareness.

At any moment, in any job or undertaking, you can leave the task to your body and embrace the witness, leaving the torment and inner agony behind.

• *Give recapitulation a try.* You can sit down and recapitulate your life from today backward right up to your birth, if you decide that is useful. This process involves imagining the people and events that have been a part of your life, including family, people you've worked with, lovers, close friends, schoolmates, neighbors and anyone else.

Begin by moving your head from left to right very slowly as you bring the people and the surroundings into your consciousness. As you move your head back and forth very slowly, you begin sweeping the energy back into you that you lost in these encounters. You are recalling the energy that you dissipated.

Some people have spent as long as two years in this recapitulation process. When they were finished, they were reenergized and able to access their new energy to transport themselves inward to new dimensions of reality—new inner worlds that defy all that they had believed possible previously.

The practice of recapitulation is recapturing energy. It gives you a much clearer picture of the need for everything that happened in your life to have transpired precisely as it did. Recapitulation shatters the belief that energy once spent is lost. You can access both your body and your energy body and know new worlds of perception. Recapitulation is the entryway to those worlds.

These ideas of recapturing energy, sweeping away useless energy and exchanging energy between people may seem absurd to you. If they do, it is because you have come to rely so heavily on your five senses that anything that is extrasensory seems unbelievable.

Everything in the universe is energy. You cannot move without influencing energy. You are a storehouse of energy, and you always have been. Give yourself permission to go beyond your senses and experience a new kind of formless energy that will put you in touch with worlds you may never have imagined.

The process of recapitulation is exquisitely exciting. You can redistribute your normal energy and enhance it in such a way as to give you a somersault into the world of the unimaginable. I recommend that you read Taisha Abelar's *The Sorcerers' Crossing* for a detailed description of the recapitulation process.

Even if you find it a struggle to cultivate the witness totally in your life, give some of these ideas a workout. More than anything, the witness posture introduces you fully to your higher self. It lets you in on the big secret: you are not your problems, your frustrations or even your physical life. You are that which is noticing it all.

You cannot firmly grasp or examine this sacred part of yourself because it resides in the invisible you. Yet it is the heart of your sacred quest.

You want to allow your sacred self, rather than your ego, to be the controlling influence in your life. You want a deeper and richer experience of life. It will elude you if you don't get to know this higher part of yourself. The witness will introduce you to this knowing. Nisargadatta Maharaj states in *I Am That*:

It is the "I-am-the-body" idea that is so calamitous. It blinds you completely to your real nature. Even for a moment do not think that you are the body. Give yourself no name, no shape. In the darkness and the silence reality is found.

As you cultivate this new awareness you will find yourself enjoying the silence even more than when you used to seek out the noise as your companion. Cultivating the witness will introduce you to yourself not as the doer but as the observer of the doer. You will come to welcome this realm as a respite from the hurry-up world that you have been living in.

The third key to higher awareness will put you further along in your quest. It is a twin to cultivating the witness.

6

SHUT DOWN THE INNER DIALOGUE

Empty yourself of everything.
Let the mind rest at peace.
The ten thousand things rise and fall while
The Self watches their return.
They grow and flourish and then return to the source.
Returning to the source is stillness, which is the way of nature.
The way of nature is unchanging.
Knowing constancy is insight.
Not knowing constancy leads to disaster.
Knowing constancy, the mind is open.
With an open mind, you will be openhearted.
Being openhearted, you will act royally.
Being royal, you will attain the divine.
Being divine, you will be at one with the Tao.
Being at one with the Tao is eternal.
And though the body dies, the Tao will never pass away.

—LAO-TZU

The more I listen, the more profound
the silence becomes.

✳

Those who measure such things estimate that our minds
have sixty thousand thoughts during the waking hours of
every day. Sixty thousand times each day something
called a new thought enters our consciousness and then
exits, while another thought enters.

The problem with this is not the enormity of that number but that today we will have essentially the same sixty
thousand thoughts that we had yesterday and the day
before that. Our inner worlds are a frenetic beehive of
activity with the same thoughts endlessly repeating themselves.

This inner frenzy I call the inner dialogue. It is an
omnipresent buzz in the form of silent thoughts. Most of
this inner dialogue is a personal inventory of beliefs we've
been trained to accept by others. Those thoughts include
all of your beliefs about everything you can possibly imagine. No limits here. Family, relationships, sex, politics,
history, your environment, criminals, God, everything.
The thoughts come and go, day in and day out in a repeti-
tive interplay of beliefs.

You may remember what I wrote earlier about beliefs. I explained that they are laced with doubt because you got them from others. Therefore, your inner dialogue is a perpetual experience of reinforcing doubt. Doubt about yourself, your ability to create miracles, your ability to manifest divine relationships, to heal yourself, to materialize prosperity, and finally doubt about your ability to know the bliss of inner peace.

The way to get to this place of inner peace and consequently to experience higher awareness is to shut down the internal frenzy.

INNER PEACE AND YOUR INNER DIALOGUE

The Chinese sage Seng T'san gave us the following piece of wisdom: "Stop talking, stop thinking, and there is nothing you will not understand. Return to the root and you will find meaning. Look inward, and in a flash you will conquer the apparent and the void." He is counseling us to simply stop talking and stop thinking. This is the third key to the sense of peacefulness that is a part of the way of the sacred quest.

I want to make it clear that peace is not the absence of conflict. There will always be conflict because there will always be others who want you to behave as they dictate. If you have a strong sense of your self as a unique individual, you will constantly be given the opportunity to strengthen that knowledge of your self. Conflict will still happen when you practice shutting down the inner dialogue and quieting your mind.

Peace is not the absence of conflict. Peace is the experience of the presence of God. As you learn to shut down your inner dialogue and become more peaceful, you will begin to know the presence of God in your life. That presence will be felt in both your body and your inner world. Beliefs are removed. Believing is replaced with knowing.

While I was preparing to write this book, I read the New Testament and came across something written by Saint Paul that was exceedingly important for me. He wrote in Philippians 2:5,6:

> Let this mind be in you, which was also in Christ Jesus: Who, being in the form of God, thought it not robbery to be equal with God.

The reason this held so much value for me is because Jesus' primary disciple, Paul, dispels the notion of God as separate from man. It seems to me he refutes the accusation of those who believe it is blasphemous to speak of God being within or a part of us. When you shut down the inner dialogue you are in direct contact with the loving presence of God. "Let this mind be within you. . . . God resides within you."

In response to how to begin to do this, the Melville quote earlier in this book is so appropriate that I'll repeat it: "Silence is the only Voice of our God." But this silence is only as worthy as what we bring back from it. The ability to go within, meet God and bring back something of value in the form of higher awareness is available when you begin shutting down the inner dialogue. Peace is what you will bring back.

At different times in my past, both alcohol and other substances were a part of my life path. Through meditation I was able to leave alcohol behind, and I have never touched it since. But with other substances, I believed I could use them when I chose to for an energizing effect beyond anything I had ever experienced. I was able to use them, enjoy increased energy and then leave them alone for long periods of time. But eventually I found myself going more frequently to this external source of energy. A time came when I knew I was making foolish and non-spiritual choices connected with seeking out these insidious substances.

My personal challenge became to rid myself of this addiction. I tried reading my way out of it. But I went back. I tried acupuncture, discussions with experts and herbal cures. But I went back. I was determined that I would no longer play around with this substance. But I went back. Then I had what I call a holy instant, which was for me a divine experience.

At 4:05 on a January morning I was meditating. In the still, quiet of that meditation, the thought of never again using the substance became real. It was my first absolutely direct experience of God. I became "openhearted," as Lao-tzu described in the display quotation at the beginning of this chapter.

My entire inner screen of awareness became a bright luminescence as I heard a voice say, "You have tried everything else, why not try me." I have never in my life known such peace and certainty that God was within me and around me. I felt overwhelmed by the bliss I experienced.

I thought perhaps that I was dying at that moment, and I didn't care because the bliss was so all-encompassing. I could see my body from a distance, like people have described in near-death experiences. Then I saw a window that was the clearest thing I have ever seen. It was like someone had cleaned the glass with a magic potion that allowed me to see thousands and thousands of miles into eternity.

I have never been so certain of anything in my life as I was that morning. It felt like I truly understood the meaning of "Being openhearted you will act royally. Being royal, you will attain the divine." I knew that my desire to reach for anything outside of myself would disappear from my life. No substance had ever given me this kind of "high."

I listened to that voice, felt the presence of God and

have not since experienced the slightest desire to go back to any substance. This is what I brought back from the inner silence. The ability to free myself from an insidious addiction and the absolute knowing that "this mind in you, which was also in Jesus Christ: who, being in the form of God, thought it not robbery to be equal with God." I had attained that mind.

It came to me when I had shut down all dialogue and given up on all other methods to send that evil monster out of my life. This is why I can write with conviction that inner peace is not the only thing you will gain from shutting down the inner dialogue. Perhaps more significant is what you bring back from that experience.

Lao-tzu further tells us that "being divine, you will be at one with the Tao." Tao is his word for God. So, we become one with God as we practice higher awareness.

I have debated with myself about putting this very personal story in this book. That is, my ego self debated with my higher self. It was from my higher self—while I was experiencing my divine holy instant, feeling the bliss of God as a part of me—that I knew. What I knew was that my experience with chemical substances also involved helping others to look within instead of outside of themselves for both the excitement and the peace their higher self has for them.

Millions of people are playing with fire when they toy with these substances, which are showing up in record numbers, threatening our children and the fabric of life. It is robbing us of our spiritual essence and "eating our bones." If, in my telling this story, one person who experiments with any substance and knows that it is out of control decides to shut down the inner turmoil and seek the help of their loving presence, then it will have been worth it.

You needn't have the challenge of getting off drugs to find value applying this third key to higher awareness. It works the same way for every experience you are ready to transcend: getting to silence and then having God be your personal knowing presence. Getting to silence requires conscious effort on your part. Knowing how your mind works as you begin practicing shutting down the dialogue can be helpful.

THE STEPS TO "NO MORE DIALOGUE"

As I discussed in the previous chapter, thoughts flow in and out of your mind all day, and you are able to witness those thoughts in lieu of identifying with them. However, you need to remember that the thoughts originate with you. No one else puts your thoughts into your mind.

In order to understand my mind, I use the metaphor of a pond with a limitless depth. I do not call this metaphor or the practice of it "meditation" because there are countless methods of meditation practice. I prefer to think of this as a simple and effective way of shutting down the inner dialogue. There are five levels to this pond.

LEVEL ONE: THE SURFACE

On the surface of the pond are all the disturbances. It is here on the surface that the wind will churn up the water, the rain will come down and pelt it, the cold temperatures will freeze the surface and the warm temperatures will thaw it back to liquid. Severe storms will cause the surface to become violent. Peaceful weather will return the surface to a smooth and glassy calm. Leaves and dirt litter the surface, people toss rocks disrupting the calm and all disturbances are visible here.

The surface of your mind is also where you note all of the disturbances. This is what I call the "chatter" level. Here is where a multitude of thoughts are constantly breezing across the surface of your mind.

The chatter is of finances, deadlines, health, children, appointments, shopping lists, retirement, vacation choices, violence in the Middle East, conflicts at work, last night's love-making, the book you are reading, the traffic, car repairs, your headache, your mother's flu, things you are afraid to say to your boss, a dialogue with your spouse in which you are the martyr. I could fill a thousand pages with these fleeting thoughts. This is the way of your daily mental life. Many disturbances are buzzing around on the surface of your mind involving virtually everything you encounter.

The storms of your life become the violence of your mind. The winds in your life create mild disturbances. These are all in the form of thoughts. Your mind becomes littered with all that drops into it from every corner of your life.

This kind of daily living at the surface level is exhausting. But more than simply tiring you out, this level keeps you from experiencing higher awareness. Unfortunately, this is probably how you have become accustomed to using your mind. It may even be true that you believe that your mind is supposed to be nothing more than the receptacle for all those thoughts.

Or you may believe that you think the way you do because you inherited that style. Until you explore other possibilities you may believe that thoughts come and go as they will and there really isn't much you can do about them. If your mind is busy, then so be it.

I encourage you to reconsider your position. Give attention to both the ecology of the surface level of your mind and to the significance of that level in relation to your mind's depth and breadth, as you would do if you were responsible for the environmental health of a pond. The surface of a pond violently whipped about by a storm is not an indication of what is happening to the entire pond. Some surface litter does not make a pond impure.

LEVEL TWO: JUST BELOW THE SURFACE

Disturbances on the surface have very little impact just below the surface. A storm is still observable from below the surface, but its presence is not felt in the same way as it is when you are in the middle of it.

Likewise, when you are able to go below the surface of your mind, you leave the stormy chatter behind. Here, the constant entering and exiting of thoughts is replaced with a different kind of thinking. You have more control of the thinking process though you are still a long way from silence.

The activity is, however, now more focused. You sit still and find that your thoughts are now on analyzing. This is akin to intellectual violence. It is here that you search for reasons for everything. You tear apart every thought and try to find out why this happened, or that failed to happen. Mock dialogues are engaged in with the people in your life whom you believe are not supportive in the way that you judge they should be.

At a rapid pace, just below the surface, the analyzing goes on. You may catch yourself analyzing something and make an effort to stop, but at this level there is a continual movement of analyzing.

Think of a pebble that has been dropped on the surface of the pond as it sinks toward the bottom. It has broken through the chatter level and is passing through the analyzing part just below the surface. Exercise the witnessing activity you learned about in the previous chapter. Watch the pebble drop and observe the analyzing thoughts.

Analyzing is the mental activity we are involved in when we automatically are making silent comments to ourselves about everyone and everything. Those silent comments will insist on analyzing your progress or lack of it even as you proceed with this meditative practice.

The difficulty is in thinking that there is something other than this moment and analyzing how to get to a place of peace and bliss. This is all to be expected. Do not judge it or become frustrated about it. Allow your mind to analyze, and know that the pebble will eventually drop right through on its way to the field of bliss. As the pebble drops, you will leave analysis behind and arrive at the third level.

LEVEL THREE: WELL BELOW THE SURFACE

The pebble is now well below the surface of your mind. The chatter is lessening and so is the need to analyze everything. You are allowing your mind to see the flow of how things are all connected and held together. To synthesize means to bring together; to analyze means to take apart.

At this level you are experiencing more of your spiritual nature. You can feel the flow of gratitude, joy and acceptance. You know that you are connected to all of life and you are using your mind to try to understand your place in the pond.

With the pebble passing through synthesis, you are still using your mind. However, you are no longer using it in a way that victimizes you. You have learned how to control the thoughts that enter and exit and you have left the chatter level.

At this level you accept that people are unique and that you cannot understand how and why everyone behaves as they do, including yourself. You are surrendering and floating into a deeper level of awareness. Here you will sense the divine flowing through everything and everyone rather than trying to figure it out. You are becoming more peaceful.

The pebble falls ever so slowly below the surface. You are beginning to know the depth of who you are without your mind having to understand for it to be personally meaningful. Until now, you have been convinced that enlightenment involves you as a seeker who must find something. Now you realize that it is not like that at all.

You surrender to not understanding and begin experiencing enlightenment. You know that God is both within you and outside of you at the same time. The pebble drops deeper into the center of your being, past that annoying chatter, past analyzing everything, beyond synthesizing, to the fourth level.

LEVEL FOUR: STILLNESS IN BLISS

You are now getting to the place where you are actually experiencing the joy of shutting down the inner dialogue. In this space, you begin to block thoughts and sink into awareness. You notice the silence of awareness, as fewer thoughts swim through.

As your mind becomes quieter, joy begins to sparkle in the depths of the fourth level. Joy is a sign of the presence of God. Joy is a particularly noteworthy feature of the sacred quest because its presence confirms that you have found your path. If you are using your mind to gain superiority over others through your emerging spirituality, you have not found your path.

The basic substance of life is joy, which pours forth from the spontaneous movement of the present moment in your life. With this spontaneity comes freedom from self-absorption and from judgment of yourself and others. This quiet mind is a peaceful mind floating in a sea of bliss. I love this passage from Tara Singh's *A Gift for All Mankind:*

> I think the most essential thing in one's life is silence. What is silence? We think if we are quiet, we are silent. But we must come to silence without desire and wanting; otherwise we are not silent. . . . Move toward discrimination and the simplicity of not wanting anything. Step out of stimulation. That would be the right thing to do.

This quieting of the mind becomes an intensely personal thing. You know the joy of not having the endless chatter and not needing anyone to confirm to you that you are or are not on the correct path. The quietness is an inner confirmation that you are experiencing a higher part of yourself.

As you grow accustomed to the stillness, you will find yourself seeking it out regularly. You will know that there is a presence with you. After a short time, the pebble will drop rather rapidly from all of that chatter to this place of quiet.

An old proverb states: "When the shoe fits, the foot is forgotten." This is the state of mind that level four takes you to—a blissful forgetting of that which doesn't fit, because the mind is at peace.

LEVEL FIVE: THE FIELD OF ALL POSSIBILITIES

This is the final resting place deep within the mind. This is beyond quieting the mind. Here is the place within, where you empty your mind of all thoughts and experience the stillpoint. It is impossible to describe with words. The best description I have ever read of this level comes from the Native American Black Elk. He put it this way:

> The first peace, which is most important, is that which comes within the souls of people when they realize their relationship, their oneness, with the universe and all its powers, and when they realize that at the center of the universe dwells the Great Spirit, and that this center is really everywhere, it is within each of us.

This is the fundamental essence of the field of all possibilities, which has been called by many names, including the unified field, the field of infinite love and the place where all things are possible.

Imagine that within you is a field, deep in the pond, where the pebble has fallen all the way to a resting point. When you are able to go to this place, through the power of your witnessing, you discover that you are not the wave but the entire sea. And remember that it is what you bring back from this center that is significant to your sacred quest.

The Great Spirit that Black Elk speaks of is within each of us. Discovering the unified field is your experience of it. In this unified field where the pebble comes to rest, you are at one with all of life. You are unified with God and the energy of love that is at the center of all. You will not be convinced of this by reading these words. You must create this as a knowing rather than a belief that I am handing to you.

I have a knowing about the unified field. The one thing I know about quantum mechanics is that space predominates throughout the universe. Everything, when broken down to its tiniest element, is not particle but space. All of us share this unified space in one way, and this experience of sharing our unified space is what it is like at the center of your being.

Rather than focusing on a single thought, I am able to put my inner awareness on the space that exists between my thoughts. This space is a mental formless thing, just as all inner considerations are. Only the focus of your awareness can shift away from a single thought and go to that space in between the thoughts.

As you begin to see yourself witnessing your mindspace rather than the thought particles, you will have a sensation of knowing God. As you experience the unified field in your daily "shutting down of the inner dialogue" practice, you will bring back a knowing about the purpose of your daily life.

The field of all possibilities is what Saint Matthew was referring to when he said ". . . with God, all things are possible." This is a magical place of miracles that you have to experience within yourself to know. "All things are possible" leaves out nothing. Within this realm of the unified field, one can manifest what previously were believed to be impossibilities.

This is my metaphor for how the mind works and what you can begin to visualize as you work toward shutting down the ceaseless, monotonous inner dialogue. The storms will continue in your life, as they do on the pond. Serenity will no longer be defined as freedom from storms but will be known as peace during that wild weather.

You can call this practice meditation if you like. Or you can call it mindfulness or simply quiet time. Some choose to call this inner serene experience prayer. Whatever name you choose, I strongly recommend that you give serious consideration to taking time each day to let that pebble come to rest in your unified field of all possibilities.

PRAYER AND YOUR INNER DIALOGUE

I recently completed reading one of the most remarkable books I have ever come across. *Healing Words: The Power of Prayer and the Practice of Medicine* is written by a man I respect immensely. His name is Larry Dossey.

Dr. Dossey is a practicing physician who has discovered the healing power of prayer. He has compiled an amazing amount of research and presents his case for the scientific value of prayer. Studies are presented in which some patients are the recipients of prayers and others are not. Prayers seem to be the independent variable in which healing takes place. The point of this excellent and readable book is that in the future, science and religion can find in prayer a common ground for exploration and dialogue.

When we think of prayer, we generally assume that it

is an activity between the person praying and God. And we generally place God both outside of the prayer and outside of the recipient of the prayers. But this does not turn out to be the case.

As Larry Dossey points out rather emphatically, "There is no evidence whatsoever in any kind of experiments on prayer that anything is 'sent,' or that energy of any kind is involved. . . . This strongly suggests that prayer does not involve any conventional form of energy or signal, that it does not travel from here to there, and that it may not 'go' anywhere at all." Of course this becomes very difficult for us to understand if we are trapped in our old belief systems from our early conditioning.

To understand the power and value of prayer we must throw out our old way of processing and look beyond cause and effect as well as time and space. The realm of God is undivided. It is not dependent on beginnings and ends. The realm of spirit is involved with wholeness, with everything existing at all times everywhere.

The quotation that I love the most concerning this phenomenon comes from the legendary author Hermes Trismegistus: "God is a sphere whose center is everywhere and whose circumference is nowhere." Try to imagine this within the framework of your personal space/time consciousness and you will find yourself stumped.

God's center (and yours as well) is everywhere, free of any external boundaries. Thus, prayer, or talking with God, puts you in touch with your center. But it is not some thing that you are forwarding out of your body and into another.

Dossey's conclusion is, "If prayer does not go anywhere, then it may simultaneously be present everywhere, enveloping sender, object, and the Almighty all at once." This is extremely important for you to digest because it will help in shutting down your inner dialogue through the use of prayer.

The practice of prayer puts you in touch with the truth that is within yourself. That innermost center is the unified field that I mentioned earlier. It is there that truth abides in fullness, and it is this center that you touch when you pray. You touch eternity, which is a magical invisible space wherein healing can occur and you know your inner divinity. Prayer is a fabulous method for shutting down that inner dialogue. It gives you a space to quiet your mind and to make contact with God.

The essence of the third key to higher awareness is simply giving yourself permission to have inner silence. If you want to call this practice meditation, by all means do so and find the bliss through your private practice. If you choose to call it prayer, and see it as a dialogue with God that excludes extraneous noise from your inner being, then by all means, pray.

The key is not in the method or the label. The key is in the practice of letting the pebble drop from the surface of your mind where you experience all the chatter, down through the depths of your mind into the field of all possibilities. Here is where we are all one, and where you will know God as a personal experience.

SUGGESTIONS FOR SHUTTING DOWN THE INNER DIALOGUE

• *When going within, use the metaphor of the pebble dropping through the various levels of your mind. While the pebble drops, be the witness. Observe compassionately all your chatter and thoughts as you descend to the unified field.*

• *When you notice your mind overly crowded with thoughts, practice not focusing on anything just for a few moments. You want to catch yourself and bring some stillness into the inner chatter.* Tell yourself, "My mind is full of the disturbance of chatter and thoughts. I'm going to try to spend five minutes without any thoughts bombarding me. I'll dismiss every thought, just for a few minutes."

- *Use your breath as a means to keep your mind from chattering away ceaselessly.* You can do this by focusing your compassionate witness on your breathing. Breathe in deeply, excluding any thoughts as you concentrate on the in-breath. Then exhale slowly and fully with the same concentration. When thoughts appear, as they will, know that they are signaling you to return to mindfulness of your breathing in and out.

  Your heartbeat can also be used as a focal point for the witness. Return to the steady rhythmic beat of your heart when you notice thoughts intruding.

- *When you find your thoughts just below the surface in the analyzing level, think of a rose.* As you replace the analyzing with the beauty of a rose, you might recall this verse by the poet Rabindranath Tagore:

  Do not carry a rose to our beloved
  because in it is already embodied a message which
  unlike our language of words, cannot be analyzed.

  This is a reminder that the habit of analyzing or picking things apart in a judging fashion keeps you from knowing the truth that is at the center of your being. The rose needs no analyzing. It simply is. The same is true of you.

- *At the synthesizing level when you are feeling the beauty and unity of life, you may discover that you are entertaining thoughts of pleasure about enjoying this spiritual space.* Let go of those thoughts too. You want to shut down all inner dialogue that muddies the way to the field of all possibilities.

The ego enjoys convincing you that you are better than others because you are more spiritual or have deeper understanding. It swims through your consciousness with thoughts like those. When it does, gently send it elsewhere for this time of meditation or prayer.

- *Make an attempt to put your awareness in the space between your thoughts.* This might sound impossible, but I assure you that you have the ability to experience this.

  When you are on a thought, slip into the gap that preceded that thought and put your awareness right there in that emptiness. In *Quantum Consciousness* Stephen Wolinsky says this about the space between your thoughts: "Experiencing the space between our thoughts eventually leads to a loosening of all the boundaries we put around things, ideas, people and so on. And as the boundaries loosen, our level of comfort increases."

  That unrestricted space between your thoughts is the gap beyond your physical and mental prowess wherein you experience the bliss of your spirituality. When you put your inner awareness there purposely, you will feel a strong sense of comfort. When you return to a thought, which is inevitable, do not judge yourself. Gently but firmly try to slip back into the gap between this thought and the next one, or this one and the previous one.

- *Sign up for a martial arts course that teaches the art of centering.* There are many forms of this activity available. T'ai chi and t'ai kwando are but two of many that are enjoying popularity because of their effective combination of physical and spiritual discipline. They actually take you through the process of centering yourself, which is another term for shutting down the inner dialogue and becoming one with your divine presence.

- *Make a call to your local Transcendental Meditation center (listed in the phone book of every major city in the world) and sign up for their introductory course.* This is a magnificent introduction to finding inner peace and shutting down the inner dialogue, conducted by highly qualified instructors.

  The purpose of TM is to teach you firsthand how to get to that unified field and to learn what your resistance to the process means. I recommend it strongly. I've practiced TM for many years.

- *In any moment of stress, go within for just a few moments and allow the pebble to drop, even if it is only a few seconds.* You can actually practice quieting inner dialogue any place. I've found the technique useful even in the middle of a tennis match. When I've done this I've discovered that some of the most important moments in athletic competition are between the points.

  That space is like the space between your thoughts where you approach a higher level of functioning. In situations like a tennis match you can stay centered by concentrating on your breathing between the points. You will become immune to external distractions this way. Try to make your activities into meditations rather than stressful competitions.

  Shutting down the inner dialogue does not have to be something you practice alone in a quiet place. You can do it in any location regardless of the external circumstances.

- *Stand in front of a mirror, look yourself straight in the eye and say out loud, "I love you, I value you, and I know there is much more to you than what I see staring back at me."* Then close your eyes and repeat the same thing. You will find yourself going beyond the physical you and removing many of your inner intrusive thoughts about defending yourself and attempting to prove your worth.

You are worthy by virtue of the fact that you have a divine eternal essence. Period. You need prove nothing. So any thoughts that you repeat which are contrary to that are keeping you from experiencing your loving presence.

- *When you make the decision to pray, rather than directing your prayer outward and seeking special consideration from God, make an attempt to be in the mind of God that Saint Paul wrote about in his letters to the Philippians.* Instead of making special and personal requests, listen for the voice of God which is present in the center of your being.

  If you are praying for someone else, have your witness focus on divine energy surrounding the person. Do not allow your thoughts to stray from the image of divine healing light. See God as your eternal divine guidance, always available to you. Make that a knowing rather than a belief.

- *Visualize a large clock whose second hand pauses ever so slightly each time it marks off a second.* I think of an old Seth Thomas clock in school classrooms that seemed to stutter each time a second went by. First focus your attention on each second, then shift your attention to the space between the seconds.

  Or visualize yourself running through a large crowd without touching anyone. Imagine you are running through the gaps between the people. The gaps represent the space between your thoughts that symbolizes the Tao. The quiet inner empty space, surrounded by form.

Marsha Sinetar, writing in *Ordinary People as Monks and Mystics,* summed up this process like this:

> Were the "average" person to take time to turn inward, to develop himself in the way under examination, his behavior, choices, activities would then also become motivated *from* within. Each act and choice would have more meaning, more fluidity. Such authentic actions are the result of a conversion process which can be experienced whether or not an individual is a grocery clerk, a grade school drop out, a nuclear scientist or a "bum." This process, happily, is the great equalizer which has little to do with where and how a person lives.

We are all ordinary people, and we are all spiritual mystics as well.

Take the time each day to turn inward and allow that pebble to drop through the levels of your mind until it settles in the place of all possibilities. All the inner noise keeps you from knowing the silence, which is the voice of God.

You can, at your own discretion, know this third key to higher awareness the moment you are willing to acknowledge yourself as a divine being. Your sacred quest is apparent in your moments of celestial silence.

As you gather the spiritual force within you in these joyous moments of silence, you will direct your ego to take a back seat to your higher self. It is this final key to higher awareness that awaits your attention.

7

FREE THE HIGHER SELF
FROM THE EGO

I come not to entertain you with
worldly festivities but to arouse your
sleeping memory of immortality.
          —PARAMAHANSA YOGANANDA

I know that my highest self is always
ready to lift me up beyond the world
I experience with my senses.

✳

The little three-letter word *ego* has had various meanings
applied to it. In Freud's system, the ego is the conscious
aspect of the psyche that chooses between the base
instincts of the id and the morality of the superego.
A person with an "ego problem" is considered to be
centered on the self. He is thought of as boastful, self-
centered and generally obnoxious. The stereotype is usually male and popularly referred to as being on an ego
trip.

There are many other interpretations of the word *ego*.
Some view it as the unconscious part of ourselves, primarily involved with hate, malice and destruction. Ego
has also been described as something that is always with
us, controlling our daily lives, but which we can do little
to change. Others define ego as the exclusive physical
aspect of our reality as opposed to the spiritual or higher
part that we define as soul.

None of these are what I mean by ego. I look upon the
ego as nothing more than an idea that each of us has

about ourselves. That is, the ego is only an illusion, but a very influential one.

VIEWING THE EGO

No one has ever seen the face of ego. It is like a ghost that we accept as a controlling influence in our lives. The reason no one has seen the ego is because the ego is an idea.

The ego is a mental, invisible, formless, boundaryless idea. It is nothing more than the idea you have of your self—your body/mind/soul self. Ego as a thing is nonexistent. It is an illusion. Entertaining that illusion can prevent you from knowing your true self.

As I see it, ego is a wrong-mindedness that attempts to present you as you would like to be rather than as you are. In essence, ego, the idea of yourself, is a backwards way of assessing and living life.

You've probably noticed the word AMBULANCE written backwards on the front of a vehicle so that a person seeing it in their rear-view mirror can read it. Think about it. When you look into a mirror, what you see is backwards. Your right hand is your left, your eyes are reversed. You understand that this is a backward view that you are seeing and you make the appropriate adjustments. You do not confuse reality with the image in the mirror.

The ego, this idea of yourself, is very much like the mirror example, *without* the adjustments. Your ego wants you to look for the inside on the outside. The outer illusion is the major preoccupation of the ego. The way of your higher self is to reflect your inner reality rather than the outer illusion.

The description given by Sogyal Rinpoche in *The Tibetan Book of Living and Dying* is a wonderful explanation of this discovery: "Two people have been living in you all of your life. One is the ego, garrulous, demanding, hysterical, calculating; the other is the hidden spiritual being, whose still voice of wisdom you have only rarely heard or attended to." He then goes on to discuss what he calls your wise guide.

Inside of you there is a wise guide, a part of your true self that walks with you as you progress along the path of your sacred quest. Rinpoche concludes: "The memory of your real nature, with all its splendor and confidence, begins to return to you. . . . You will find that you have uncovered in yourself your own wise guide. Because he or she knows you through and through, since he or she is you."

This inner wise guide is you, not the idea that you have of yourself. Think of this inner guide as your true self and allow yourself to listen to this wise guide. Instead of listening to the gossip of the ego, you will hear clear and inspiring messages of wisdom. Eventually you will free yourself from the demands of the ego.

I am not suggesting that you conquer, defeat, or despise the ego. It is important to honor and love all aspects of ourselves. This includes the visible world of sensory perception and the invisible world of divine spirit.

This fourth and final key to higher awareness is about freeing yourself from the ego-sponsored illusion that the ultimate meaning and gratification of your life will be found outside of yourself. Taming the ego is a way of inviting the higher aspects of yourself to function in their natural, loving and integrated design.

A Course in Miracles makes this point clear: "Your mission is very simple. You are asked to live so as to demonstrate that you are not an ego." If you are not feeling a deep, rich sense of yourself and your purpose in now-here, it is probably because you believe you are your ego.

Seven Primary Ego Characteristics

Freeing yourself from the illusions of the ego will be easier when you recognize ego's characteristics.

1. *Ego is your false self.* Your true self is eternal. It is the God force within you that provides the energy for you to roam around in the clothes you call your body—a quiet, empty space surrounded by form. Believing you are only the physical self, the body enclosing the energy, is a false belief.

You needn't repudiate the ego when you recognize it as a false self. What you are really recognizing is the ego as an idea of the self that is inconsistent with your true, sacred identity.

We are more used to thinking we are a body with a soul than we are to realizing that we are a soul with a body. Viewing yourself in the way of the ego—with the emphasis on you as a physical being—is a form of amnesia, which is cured when you recognize who you truly are.

Tagore touches on the falsity of the ego in this telling passage:

> He whom I enclose with my name is weeping in this dungeon. I am ever busy building this wall all around; and as this wall goes up into the sky day by day I lose sight of my true being in its dark shadow. I take pride in this great wall, and I plaster it with dust and sand lest a least hole should be left in this name; and for all the care I take I lose sight of my true being.

The wall is the ego that we construct. It imprisons us in a dungeon of frustration. Notice that Tagore uses "true being" to describe that which the ego shields from his awareness. The ego is the opposite of that true being. It is the false being—only an idea about the true being.

This idea has been with us ever since we began to think. It sends us false messages about our true essence. When we listen to it without the loving presence of the witness, we enter darkness. We make assumptions about what will make us happy and we end up frustrated. We push to promote our self-importance as we yearn for a deeper and richer life experience. We fall into the void of self-absorption repeatedly, not knowing that we need only shed the false idea of who we are.

2. *Ego teaches separateness.* Ego wants to convince you to believe the illusion of separateness. With each painful experience of feeling alone, apart or separate, ego tightens its hold. This false belief is continually reinforced by our outer culture.

Convinced of our separateness, we view life as a competitive exercise. The competition increases the feeling of separateness and fosters anxiety about our place in the world. Unable to see ourselves connected to the invisible intelligence, the God force, our anxiety mounts and our sense of aloneness drives us to seek outer connectedness.

Substituting outer for inner connectedness is what you are attempting to do by needing to prove yourself better than others. Your need to look better, achieve more, accumulate more, judge others and find fault are all symptoms of the erroneous belief that you are disconnected and separate.

The idea of separateness begins early in life. Without someone to model a rich inner life, we grow up experiencing the pain of loneliness, injuries and peer criticism, which intensify feelings of being apart from rather than a part of our true self.

The ego's development is reinforced with the central belief in our separateness. We become convinced that the physical life is all that there is; we spend a lot of time believing we are better than others; our interpersonal philosophy is to get the best of the other guy first. Lack of purpose and meaning in life is countered with the belief that you are born, you shop, you suffer and you die. Since this ego illusion is all there is to life it becomes important to fight for what one wants and to defeat others.

The feelings of separation are so deep with this ego attitude that convincing someone otherwise is a major undertaking. However, you know inside yourself whether what you have just read describes you. And you can make the choice to no longer allow your ego to insist that you are separate from your sacredness.

When you drop your ego beliefs, you are on the way to becoming one of those people Jean Houston describes who have managed to grasp their spiritual identity and fulfill their sacred quests. In a taped interview from New Dimensions Radio, Houston says of these people: "They all had little of narcissism, little of self-interest. They actually had very little self-consciousness at all. They simply didn't waste time worrying about their self-presentation. They were in love with life. They were in a state of constant engagement with all fields of life, whereas most people are encapsulated bags of skin, carrying around little egos." In order to get to this place you have to shatter the illusion of your separateness.

Your idea of yourself, which is what your ego is, will make itself known over and over as you attempt to shatter the illusion. And when you know that you are not separate, when that idea of yourself has shattered, you will experience a new kind of peacefulness.

No longer will you have to compete or be better than anyone. No longer will you need to accumulate, achieve or seek outer honors. You will have left behind an idea that you had cultivated most of your life. Rather than view yourself as distinct from God and everyone else, you will experience your life as connected rather than separate.

The eternal aspect of your self will know its freedom to influence your life. You will experience the connectedness to your self and all life in a way that ego's illusion couldn't begin to comprehend.

3. *Ego convinces you of your specialness.* The ego cannot recognize that the loving presence sees everyone as divine and lovable. "No one is special" is not an idea that the ego takes lightly. As a culture we tend to agree with ego that there are special people and special situations.

This attitude of specialness contributes to our social and economic problems by putting our country into debt and maintaining life support systems that mock the meaning of life.

Specialness implies that some are more worthy than others, as if God has favorites. When we offer this belief to our higher selves, we quickly see that it is preposterous. However, we allow our egos to create special categories and we ask others to honor them.

Specialness denies the perfect equality of creation. It also denies the totality of God's love. Your ego may insist that God loves you more than someone else, denying the totality of unconditional love that is God and that is you. Your ego's insistence also subjects you to the fear of not being special.

That fear of not being special then keeps you from knowing the peace of God, the harmony of oneness that leads to the bliss of your higher self. Ego specialness prevents you from authentic feelings of your sacredness by creating an inner experience of fear. Self-esteem, which is a given because you are a spiritual being having a human experience, becomes dependent on believing you are special or virtuous in the eyes of God.

Who you are is not special. It is eternal, invisible, blissful and sacred. Your self-esteem is not something you have to earn. A self-realized person does not ever think about self-esteem because he or she cannot doubt their value. They know to do so would be to doubt the value of God.

Attachment to your specialness creates enormous blocks to awakening to your true identity. It cultivates fear and resentment and prevents your awareness of unconditional love.

To discover your sacred self is to let go of any attachment

to specialness or identification with the ego. These are mere symbols of what you have come to regard as success. The ego encourages you to accumulate, believing you will increase your happiness.

But you know that happiness is not found in the more-is-better lifestyle. You know that something outside of yourself cannot give you inner peace. You know that this is backwards thinking.

Turn those thoughts around. Look at the inner path, where you see yourself connected to God and all of life.

4. *Ego is ready to be offended.* Whenever you are offended, you are at the mercy of your ego. Setting up external rules of how you are to be treated is a way of guaranteeing a terminal state of being offended. It is the ego's way.

A favorite story of mine concerns Carlos Castaneda and his spiritual teacher, the Nagual don Juan Matus. After having been chased by a jaguar in the mountains for several days and being thoroughly convinced that this jaguar was going to tear him from limb to limb and eat him as his prey, Castaneda was finally able to escape the fierce beast.

For three days he had lived with the horrible fear that he was about to be shredded and devoured by the jaguar. When his teacher asks him about this experience, Castaneda, writing in *The Power of Silence*, replies:

What had remained with me in my normal state of awareness was that a mountain lion—since I could not accept the idea of a jaguar—had chased us up a mountain, and that don Juan had asked me if I had felt offended by the big cat's onslaught. I had assured him that it was absurd that I could feel offended, and he had told me I should feel that same way about the onslaughts of my fellow men. I should protect myself, or get out of their way, but without feeling morally wronged.

All the things that offend you in some way play to your sense of self-absorption. That which offends you doesn't offend the real you—it offends your idea of who you are. In the world of the eternal you, nothing ever goes wrong, so there is nothing to be offended by.

But in the world of your ego, you are immediately jolted out of the blissful place of higher awareness into a world where you determine how others think, feel and behave. When they are not the way you believe they should be, you are offended.

When you have sufficiently restrained your ego, you will be able to treat the onslaughts of others in the same way that Castaneda was taught to think about the jaguar. It obviously makes no sense to be "offended" by a jaguar's attack, because it is just doing what jaguars do.

Whether you like it or not, your fellow human beings are in some ways like the jaguar. They are doing what they do. If you can allow that without being offended, you will have put your ego's idea of who you are in its proper position in relation to the loving presence within you. Then you can be motivated to make the world a better place, without first needing to be offended.

When you have tamed your ego, you are no longer offended by your fellow humans. Free of ego's illusions, you see your fellow human beings as they are rather than as you think they should be. The way of your sacred self becomes clearer.

5. *Ego is cowardly.* Your ego thrives on convincing you that you are separate from God. To keep this belief strong, it promotes the illusion of your guilt and sinfulness in a cowardly attempt to avoid the face of God, which is your true self.

The ego thrives on keeping you convinced that you are separate from God and will do anything to keep you in that mind-set. It will even take the coward's way of dealing with fear by encouraging your belief that you are a worthless sinner.

Your higher self knows better. That loving presence knows that at the core of your being is a divine spirit, drenched in the light of love and bliss. When you find ideas of guilt continually surfacing, they are the cowardly acts of the ego, trembling in fear at the idea of your knowing that you are an extension of God.

But just as fear of the dark is transformed by turning on outer light, so is the cowardice of the ego transformed by your inner light. Cowardly behavior is simply a symptom of great fear. The antidote to fear is courage.

You can courageously deal with ego's fear and cowardice if you *know* that the part of God that you are is not separate from divine energy. That knowing provides the courage to shine the light of your inner love on the darkness of ego's fear. Thus illuminated, ego's idea—its illusion of you as exclusively a part of the physical world—is enlightened.

6. *Ego thrives on consumption.* The false self will continually bombard you with the idea that you must have more in order to have peace. The ego pushes you toward external validation of yourself and is threatened by the notion that you can find peace within yourself. This push toward looking outward is what I have called "facing the wrong way."

The ego tries to keep you looking outward for your sense of peace and for a deeper and richer feeling of love. Its position would be weakened if you were to become acquainted with the love and richness within you. The ego is thus involved in a major endeavor to keep you facing the wrong way.

As you look outward in this futile attempt to find peace, you convince yourself that possessions will bring you the peace and fulfillment you yearn for. The ego has succeeded at this point in directing your life energy outward toward external pursuits, and it rejoices as you focus all your energy on acquisitions.

With your attention centered on what you see as

wrong, you attempt to fix those wrongs by getting more of something outside of yourself. Those circumstances distract you from knowing the decision-making power of your mind to choose peace and love over anxiety and fear. This is how the ego system stays intact. It is imperative that you reclaim the power of your mind in order to transcend ego's false beliefs.

It is impossible to consume your way to peace. You cannot buy love. There is no peace in more-is-better, as I've already written. That way leads only to a lifetime of striving without ever arriving. The ego is threatened and frightened of your arriving. It wants you to consistently push yourself to new and more elaborate ways.

When you discontinue seeking what cannot be gotten from outside of yourself, you arrive and relax in peacefulness. Your false self will be tamed.

7. *Ego is insane.* My definition of an insane person is someone who believes that they are something they are not and acts on that belief in the world. This is precisely what the ego believes. And it is constantly attempting to convince you to believe that too.

The insanity persists because ego fears death. We could say that ego has an insane belief that it has to die if you start knowing your true self. As this insanity takes hold of your life, you absolutely come to identify with this false idea of yourself. Unaware, you involuntarily join most of the rest of the world who also practice this insanity.

Keep in mind this quotation from *A Course in Miracles:* "This is an insane world, and do not underestimate the extent of its insanity. There is no area of your perception that it has not touched." Yet, the world is filled with people who are convinced that the holy spirit is something separate from them. And they spend their lives attempting to convince others of this insanity as well!

All human violence is a reflection of the belief in our

separateness. If we knew we were all one and that God is within us, we'd know that any harm to another is a violation of God. We would not be able to behave as we do to each other. But the insanity of the ego has convinced us that we are separate and encouraged us to pursue our vendettas of hatred.

Pierre Teilhard de Chardin, the French theologian and paleontologist, wrote: "We are one, after all, you and I; together we suffer, together exist, and forever will recreate each other." This is sanity—knowing that you are one with God.

For the ego, this is a dangerous proposition to announce because it threatens ego's importance. Total capitulation to ego's fears is insanity. For instance, Teilhard de Chardin was forbidden by his Jesuit order to publish his metaphysical and philosophical papers. His pain must have been deeply felt, but his sanity was not compromised by an untamed ego. His knowing was stronger than ego and the church authorities. Today his published works are accepted classics.

One of the most insane ideas that your ego offers you is that you are morally and spiritually superior to those who are not consciously seeking their sacred selves. This idea of spiritual superiority is a separatist belief.

According to this belief, those who are spiritual are separate from those who are ego-bound. This is another ego trick attempting to satisfy your longing to know your higher self, by creating a false dichotomy in which you are better than others. The reality is that there is no inherent superior/inferior dichotomy in humanness.

Each of us has our own path to traverse, and each of us will be tested in many ways. Your inner awareness of God does not make you superior to anyone—it simply brings you a deeper, richer sense of your purpose. Those who have not yet seen their inner light are still a part of you. They are you in other forms—different shapes with different behaviors.

The essence of you and of them is still the one source:

the celestial light of God. It is insane to let ego convince you to attach labels of inferior or superior to the loving presence within us all.

The above seven characteristics of the ego are merely an introduction to this topic. They are the primary general characteristics of how ego is involved in our individual lives.

You will experience a new kind of spiritual awakening as you become aware of ego's influence in your life. Real freedom is a result of freeing oneself from the power of the ego. However, ego will try to tempt you with many counterfeit freedoms along the path of your sacred quest.

AUTHENTIC VERSUS COUNTERFEIT FREEDOM

You will recall that in my earlier discussion I described freedom as an unconcern about oneself. When you have succeeded in taming your ego, freedom, in this sense, is accessible when your inner world is not focused on being offended, being separate or feeling special. Detachment from self-absorption, from the ego, is authentic freedom.

The opposite of authentic freedom is counterfeit freedom. This is the freedom that the outside world tries to sell us. It is just as much of an illusion as is the existence of ego as a separate entity. Counterfeit freedom, like ego, is nothing more than a false idea.

The idea is fed by the ego when it convinces you that to be truly free you must "get" something external to yourself. This is the freedom that society offers and your ego seeks in order to strengthen the illusion and keep itself alive.

To get to the joy of authentic freedom, you first have to examine the kind of freedom you have been pursuing. You need to see what kind of freedom you are continually being encouraged by your culture to pursue. You need to recognize the freedoms you believe you enjoy, which are inauthentic.

Here are several of those freedoms that are being offered to you. Notice how they contrast with the authentic, pure freedom that comes from transcending the ego and knowing God.

CHEMICAL FREEDOM

The United States has been the most chemically dependent country in the history of the world. Using a chemical in order to be free is the ego at its very worst—an illusion feeding an illusion. Using chemicals results in hallucinations and delusions in your daily life. The cost of this approach to freedom is freedom itself.

The price of brief experiences of freedom found in the physical ecstasy of drug use is being paid by far too many human beings. Babies are born addicted to crack cocaine; young girls and boys prostitute for drugs; families and lives are destroyed and broken; escalating crime affects everyone; productivity declines; poverty increases; living conditions become inhuman.

The search for freedom through chemicals has trapped users into lifestyles of never getting enough of what they don't want. The ego is telling the user, You'll be free when you experience the fantastic high that comes with this chemical or this bottle of booze.

But the pleasure is only physical. It lasts only a moment or two. Then there is the ego, demanding more. You never arrive with this approach to freedom. You must always strive for more of what you have come to despise.

Is this kind of life authentically free? If you were free,

you would experience a sense of arrival. You would say, This is it! I need nothing else.

When you transcend the ego, you will simultaneously begin to cultivate a friendship with the loving presence that resides within you. Then you will announce to yourself, This is it. I *need* nothing more. I *want* more love, more life, more purpose, all of which feel attainable with the partnership of my higher self and knowing about my sacred path. I want authenticity; I do not want a drug fix or a hangover or to impoverish myself to feed my habit.

The idea that a chemical provides freedom is a counterfeit idea. All you will get from that counterfeit idea is a need for more and an internal boost to your false self, your ego.

SEXUAL FREEDOM

The practice of sexual freedom has produced the exact opposite of authentic freedom. The idea of sexual freedom has created a counterfeit freedom that has immense appeal to the ego.

The pursuit of sexual freedom has resulted in shattered lives. I am not taking a moral position on sexual promiscuity. I am pointing out that it is the work of your false self to convince you that this kind of sexual activity has something to do with freedom. A key test of whether you are on the inner path of the higher self or the outer path of the ego is the amount of peace and harmony that a pursuit brings to your life.

Our pursuit of sexual freedom has brought the largest increase in sexually transmitted diseases in the history of humanity. Clearly, sexual freedom has created a lot of disharmony. God is peace. Ego is disharmony. The biblical admonition could just as easily have been written, "Lord deliver me from ego."

Ego-driven sexuality is the outer reflection of our longing

to know our spiritual self. Ego convinces us that sexual freedom will bring the peace and bliss and ecstasy that we know is somehow available to us. When we accept ego's solutions, we get a counterfeit freedom.

Authentic freedom allows you the freedom to know and experience the love of God within you, and to share it in the physical world as an expression of that love rather than as an end unto itself. This kind of freedom is found by facing in the opposite direction from ego, where your higher spiritual self is waiting to be known. Sharing both your physical self and your higher self is true sexual freedom.

Pleasure is a glorious experience and I encourage you to have as pleasurable a life as possible. But don't mistake that pleasure for freedom. Ego-inspired freedom is always based on a false sense of security because the ego itself is a false idea.

FINANCIAL FREEDOM

Remember that the ego thrives on consumption. The false belief is that the more you have, the more you will acquire and ultimately the more freedom you will experience. You can buy freedom, says your ego, and you are free to spend money you don't even have yet. Ego insists that all you have to do is want it and that your specialness entitles you. You don't even have to earn it, only want it.

Any freedom experienced this way is counterfeit and generally involves credit cards. You are not liberated—you are actually in a form of bondage to creditors. Owing usurious interest rates, mortgaging your future and your happiness, infecting your life with worry and fear—these definitely do not bring authentic freedom in any form.

Objects cannot give you freedom. This is an ego-designed trap to keep you chasing and consuming, always feeding this false idea. Your ego insists that you will find "it" as long as you continue working toward increased financial success.

But what is "it"? When I was a young boy I thought it was being on the hockey team. I made the hockey team and that wasn't it. Later I thought a date with Penny would be it. She was great, but she wasn't it. I thought having my own car would be it. Then being in the Navy. And then being out of the Navy and in college. Then I thought having a degree would be it for me. But, with each acquisition, it was still out of reach.

So I thought it would be my wife, then a child and perhaps more children. These were all wonderful events in my life, but they weren't it. Later I thought it would be my first professorship, then my first book, and then, for sure, my first bestseller would be it. It, however, kept eluding me.

Authentic freedom cannot be purchased or found outside of you. There is no discovering the elusive "it" in money, fame, prestige, possessions or even family.

These are three of the most common pursuits of the ego in its effort to sell you on its idea of freedom. Authentic freedom is actually the freedom of knowing who you are, why you are here, your purpose in life and where you are going when you leave here. It is knowing that your identity is not located in the physical world but in the eternal, changeless world of God.

Self-realization is authentic freedom. Self-realization is not an acquisition but an understanding that, once found, cannot be lost. All of the fruits of false freedom can and will be lost eventually. They demand specialness and separateness from you, and they all will turn into dust in your hands.

Authentic freedom is permanent. It is beyond all comings and goings. And it comes with a knowing rather than a belief. Once you know within that this inner experience of your higher self is the source of your freedom, you automatically have it. You are free from anger, hatred and bitterness. In essence, you are free to love. Your life will be filled with joy because you will have attained self-realization.

The self in self-realization is not the ego. So know that losing counterfeit freedom is no loss at all. Your sense of authentic freedom is egoless. You are no longer self-absorbed.

Freed from self-absorption, you enjoy authentic freedom. This new kind of freedom will provide you with a knowing that forever precludes any question of uncertainty. Instead, you will know freedom as an inner connection to the divine—your personal loving connection with God.

SUGGESTIONS FOR TRANSCENDING THE EGO AND KNOWING HIGHER AWARENESS

The following suggestions will help you get in touch with and transcend your ego. In the next seven chapters I will offer more specific ways of freeing your sacred self from the power of ego self.

- *Make an attempt to know your ego.* Try to determine when it is operating as the dominant influence in your life. Ask yourself, "Am I listening to my false self or my higher self?"

  The more you can be aware of the presence of ego and how it is manipulating you, the less influence it will have over you. For example, if you are boasting to someone about yourself, or in any way feeling superior about your appearance, abilities or possessions, recognize that this is your ego at work trying to convince you of your separateness from God and of your superiority to other human beings.

As you become aware of your ego, make a shift away from self-absorption into your higher awareness. As Cicero put it centuries ago: "In nothing do men more nearly approach the Gods than by doing good to their fellow man." The awareness of your ego at work is the first step to taming it.

- *Start keeping track of how frequently you use the pronoun "I."* Self-absorption is the ego at work. It keeps you from the kind of blissful inner freedom that characterizes your sacred quest. By catching yourself when you persistently use "I," and then making a decision to take the focus off of yourself, you will be transcending your ego.

  You may be surprised at how frequently this self-referencing takes place. The more you can check yourself by cutting back on "I," the more personal freedom you will experience.

- *Begin to view your ego as an entity that sits on your shoulder with a purpose.* This invisible companion is always with you. It tries to convince you of your separateness from God, your superiority over others and your specialness in the universe. The more you listen to this entity, the more you are off your sacred path.

  As you begin to recognize the signs of ego's presence, gently say to yourself, "There you go again. You allowed me to take the bait and I got trapped in my self-importance." You will find that most of your thoughts and actions are prompted by this invisible entity perched on your shoulder.

  It wants you to feel outraged when you are wronged, insulted when you are not stroked, offended when you don't get your way, hurt when you lose a contest or an argument. As you recognize and name this entity, you eventually will be able to ignore it. Ultimately it will no longer play the dominant role.

First you recognize it. Then you acknowledge that it is at work. Finally, you retire it with a full pension!

- *Practice listening to others and keeping the focus off of yourself.* Concentrate in your conversations on what the other person is saying and what they are feeling. Then, respond with a sentence that begins with "you" rather than "I."

  For example, if someone is telling you about a hospital experience, don't respond with a story about your hospital experience. Instead, say something that either paraphrases what they said or that convinces them that you really heard both their words and their feelings. You might say, "You really had a scary experience, didn't you?"

  This is called active listening. You will be pleasantly surprised at how much you will learn and how purposeful you will feel. This is a way of restraining your ego and allowing your higher self to participate.

- *Actively resist the habit of letting your ego run rampant in your life.* Nisargadatta Maharaj told a questioner in one of his dialogues: "Resist old habits of feeling and thinking; keep telling yourself 'No, not so, it cannot be so; I am not like this, I do not need it, I don't want it,' and a day will surely come when the entire structure of error and despair will collapse and the ground will be free for a new life."

  The more you resist allowing your ego to be authoritative, the sooner the day will come when your higher self fills the space previously occupied by the demands of your false self.

- *Practice daily meditation or quieting the mind to shatter the illusion of your separateness.* The more time you spend shutting down the inner dialogue, the more you come to realize that you are not separate from God nor any of the billions of souls that are extensions of the God force.

You will begin to treat others as you would love to be treated. You will have the inner knowing that you are connected to everyone in the universe. Meditation, more than any other practice, breaks down the illusion of separateness.

- *Try to remove the word "special" from your consciousness.* Special implies better than or more important than. It denies the existence of God that is in all of us. We are all special—therefore, none of us need the label "special."

   You are divine, eternal and purposeful, and when you recognize this, you will not need to compare yourself with anyone or to waste your time checking on how others are being treated. This is the hard work of the ego. It is constantly prodding you to prove your specialness.

   Have the inner knowing that the living spirit is in all things, and that is what you have to offer. When you know this, you are secure and serene, with no need for compliments or reassurances that you are special or in any way distinct from others. We are all children of God. No favorites. No outcasts. All one.

- *Keep a journal.* In it, describe what offends you about other people. Try to discover what being offended does for you. If you can be objective about it, viewing it from the perspective of the witness, you will find that what offends you is really a judgment about how others should be behaving. Yet, by itself, being offended in no way alters the offensive behavior.

   So try to take an instance of your being offended and merely witness it. Just notice that you feel offended and observe how it plays out in you. As you get proficient at observing your ego at work, you will find that this act of observation will defuse the inner angst.

With the technique of observing yourself, you will come to see that what offends you is your ego at work, hammering into your mind over and over that the world should be different, that people have no right to treat you in ways that you find offensive. Your ego insists that you have a right to be offended, hurt, miserable.

These judgments are that false idea of yourself, working hard, convincing you that the world ought to be as you are rather than as it is.

- *Give more of yourself and ask less in return.* This is a wonderful way to tame the ego. For example, Leo Tolstoy, toward the end of his life, had gone from being self-absorbed to becoming a servant of God, learning many of the lessons on the path of the sacred quest. He wrote: "The sole meaning of life is to serve humanity." So simple. So profound.

When serving others becomes a priority, you will start asking, in the form of a mantra, "How may I serve?" You have found spiritual enlightenment, and you will know bliss. Donate your time to a children's hospital and help those tiny souls struggle with their infirmities. Notice whether your ego wants to pump you up and take credit.

Suspend the false idea of yourself as a separate entity in need of special caressing. Become the one who does the caressing. When you cherish others first, you will know what it is like to be cherished through your own selfless acts. Try not to tell others about your philanthropic deeds, even when your ego pushes you to publicize your activities.

- *Remind yourself every day that the highest worship of God is service to mankind and that it is through those acts that your sacred self will be realized.*

You do not need to convince others or yourself that you are divine. Do it in deed. Your inner awakening of joy and bliss will be reward enough.

- *Stop the external search for freedom and come to know the flavor of authentic freedom that is communion with your highest self.* Every time you find yourself seeking out something else in order to feel free, ask yourself out loud, "Will this be the thing that finally liberates me?"

  Picture yourself having that which you so desperately crave. Create the feeling within you of having the car, house, drug, promotion or whatever it is that you imagine is your ticket to freedom. Are you now free? Or are you merely one step further removed from being authentically free?

  The exercise of visualizing yourself with what you desire, and then asking yourself if you are free, will put you directly in touch with what it means to be authentically free. Authentic freedom needs nothing to prove its existence. Counterfeit freedom demands something in your hand to validate its existence.

  Knowing this will disengage you from the directives of the inauthentic ego, which fears that inner celestial light of authentic freedom.

Higher awareness demands a new agreement with reality. You've read about banishing doubt, cultivating the witness, shutting down inner dialogue and freeing your higher self from ego. You can practice these four keys to higher awareness anywhere, anytime, regardless of who is around. I guarantee you that if you do, you will begin to see a new, miraculous awakening happening in your life.

As you apply these keys to higher awareness, keep in mind that your sacred quest is really all about having your highest self make the daily decisions of your life rather than being dominated by your ego.

In Part III I will present the major conflicts that arise in the dichotomy between the holy spirit within and the false idea of ego. In each chapter I will provide you with distinct insights for allowing the higher self to surface as the dominant spiritual force in your life.

When you feel yourself attaining your sacred self, these will no longer be considered conflicts. You will have the knowing that you are awakening to your divine mission. You will know God on an experiential level perhaps for the first time since you left no-where and arrived in now-here.

Part III

TRANSCENDING OUR EGO IDENTITIES

The blossom vanishes of itself as the
  fruit grows
So will your lower self vanish as the
  Divine grows within you.

—VIVEKENANDA

8

From Turmoil to Peace

All God wants of man is a peaceful
heart.
—Meister Eckhart

I know I can connect my mind with
the divine mind and guarantee myself
peace in any moment.

✳

The question I am most frequently asked concerning the
role of the sacred self and the ego is "How do I know
whether it is my ego or my higher spirit beckoning me at
any given moment in my life?" Part III, beginning with
this chapter, is written to guide you to your personally
authentic response to this question.

At any given moment in your life, you are choosing
between two pictures or evaluations of yourself. Your
choices include the one offered by your soul, or higher
self, which I think of as the voice of God, and the one
offered by the ego, or your false idea of yourself. You
decide how you view yourself and how you view others as well. Essentially, you accept either ego's picture
of yourself and others or that of your higher spiritual
self.

The first answer to the question posed above is, "If it
brings you a sense of peace, then it is your higher self at
work." Your higher self is always nudging you toward a
resolution of the conflicts that you experience in your

life, so that you will have room for serenity and harmony. I encourage you to pay strong attention to those feelings.

The only peace in your world, in your personal life, is the peace of God. If you are living with inner turmoil, continually quarreling with yourself and feeling anxious and fearful, then you are allowing ego to dominate your life. If you feel serene and peaceful, ego has been replaced by your higher self.

So you can always ask yourself, "Will this bring me peace or will it bring turmoil?" If the answer is turmoil, either in your thoughts or in your physical world, then you must examine how and why you are allowing ego to dominate your life. If the answer is peace, then you know what to do and how to think. And you know that your higher self is actively working for you at that moment.

REPLACING TURMOIL WITH PEACE

In every moment of your life, you have the option to choose peace for yourself. Your false self thrives on your inner anxiety because that is what it thinks it needs to stay alive. Ego promotes thoughts like these: I cannot be happy or content; I must be a sinner and an evil person; If I am feeling peaceful then I will simply vegetate; I must constantly look at how others are living and performing in order to assess my value. This constant state of comparison keeps the turmoil alive.

The ego wants you in a constant state of agitation to keep you from embracing your higher self. It convinces you that if you are not always on edge, you can't grow. But you must keep in mind that experiencing this inner turmoil is a choice that you have made by allowing your false self to dominate your life. When you make the choice for peace, you are literally allowing God into your life. Rather than vegetate, you will discover that you can be busy, purposeful and blissful and still have peace.

We all long for the peacefulness of being without turmoil and angst. There is a feeling of an inner glow when we know that we are on course, on our sacred path. So why do we frequently choose the opposite emotions, thoughts and inner beliefs, which agitate our minds, cloud our perceptions and distort our relationships?

You need to carefully examine your choices that block your experience of peace, of God. Just knowing that peace is always an alternative is a significant awakening. These tools will help to tame the ego when it demands that you pursue separateness or specialness.

Replacing the turmoil that you so often choose is then a simple matter of allowing your higher self to take over in any situation where you are about to allow turmoil to enter. Your ego will push you in the direction of the fight—away from peace. You must be ready to see it as it is about to happen and invite your higher self to send your ego a not-wanted-right-now message.

I'm fond of this *Course in Miracles* quotation concerning ego replacement: "You will not find peace except the peace of God. Accept this fact, and save yourself the agony of yet more bitter disappointment, bleak despair, and sense of icy hopelessness and doubt. Seek you no further. There is nothing else for you to find except the peace of God."

Give these words thoughtful consideration as you read the remainder of this chapter. Just know within that you always have this choice, and that when you opt for anxiety and turmoil you allow your ego to take over. You can instead be peace's home.

SOME TYPICAL PEACE AVOIDANCE BEHAVIORS

When you have an absence of peace at any time in your life, know that your ego, the false idea of yourself, is responsible. Here are some of the more common and acceptable behaviors that contribute to the absence of peace.

- *Confronting and arguing.* Nothing will bring about an inner feeling of turmoil faster than allowing yourself to be seduced into fighting or arguing. You always have a choice. Always! To argue or not to argue. To confront or not to confront.

  When you opt for arguing or confronting, you're allowing the ego to push your higher self into the background. Here is your ego speaking to you: "You are separate from your spouse/that clerk/those bureaucrats. You need to show them how special you are and that you can't be pushed around. Go ahead and tell them your point of view and don't listen to what they have to say."

  Behind this approach to life is the ever-present need to be right. When you give up the need to be right, you no longer need the turmoil.

- *Competing and comparing.* When you compare yourself with others as a measurement of your performance or feelings of success, you are at the mercy of your false self. You have bought into the erroneous idea that God plays favorites and that you will in some way be better when you are ahead of someone else.

  Ego is talking to you in a style that you've probably been taught to believe is important to your success in life. Ego tells you: "If he/she can, so can you. You are much smarter/prettier/ stronger/more spiritual/more stable than he/she is. You must assert your superiority and show her/him the truth. You are the best. Now get out there and prove it to everyone. You must purchase something they can't afford, to demonstrate how successful you are."

This inner dialogue, originating with ego, guarantees that peace and inner harmony will not be within your reach.

- *Chasing and striving.* The popularity of movie chase scenes speaks to an inner part of ourselves. The more intense the chase, the more popular the movie, the more secure ego feels. Up stairs; over cliffs; cars, planes, trains; through guns, robotic devices, violence and crash scenes. Over the fences and through the woods to ego's house we go. This is also the movie of your inner life when ego is in charge. Chase after success, prove that you are better than all those lazy bastards who are expecting something for nothing.

Go after the symbols of success and the merit badges of striving and your rewards will be more badges, more badgering from your ego and a void inside where peace might otherwise reside.

Here is the talk of your false self: "You are special. The way to prove that is to maximize your achievements. You are different than everyone else. Now prove it by getting that promotion, regardless of what your feelings are saying. You should be offended when someone else gets ahead of you. Do you want people to think they are better than you? Chase those incentives. When you get all of them, you'll be the best. Remember, if you don't know where you're going, how will you know when you get there?"

The ego loves to see you striving. It doesn't want you to be content, peaceful and knowing the God within you. Then you might not need ego, so it prods you to forget that rubbish and keep on striving. Ego instructs you to forget about arriving, whispering that there's a casket waiting for you when you arrive.

- *Worrying.* The more your inner world is focused on worry, the less time you have for experiencing peace. Worry is the absence of peace, and ego finds it extraordinarily easy to eliminate peace with worry thoughts.

  Ego's worry program informs you: "You should be worrying. There's a lot to worry about. You could get sick. One of your loved ones could have an accident. You might lose your job. You might get a divorce. You could go bankrupt. Your hair could fall out. You might be audited. You could get a disease."

  Ego thrives on this kind of thinking, happy that you are using up your inner energy to worry, not leaving any room for all that peace nonsense.

- *Saying, "Notice me!"* All of the time you spend practicing this two-word sentence is time spent away from peace and harmony. The need to be noticed and approved of is almost a full-time job for some people.

  Ego effectively uses this tactic to avoid the higher self with statements like these: "If they don't notice you, there is something wrong with you. It proves that you are inferior. Ask others if they think you are special. If they don't acknowledge your specialness, do something to get their attention. You must be noticed, and you will be if you spend a lot of your life energy securing approval. Beg for it, steal for it, cry if you don't get it, feel insecure and anxious if it is refused."

  When you need to be noticed and approved of, you will automatically experience turmoil and anxiety. Harmony cannot reside with these ego activities.

- *Giving yourself deadlines and pressure.* When you find yourself feeling the pressures that you have opted for, you are shutting out the potential for peace and allowing your ego to tyrannize your higher self. This is your false self working hard to keep you from knowing the loving presence.

It does it with these sentences: "You must prove yourself by not only doing better than everyone else but also doing it faster and without flaws. Give yourself a multitude of deadlines. Remain dedicated to those pressures no matter the cost. The closer the deadline gets, the more anxiety you should feel. This is good. It will keep your attention where it belongs—on your physical accomplishments and your specialness and separateness rather than on that silly notion of feeling serenity. Serenity is for losers. You have something to prove and you have to get it done now."

The ego is masterful at convincing you of your need to work faster—that is, if you believe that time is money and that money is everything.

- *Accumulating and acquiring.* The more you have, the more special you are, according to ego. The more special you are, the more you prove how separate you are from all of those others who have less than you have.

  There is no peace in measuring your worth in terms of your acquisitions. Therefore, your ego convinces you that peace is not what you want. Ego wants you to believe that things are more important. It tells you: "Store as many possessions as you can, and feel attached to them. You will feel a sense of pride and accomplishment when you polish those trophies and fondle all of those items in your valuable collections. How else will you know you've been successful if you don't have something tangible to show for it? Now get out there and consume, collect, acquire and accumulate as much as you can. These are the true tests of your specialness."

- *Chattering to yourself.* "Forget about all of that meditation stuff. It will just put you in danger of being seduced by the evil spirits that are the real bedrock of your personality. Keep your mind busy. Think about as many things as possible. Keep those thoughts coming, even if the previous one had nothing to do with the one you are now thinking."

This is the language of the ego, keeping your mind chattering away all day long, even disrupting your sleep. The more you chatter and keep your mind engaged, the less space you have for peace and harmony. Again, this is the job of the false self.

The false self is busy convincing you that you are something that you are not. To keep this illusion working, it does not want you getting into anything even resembling silence and inner peace. Your ego constantly pushes you toward inner noise and disruption, in the hope of keeping you from knowing the higher self, which thrives on harmony and silence.

- *Rejoicing in the troubles of others.* When you find some happiness in the suffering of others, including your so-called enemies, ego has its stronghold on you. It wants you to think of yourself as separate from everyone else. When others are having troubles, ego has an opportunity to solidify those beliefs.

  All of the tabloid gossip that provides people with a sense of titillation or amusement is ego at work. Preoccupation with others' miseries shows that you do not want to serve them but to savor their difficulties and feel amused at their humiliation.

  Your ego confides: "Those people deserve what they get. They are not your friends. They are obviously evil because they are on the wrong side."

  Your ego supports your separateness. Preoccupation with gossip, belief that the bad guys are getting theirs and the horrors of daily life that provide reading and viewing entertainment—these are all data supporting your separateness from those "others."

These are some of the more typical daily beliefs, attitudes and behaviors that the ego manifests to bring about an absence of peace. If you find these elements present in your life, you will very likely notice that these ego-producing behaviors also result in many physical manifestations.

Keeping in mind that every thought has a physical counterpart, you can see that these ego-produced elements materialize in your body in specific ways. The presence of this constant state of tension that comes with proving yourself, hurrying, chattering, worrying, chasing, acquiring and competing produces the same kinds of results in your physical body. The accompanying tension that goes with all of these ego-engendered thoughts involves tension in the body.

High blood pressure, ulcers, skin disorders, headaches, back pain and even more serious ailments such as cancer, strokes and liver disorders are the payoffs for the dominance of the ego. These disorders manifest because you allow ego to create turmoil to avoid the peace that is found within. This awareness of the ego's program should help as you move toward restraining ego and getting to know your higher self.

THE PAYOFF PICTURE FOR THE EGO IN PROMOTING TURMOIL

The ego—that false idea that we all have of ourselves—wants to maintain this persistent state of inner confrontation for some very solid reasons. When you understand your ego, you are much more apt to work at restraining it. When you know why your ego behaves as it does, you will then be able to make the adjustments necessary for your higher self to have a greater influence in your life.

Here are some of the most obvious reasons why your ego keeps you in this state of inner turmoil:

- *Most important, your ego has been with you since childhood.* It has been nurtured by almost everyone you've ever known. Generations of those nurturers have also been dominated by their egos.

    Your ego wants to survive. If it can keep you in a state of inner tumult it will block you from knowing your spiritual self. From the ego's perspective, God is a huge threat. So it will do all that it can to keep you from experiencing that inner peacefulness where God's voice is so beautifully clear.

- *Your ego does not want you to change.* The idea of yourself as self-important and special nourishes ego, keeping it healthy and operating at full strength. Even though ego is itself an illusion that you carry around with you, it behaves as if it had a life of its own.

    Your ego will make every effort to convince you that you do not need to change. In fact, if you are asking yourself why you shouldn't feel special, you may be listening to it right now. These are the kinds of thoughts that have kept you from making the changes leading to inner peace. The more you have these conflicts, the happier your ego is.

- *The ego thrives on fear.* When you are afraid, you are at the mercy of ego. Fear will drive you to behave in ways that undermine your sacred self.

    Your higher self tells you that there is nothing to fear, that love is the answer to everything and that God is what love is about. Your loving presence assures you that you do not need to feel guilty or fearful and that if you do it will subside when you experience inner peace.

    But your ego wants you to maintain that sense of fear. Living in fear is a manifestation of your belief that you do not trust in the divine force or in your inner knowing. This presence of fear confirms an abdication of your higher self and an admission that God does not know what she is doing. The opposite of fear is not courage—it is love.

When you experience love within, you have no guilt and no fear. You know that everything you are experiencing is in order, including your woes, which are your greatest teachers, and the death of your body, which is ordained for all the world of the manifest. You know that death is a reward, not a punishment. Therefore, you have nothing to fear unless you listen to your ego encouraging fear and dismissing God.

- *Your ego wants you to be on the move, looking for more things to consume and more possessions to own.* The more you are on the move in your life, the less time you will have for knowing your spiritual base. Ego cheers you on to stay busy, keep moving and avoid the inner quest where your ego faces restraint.

- *Your ego wants you to face outward.* It wants you to continue facing the wrong way so that you cannot experience the presence of God in your life. By facing away, rather than inward, you ensure the strong presence of your ego forever.

The consequences are that you will continually feel the pressure to compare yourself with others; the need to defeat others in order to feel powerful or even worthwhile; to have more and better toys; to accumulate more trophies. All of this facing outward is the work of the ego. When you refuse to listen, it shouts that you must be upset when others get ahead of you; that you are worthless when you lose; that being number one is more important than anything; that to settle for less is to admit to being a loser.

All of these beliefs are deeply ingrained within you. It is very difficult for you to even imagine not having them because the efforts of your ego and the egos of so many others have been working overtime convincing you that this is the only way to be. Facing outward brings about a sense of inner conflict and agitation that keeps you pursuing the gold stars that the ego offers.

A feeling of peace would challenge those long-held traditions and could mean the death of your false self. Your ego is in a survival contest with your desire for peace, and it will not loosen its grip willingly. It gets louder and louder, but remember that it will wilt when it faces the light of God on the path of your sacred quest.

These are a few of the more obvious payoffs your ego uses to keep you in a confrontational rather than a peaceful mood. I have provided some alternatives to the persuasive tactics of your ego. Keep in mind that you can restrain this ego simply by the power of your own will. All it takes is a determination to live by the dictates of your higher self and a willingness to act on that determination rather than succumb to the easier path of the ego.

SOME IDEAS FOR PUTTING PEACE IN YOUR LIFE PERMANENTLY

- *Remember, you must offer peace to have it.* You must teach peace to know it. Make it a practice to offer peace in as many quarters as possible.

    Thinking of yourself as a peaceful person is the first step, but it is only the first step. The thought must translate into action in order for you to know peace.

Work at curbing your inclination to create confrontation and disruption in the lives of others.

A simple practice of pausing and asking yourself whether your ego, which loves turmoil, or your higher self, which loves peace, is about to act will help you to send out a peaceful response, even in situations where you are feeling impatient or misunderstood.

In those situations you will be able to state simply, for example, "You are really having a rough day," to a hassled clerk, rather than, "I've been waiting for fifteen minutes already and I'm really feeling abused." Send out peace by catching yourself and then consulting your loving presence for a response rather than relying on your ego.

- *Remember that your past must have taught you the wrong messages if they do not bring you peace and happiness.* Do not be afraid to let go of those beliefs if they do not promote a sense of peace for yourself.

  For example, if you've been taught to win arguments and debates at all costs, but those behaviors have not brought you a true sense of peace, try abandoning that posture and encouraging others to feel joyful rather than defeated about being in your presence. See if their joy brings you a stronger sense of peace than winning the debate.

- *Practice releasing the emotions of fear and guilt and replacing them with love, forgiveness and kindness.* You will experience peace when you let go of those emotional responses. If you are feeling guilty about your past conduct, remind yourself that you are inviting turmoil to be with you.

  Release the guilt by forgiving yourself and vowing to avoid that kind of conduct in the future. You do not need the guilt, unless you are going to allow your ego to continue its dominance over your life.

  For example, make a list of all the things that keep

you from loving yourself. Your list might include being overweight, jealous, nervous, addicted, incompetent or uncoordinated. Then, regardless of how much effort it takes, reverse your mental sentences and state that you love yourself while being fat, addicted, and so on.

This will help you to feel peaceful about the choices you've made and to realize that you are not that body or those desires. You are the invisible chooser. As you become more peaceful with the chooser you will begin to replace the unhealthy choices in a spirit of love.

- *Examine everything that offends you and see if you can get your ego out of the picture.* If hunger and starvation in the world offend you, try shifting to a new awareness.

Somehow, in some way that I do not comprehend, these things occur in divine order, and so too does my desire to change it exist in divine order. Shed what offends you, and act on your desire to make corrections.

When you are offended, you are actually thinking, "This is awful, it shouldn't be happening. How could God allow it?" Get your own ego out of the picture, then act upon that which you are for. There will be no need to fight.

Similarly, if you find someone's behavior offensive, you are interpreting that behavior from your own self-absorbed position, which is that they shouldn't act the way they do. You choose to be offended, hurt or angry by their behavior.

But they are acting the way they are. Your being offended is your ego talking to you to keep you anxious and upset. If you don't take it personally, and if you see the behavior for what it is, you can work to eradicate the evils of the world unimpeded by your ego's encouragement to be offended.

- *Keep in mind that grievances bring turmoil while communication brings peace.* If you want peace in your life, rid yourself of your grievances.

  The way to shed these grievances is to let go of your own self-absorption and to practice forgiveness rather than revenge. As you let go, you will feel a sense of peace overtaking you. If you are angry toward someone in your life, no matter how difficult you may find it, work at communicating with that person about your aggrieved feelings.

  Your resistance to communicate is your ego's strategy. If you allow it to fester, you will keep the turmoil alive and never experience the bliss that peace brings. When you resist communicating with someone, remind yourself that this is your ego at work, and that you are determined to have peace. A few moments of discussion or even forgiveness will send the turmoil away and will weaken the influence of your ego.

  Your embarrassment or inner anguish over being wronged is just what your ego wants you to experience, since it will keep you away from your sacred quest and keep you in the clutches of your anxiety-loving ego.

- *Keep this little sentence ready to consult: "Judgment and peace are antithetical."* A Course in Miracles says, "The strain of constant judgment is virtually intolerable. It is curious that an ability so debilitating would be so deeply cherished."

  You must make a daily effort to look upon others without condemnation. Every judgment takes you away from your goal of peace. Your ego loves your judgments, because with them you remain in a constant state of anguish and remorse. Keep in mind that you do not define anyone with your judgment; you only define yourself as someone who needs to judge.

  Judging others with condemnation removes the possibility of your experiencing love. If you can practice just being still, rather than condemning, you will get to the bliss I am writing about. You do not have to pretend that you love something that you loathe. Just get still and let the judgment subside.

Peace is not found in being right or being hurt or angry. By all means, work toward righting the wrongs you perceive, but do it with an understanding that an angry heart keeps you from knowing God on the path of your sacred quest.

Peace will come to you when you are a healer rather than a judge.

- *Give yourself the gift of a silent retreat every day.* Even if it is only for a few moments. Go back to that key to higher awareness, shut down the inner dialogue and know the difference between the constant chatter and the bliss of the unified field. When you begin to have silent time on a regular basis, you will covet it and insist on it being a part of your life, regardless of how busy you are. This is the surest way to ease control away from ego and move into the inner vision of peace that is your birthright.

- *Once again, the greatest technique for bringing peace into your life is to remind yourself to always pick being kind when you have a choice of being right or being kind.* This is the single most effective method I know for having a sense of peace. And remember, you have that choice in all of your interactions.

- *Keep uppermost in your mind that there is a place within you where there is perfect peace and where nothing is impossible.* If you give yourself the right to pray regularly, you will get to that place. Peace is yours just for the asking.

When your higher self is present, it always promotes peace. If you have a question about whether it is your ego or your higher self prodding you, the answer becomes obvious when you ask yourself, "Will this bring peace or turmoil to my life?"

In the *Yoga Vasistha,* we are reminded of the need for peace:

This worldly life is not conducive to true happiness,
So reach the state of equanimity
In which you will experience peace, bliss, and truth.
If you stay within the unsteady mind,
Then there is no peace, there is no happiness.

This notion of an unsteady mind will be helpful to you. Unsteady translates into turmoil; equanimity is peace. This state of equanimity is unreachable with your ego. You must purchase the ticket to bliss from your higher self.

If you continue to look for that passage via ego as your travel agent, you will stay in that unsteady mind eternally. Your higher self—and only your higher self—promotes peace. It desperately wants you to know the bliss of this inner state of equanimity.

9

FROM DECEPTION TO TRUTH

The truth shall make you free.
—JOHN 8:32

> I know I am strengthened as I seek to
> make truth my personal reality.

✳

The words of Saint John are enormously significant for me. I work each day at allowing my higher self to be where my ego has been dominant for so many years. When I am successful, I am able not only to speak the truth but to think truth and be truth. Then I feel the bliss and fulfillment of being on my own sacred quest.

The intention of this chapter is to help you move truth into your life by identifying behaviors and rationales that are keeping you from that divine truth. A commitment to truth means a huge step in the direction of curtailing ego, which thrives on deception and phoniness.

Essentially, embracing the truth is welcoming your higher self and coming to know God. All that is not authentic will drop away automatically.

Your ego works hard to convince you that you are separate and better than everyone else, and you know that it does not take kindly to your embracing anything that threatens its existence. But remember that this is your inauthentic self, your false self. Deception is going to play a big role in your life when you embrace ego as your guide.

Therefore, in order to abandon your reliance on that false self with all of its deception, you will have to make a new agreement with truth. I encourage you to actually write yourself a contract in which you agree to include truth as your companion in your thoughts, in your conversations and in your life.

This is a big challenge and perhaps difficult for you. But it is guaranteed to lead you to the path of your sacred self. Begin by looking honestly and fearlessly at who you are beneath all the surface trappings that you have surrounded yourself with.

THE TRUTH BELOW YOUR SURFACE

You have a human story line, as does every person who has ever lived on this planet. That story line begins with your conception, continues through your childhood and all of your personal triumphs and tribulations, right up to this moment.

Your ego tells you this is your kingdom, your true identity, and therefore you must do whatever it takes to make this story turn out to be a good one for you. But you already know, by virtue of having read this far, that this is not so.

There is a divine whisper within you telling you that this is not your ultimate home and that the things this life offers are unfulfilling to a part of you. You sense that the real you does not value appearance, possessions, achievements, physical strength, talent or intellect because all these things eventually atrophy and disappear. You know that there is an eternal aspect of you beneath the surface and that for this part of you, only the truth will suffice.

It is similar to the truth Michelangelo knew as he sculpted the statue of David. He described knowing that the statue of David was already inside the block of marble. Part of his artistic life was spent chipping away the excess to reveal God's creation. Try to visualize your inner life in this fashion.

What exists within you is not some kind of hideousness that needs to be lied about. There is nothing imperfect about you that requires you to create a whole world of deception in order to make you worthy in the eyes of others. There is a loving presence residing within you. It is as perfect as Michelangelo's David, just waiting for you to allow it to emerge.

YOUR EGO DESPISES TRUTH

I have worked very hard on this matter of truth in my own life. For a large part of my life I have had only a very casual relationship with truth. It was never my intention to be malicious or harm anyone, but I allowed myself to reach into my ego's large repertoire of deceptions. This casual relationship with truth kept me from knowing my higher self.

I had learned to listen to my ego rather than to my higher self whenever it was convenient to explain away my own weaknesses or inadequacies. If I wanted to have an affair, I found it easy to explain it away as my entitlement to the pleasures of the moment. Lying to protect that pleasure was simply what my ego demanded. The ego was very strong in this direction.

A friend told me that he had once come home at 5:00 A.M., still drunk after a night of partying. His wife had locked him out, so he went back and partied some more, finally arriving home at 8:00 that morning. He told his wife that he had fallen asleep in the hammock in the back yard and had really been in the yard all night. When his wife told him that the hammock had been removed three days earlier, he responded at the behest of his ego: "That's my story, and I'm sticking with it."

That is ego at work, encouraging a false identity with lies and deception if need be to maintain the image.

I found myself on the spiritual path as the result of a calling rather than as a conscious choice. As this happened, I saw that deep within me I did not accept myself as a divine being. I was at the mercy of my false self, which told me to project an image to the world and did not want me to know God or the truth that is embodied in that knowing. Consequently, I was deceiving myself to maintain that false self.

Gradually, it became intolerable to live with the lies, even the small distortions. The truth terrified my ego in the beginning. Then, as I tamed my ego, truth became an enjoyable feeling of freedom. Truth does literally set us free, as Saint John told us in the New Testament.

Truth sets you free because you no longer are focused on yourself and what kind of an image you are projecting or protecting. In fact, you are no longer of this world even though you are in it. You find your identification in the world beyond, with that which is eternal.

I've had many discussions with my good friend Stuart Wilde on this subject. He tells me that it took him eight years of daily corrections and reminders to move away from distortions and live the absolute truth. Eight years of correcting himself and learning to be independent of the good opinion of others. His ego kept telling him that what others in this world thought was more important than anything. This meant that he had to create the scene as he felt "they" wanted it.

I did the same thing. What I thought of as little white lies or meaningless exaggerations were in fact the work of the ego constantly reminding me that I needed to protect myself by giving the world what ego said was wanted. Why? Because deep down, according to ego, I was hideous. That has all changed dramatically since I made an agreement with God that truth is my way to higher awareness.

My experience of this change is echoed in the words of Stuart in *The Whispering Winds of Change*:

> Over the years, as your spiritual energy grows, lies go from a part of everyday life to unfortunate necessities, to uncomfortable experiences, to extremely painful burdens that you will do anything to be rid of. If you have taken to the spiritual path you will know what I mean. . . . Transcendence is partly the process of moving from phony to real.

I am confident that as you travel the path of your sacred quest, you will have a similar experience. This transformation will take place in yourself as you witness and recapitulate your personal experiences. You will begin to find even the smallest distortions too burdensome. Then you will know that your higher self is winning the conflict with ego.

MOVING FROM PHONY TO AUTHENTIC

We see and hear lies all the time. The media is filled with advertising claiming all manner of things that have nothing to do with reality. According to advertising, you can recapture your youth if you drive a certain car, find love if you wear the advertised fragrance, gain new energy if you eat a certain cereal or regain lost intimacy if you use a certain deodorant. Our government promotes its policies with lies and spends money it doesn't have. It distorts unemployment figures for politically advantageous sound bites on the evening news. Legislators tell us that we cannot have health care because we cannot afford it, yet they legislate themselves comprehensive care. We are supposed to believe that there is no money available to assist the poor and ill, yet we eagerly finance wars in faraway places.

We've all become used to lies. You may even have convinced yourself that to tell lies is a worthwhile activity. When you adopt distortion and deception, the problem is that you will always need more of the same to keep covering your tracks. The same is true for our society. Ultimately, as we move toward a more spiritual base, the lies will decrease, both in our culture and in our personal lives.

At first, when you discontinue lying, it stings. It is like a new remedy on an old, open wound. Your willingness to think, feel and act truthfully will expose some warts. The warts are you. The mistakes are you. They are not unique and they do not say anything ugly about you. The sting and the discomfort will be soothed as you let go of the need to deceive.

The ego will suffer whatever anxieties it will, but you will bask in the warm light of the truth.

I want to share a letter with you that I received recently. It illustrates how truth can come into your life in ways you might not imagine when you allow yourself to consult your higher self rather than succumb to the demands of your ego.

Dear Dr. Dyer,

I hardly believe I am writing this letter to you. I have just started reading for the second time your book *Real Magic*. Many of the ideas in it were already familiar to me, but it seems to be the kind of thing that has awakened in me—indeed really pushed me—to reach out of myself and begin to live and realize some dreams. I appreciate the work you put into it for us.

I am writing you for a purpose. I have a question. Now I don't really suppose you can pay much attention to every letter that comes your way, but if you have an answer for me, I am sure I will get it.

After a couple weeks of putting some of the things in your book into practice—affirming myself, affirming my life, affirming even my purpose, and visualizing, not just visualizing, but putting love into my imagining it came to me one night just before I fell asleep, that the answer to my dream longing, that my miracle would come in the mail the next day. This knowledge was absolute, and I went to sleep feeling very peaceful. Now, I am a single parent of two children; it is a sheer monthly miracle we scrape together enough to survive—but I have dreams of a peaceful world and I have intentions of transforming it.

The next day my miracle did arrive in the mail— in the form of immediate credit of $7,500—from a bank card. Just imagine, my financial woes temporarily diminished and the ability to purchase the things I needed to begin our family-based company. (We want to manufacture children's clothing and toys all produced from 100% natural sources and regionally sustainable.) And here it was—enough credit to put out a catalogue and purchase fabric. There was only one problem—the credit wasn't for me. I had mistakenly opened a letter addressed to a former occupant of our duplex. All I had to do was sign his name and send it back.

So I did. I dashed off a fake signature and sealed the reply envelope before I could think about it. I headed for the mailbox. Oh, I can't tell you what it felt like to think our dreams were going to become a reality. And I didn't think my wrongdoing was that great—after all, the person would never know, and of course I would pay the bills on time.

During my bus ride to the mailbox, however, something began to form in my mind. My conscience, of course, but something else. It somehow became very clear to me that refusing to do this dishonest deed meant I was not only doing the right thing but something even deeper—sending a message to my subconscious of trust. That I didn't need

to do this dishonest thing to realize my miracle—
that I could trust in my self to do what needed to be
done. Now this may not sound like much to you, but
Dr. Dyer, for me to realize I could trust in myself is
about as victorious as landing on the moon was! I
ripped up the poison letter and went home. I spent
the rest of the day on a victory "high."

But now the days have gone by and I'm starting
to feel a vague doubt. I'm still visualizing and trying
to trust, but occasionally I feel that maybe that
credit was a gift from God, and I should have taken
it. Dr. Dyer, do you think I did the right thing? If
so, can you discern where perhaps I am now going
wrong?

Thank you for the time, energy and hope you
bring for a transformed world.

Peace,
Rebecca Roberts
St. Paul, Minnesota

Many times what we think we need is not what God is
trying to teach us. Rebecca needed to know the value of
truth in her life and she received this message by listening
to her higher self rather than her money-based ego. In
this case, by going with the higher self, she allowed the
truth to reign in her life.

I was so touched by her honesty and the questions
posed by her ego (guilt over having been so stupid, ratio-
nalizing dishonesty as what God really wanted) that I
made arrangements for Rebecca to get that line of credit
interest-free.

As we know, God works in mysterious ways, but the
higher self knows when it is being untruthful. Rebecca's
insight the night before—that her dreams would be
answered in the mail the following day—turned out to be
true. But she had to pass the test of truth before her
dream was answered.

The movement away from phony to authentic begins

with the self. You—the invisible presence within, who studied those four keys to higher awareness—in the silence of your being make a new covenant with reality.

You hear the loving presence telling you that you are divine and need not hide by portraying yourself as anything other than what you are. You become able to love any other who finds this difficult and you do not have to alter who you are because you know that deep within you is that unified field of all possibilities. You know your holiness.

Then, as you gain this self-awareness you also grow in the awareness of not being your physical body. You no longer need to project anything other than your peaceful divineness to friends, family and even strangers. You've made the transition from phony to real in a holy instant. You recognize your inner sanctity and are willing to forgive yourself for any and all mistakes-now-viewed-as-lessons. You have moved to truth.

The inner knowing that you no longer have to lie or distort anything for the sake of the approval of others or to elevate yourself in others' eyes is the freedom that truth brings. It took Stuart eight years to get to this point. It has taken me a longer time to come to grips with the value of truth in all circumstances, but it has come to me in moments of satori.

I figure that if Saul of Tarsus, a murdering thief, can be transformed in a moment of holy insight and become the apostle Saint Paul simply by letting in the truth and living it, so can Wayne Dyer admit to his mistakes of the ego and live the truth, and so can you. As Thomas Merton put it: "We must be true inside to ourselves, before we can know a truth that is outside of us."

Moving from phony to real is first being true inside and then experiencing the truth of living it. As you begin to live these truths, you not only turn your own world around, you also affect the transformation of the world around you. The truth not only sets you free, but it will set the world free as well.

The world's ego cannot stand up to the celestial light of the truth any more than your personal ego can. The distortions that you see around you—the cheating, lying, stealing and killing—will begin to disappear as we reach within our own individual selves and transform the ego energy.

The distortions and deceptions created by ego are many. In the following paragraphs you will find some of the more common forms that appear in all of our lives.

How Avoidance of Truth Shows Up in Your Life

This section is not addressing con artists or those who lie for personal gain, commit criminal perjury or engage in nefarious deceptions of that sort. What I am presenting here are the ways ego convinces us to consult our false self rather than our higher self in our daily life.

This is not evil double-dealing but rather the learned ways we have adopted of allowing ego rather than higher self to guide us. Here are some of the more common forms that this avoidance of pure truth takes in your life.

- *Boasting or bragging.* An inclination to draw attention to yourself and to misrepresent your accomplishments so that others might view you in a positive, special and separate way.

- *Factual distortion.* Stating facts as you would like them to have occurred rather than how they actually did occur. These little white lies or petty exaggerations, when defended, become a way of life.

- *Deception to save face or embarrassment.* Making up a scenario for the purpose of convincing another that you are innocent of some wrongdoing. This kind of deception means having to keep track of what was told to whom and when. Further distortions get piled on to the original to keep the phony story line going.

- *Creating an imaginary future scene.* Lying about your future whereabouts to hide the truth. You live out your future moments in a false way, knowing before the time comes that you will be living a lie. Your life is a lie in the now and in the future.

- *Exaggerating facts to gain attention.* An example of how difficult it is to discontinue this distortion is found in this little story from *Illustrations Unlimited*, edited by James S. Hewitt:

  A little girl developed a bad habit. She was always lying. Once when she was given a St. Bernard dog for her birthday, she went out and told all the neighbors that she had been given a lion. The mother took her aside and said, "I told you not to lie. You go upstairs and tell God you are sorry. Promise God you will not lie again." The little girl went upstairs, said her prayers, then came down again. Her mother asked, "Did you tell God you are sorry?" The little girl replied, "Yes, I did. And God said sometimes He finds it hard to tell my dog from a lion too."

  The practice of changing the facts for the purpose of impressing others can be cute when a small child does it. For adults, it is a way of relying on the ego to keep illusions alive. It will keep you from knowing your higher self, which needs no exaggeration to feel important in the eyes of others.

- *Overlooking something for your advantage.* This story reveals how this can operate in anyone's life:

  A man was given his paycheck and he noticed that he had been overpaid by twenty-five dollars, and he didn't say a word to the paymaster. The paymaster realized his mistake and the following payday he deducted the twenty-five dollars from the man's paycheck. The man immediately went to the paymaster and told him that his paycheck was short. The paymaster replied, "You didn't say a word last week when you received too much money." The man replied, "I don't mind overlooking one mistake. But when it happens twice, it is time to say something."

  The practice of spiritual honesty requires one to speak up regardless of whether one is to benefit from a mistake.

- *Deliberate cheating for your own gain.* The practice of gouging others or misrepresenting costs and then putting in hidden charges seems to be a normal practice for those who allow their egos to run their lives.

  It has been estimated that American hospitals add excess charges and erroneous amounts on 99 percent of their invoices. Imagine, ninety-nine out of every one hundred bills contain errors that favor the hospital!

  This practice is far too common in many businesses and in personal lives too. The feeling that it is alright to cheat others if you can fool them is a way of being that will keep you far from the path of your sacred quest. Instead you will find yourself being cheated by others as you cheat them.

- *Macho and bravado behavior.* The ego's need to appear better or stronger or more important creates behavior that frightens or manipulates others. Bullying, bragging, strutting, cajoling and the like are all acts of deception that the ego believes will convince someone of your uniqueness and specialness.

• *Inner dialogues about the dangerous world.* Using your mind to have dialogues about how scary the world is is a technique of the ego. The more you can be convinced that the world is dangerous, the less you are able to know your higher self. Preventing contact with your higher self ensures you will not know that you are safe and divine.

• *Self-deception.* Ego convinces you that others are special and that you haven't a chance because of your inferiority. When you put yourself down with self-deprecating statements and shy away from risks, you are in agreement with ego's claim that you are weak and unimportant. This deceptive and unrealistic self-appraisal is an avoidance of truth and a tool of the ego to keep you from your sacred quest.

To transcend the inclination toward deception you need to understand why you allow this scenario to rule your life. There is always a payoff for your behavior and thoughts, even the false ones.

THE REWARD SYSTEM FOR YOUR EGO WHEN YOU CHOOSE DECEPTION OVER TRUTH

• *Your ego is attracted to what makes it special.* When you create a picture that accomplishes that objective, false or not, your ego is enjoying a payoff. The more attractive you make the picture with distortions, the more your ego is rewarded. Remember, your ego is your false picture of yourself. It is not your true self.

This inauthentic self thrives on falsity. The more you practice this ersatz thinking and behavior, the less likely you are to consult your higher self and be on your sacred quest.

- *The use of deceit and deception is a way of ensuring the survival of the ego.* The presence of your authentic self would send the ego scurrying away because it would have no purpose. When you are in tune with God, living your spiritual life, you have no need for anything that is not authentic. Your ego needs the deceptive behavior to maintain its own survival.

- *When you rely upon deception, you are falling victim to the approval-seeking game.* Your false self is what you want others to see of you, so you project an image of yourself that is based on distortion rather than reality. This is the same as saying, What you think of me is more important than what I think of myself.

  With this attitude, your ego can keep you from taking any risks, including making any spiritual changes in your life. The more you stay in the same skin, wearing the same masks, the more ego succeeds in keeping you from your higher self.

- *The truth shall set you free is a scary idea for your ego.* By keeping you in bondage with all of those distortions, the truth remains unavailable. When truth is unavailable, freedom is too. No slaveholder likes the idea of freeing his servants. Your ego is the slaveholder and those distortions are your chains.

- *Your ego can convince you of your worthlessness.* Who you are is divine and eternal, flowing from a base of love and peace. But your ego persuades you otherwise.

You are convinced by your false idea of yourself that you are without worth, and so you conceal your worthless self with ego's facade. Otherwise your worthlessness would be revealed for the world to see.

Your ego keeps itself in business by convincing you that you are not loving, not peaceful and not a perfect extension of God. It will encourage you to say or do anything to reinforce this false belief.

- *Ego loves to see you in a tenuous, self-doubting attitude.* You can send ego out of your daily life when you have a strong sense of certainty about your value and do not allow doubt to infiltrate your inner world. Certainty about yourself and your connection to God is blasphemy to the ego.

  Remaining uncertain and unsure of yourself is what that false self pressures you to embrace. It will continue to send you messages of distortion in order to guarantee its existence.

These are the payoffs that you receive for allowing your ego to take over and talk you into embracing the false self. Once you have a sense of what it is that you receive from this behavior, you can begin to adopt new ways to bring truth in and get rid of deception and deceit.

Some Suggestions for Ridding Yourself of Deception and Embracing Truth Full-time

- *Make an inner commitment to establish a new relationship with truth.* The way to make this happen is to catch yourself when you are exaggerating or deceiving anyone, including yourself. Then silently tell yourself that you were about to puff yourself up by overstating the truth. Decide to simply relate exactly what happened—no more, no less—and see how that feels.

You will discover, as you catch yourself immediately before the lie, that you are consulting your higher self, which flourishes in truth instead of giving in to ego demands to be false. You will enjoy a deeper, richer experience of life that feels refreshing compared with the phony presentation of yourself seeking approval.

- *Become conscious of inner dialogue that convinces you that the world is a scary and dangerous place.* Use one of the techniques for engaging in dialogue with the fearful part of yourself. Or, seek a friend or relative, or a support group, where it is safe to be honest about your fears. That scared inner dialogue is an aspect of yourself whose truth needs to be loved and heard, too, rather than obscured with ego camouflage.

As that scared inner dialogue is permitted its truth, you will be able to replace those thoughts with the loving presence that is your higher self. Instead of presenting fear thoughts, your inner dialogue will remind you that God is with you and that you are in a divine universe and are an extension of the divine truth.

With fewer thoughts of fear and danger, there will be less need to distort your experience of the world or to employ deceit.

- *Be on the alert for inner dialogues that dwell on your accomplishments rather than the path of purpose.* Recently I gave a speech to a large group of radio broadcasters and was very pleased with my performance. After the lecture, as I was jogging, I was reliving the lecture experience.

At the very moment that I was seeing in my mind's eye the crowd getting to its feet and applauding, I turned a corner and smacked my elbow into a wall so hard that it sent a sharp pain through my arm that lasted for several weeks. Every time I felt that pain I was reminded to get my ego out of the way and stop focusing on myself. I was reminded of my purpose and my service and not to get caught up in the applause.

Self-flattering inner dialogue is generally ego chatter, which can make you lose your way. Inner dialogue about your purpose in life will keep you on the path.

- *Engage in mental discipline.* Tape this Stuart Wilde quotation to your mirror:

> In controlling your ego you tend to melt it. It feels very threatened by its loss of power. But you have to lose yourself in order to rediscover yourself again. Once the security of spirit flows through you, you see how mental discipline heals your life. Eventually the ego relaxes when it sees that the new driver of your personal bus is as steady as a rock.

Mental discipline is what you are after. Suppress ego's inclination to push you toward a deception. Either say nothing or let the truth tumble out. Soon it will become habitual and you will have removed your ego from its dominance.

- *Be silent.* When you are unsure about whether to tell the truth or distort because you feel that the truth will be more painful than it is worth, then do and say nothing. You are not obligated to anyone to reveal every detail of your life. You have the right to remain silent and learn your lesson in that silence.

In this way you strive to bring the truth that you want to embrace back from the silence. Doing nothing is far more spiritually gratifying than distorting or lying. If the Constitution protects you from self-incrimination, certainly you are spiritually exempted as well.

- *Develop a personal truth that is unassailable from outside forces.* Simply declare your own agreement to practice truth and to be independent of the good opinion of others.

  When you do not fear rejection because you know you always will encounter some disapproval, whatever your position, then you are free to be yourself as God created you.

  Keep turning to the sacred and holy nature of your loving presence whenever you feel tempted to camouflage yourself. You do not need outside approval. More important, you need the truth so you can be in alignment with your higher self.

- *Resist the need to boast and talk about yourself.* Strive to be interested rather than interesting. This is the way of the higher self. Become the listener—the one who is interested in the accomplishments and activities of others—and you will not need to boast and to distort your personal story line.

- *If you find yourself exaggerating, stop.* Just stop and verbally correct yourself. You don't need to explain that you are breaking your habit of exaggeration. Just correct the statement. Make this personal attempt to bring truth into your conversations by removing the petty distortions. As you do this you allow ego to know how unnecessary its exaggerations are.

- *Write your own personal honor code.* In your words, describe your intention to make truth the way of your thoughts and actions by suspending your need to deceive yourself and others. Then internalize your code of honor by reading or reciting it to yourself on some regular basis.

You will eventually radiate your inner spirituality and you will have discovered a blissful way of being in this physical plane.

• *Know that being credited is unimportant.* Finally, remind yourself that when you are fulfilling your life mission, credit and accolades are unimportant.

The irony here is that the more you seek approval, the less you receive. No one really approves of an approval seeker. Letting go of the need for approval leaves you open to embrace the truth.

The journey of the sacred quest involves letting go of the ego. Your ego has been entrenched in many of the behaviors you have read about in this chapter. Even admitting that they are true about you is a step in the direction of your higher self.

Rumi's words sum up this subject of truth versus deception:

When you eventually see through the veils to how things really are, you will keep saying again and again, "This is certainly not like we thought it was."

The veils are the distortions. Use your personal honor code to shed them. Then you will agree with Rumi, "This is not like I thought it was." It will be more than you ever might have imagined when your ego was leading you away from the way of your sacred self.

10

FROM FEAR TO LOVE

I have seen the truth
It is not as though I had invented it with
   my mind.
I have seen it, SEEN IT,
and the living image of it
has filled my soul forever . . .

If in one day, one hour,
everything could be arranged at once.
THE CHIEF THING IS TO LOVE.
                    —FYODOR DOSTOYEVSKY

I know that the very essence of my being and the way of transforming my life is love.

✳

You may believe that the opposite of love is hate. I do not see these two emotions as opposites. In fact, love and hate are often closely aligned. To me, the opposite of love is fear.

Love and hate are powerful emotions that can be present simultaneously. There are things that we love. There are things that we hate. Why pretend otherwise? There are times when we love what we hate and times when we hate what we love.

But when you have fear, you do not have love. Ego uses fear as a way to keep authentic love out of your life. When love is not present in your life, you have succumbed to ego and allowed fear in where love could be. You have allowed ego to replace God.

Love, as Dostoyevsky alluded, is the chief thing in life. It is the essence of the universe. It is the glue that holds everything together. It is the substance of your higher self. "God is love" is a tautology because the sentence has exactly the same meaning when read forward or backward.

Ego tries to keep you disconnected from the loving

presence inside of yourself because ego's area of concern has become focused on the outer world. Ego is afraid it will die if you begin to develop a relationship with the inner part of yourself. To be able to love fear-based ego even while it is promoting fear as its survival technique could be one of the most difficult challenges of your sacred quest.

Causing fear is a tactic of the ego, whether it be your own ego or the world's ego. The world's ego is a reflection of individual ego power and the amount of fear that is active. Fear is present when we do not know we are a part of God's divine design. Ego causes us to transmit fear energy instead of love energy. This is a part of the divine plan we've all signed on for during our brief visit in now-here.

Learning to experience authentic love means abandoning ego's insistence that you have much to fear and that you are in an unfriendly world. This begins with an assessment of your reluctance to embrace love.

So What's Not to Like?

Mother Teresa says that love is the central point of our existence. She has written: "For this purpose we have been created: to love and to be loved." These are helpful words to recall as you begin to restrain your ego. You are here for the purpose of loving and being loved.

If you are not experiencing love in your life, it is because you are, in some way, afraid. You need to examine your fears with honesty and with love. When you do, you will transform your fears with love into love. You will open up a space within you that can only be occupied by love. In this space you are on purpose, walking the way of the sacred self. But first you must see how you substitute fear for love.

Your ego steadfastly promotes fear because it fears authentic love itself. This false self helps you convince yourself that you are in some way incomplete. That is the source of all fear. So you, like many people, attempt to fill that emptiness with ego's solutions.

Afraid of having your emptiness, your incompleteness, exposed, you expend a lot of energy creating a false image of happiness. But if you were to stop and do a realistic assessment, you could sense that the feeling of incompleteness is a call from a disowned part of yourself.

What's not to like about the universal intelligence that flows through you? Greeting the spiritual being that you are, having a human experience and feeling the love that is there—what's not to like about that?

The fear about exposing the emptiness keeps you seeking relationships that ego tells you will satisfy the longing within you. What happens is that you enter a relationship, starved for the love that is your higher self. Your inner hunger is masked, pretending to be something else. No wonder so many people repeatedly think they have found love and repeatedly declare they've lost it.

How different it is when you can notice the inner emptiness and think, "What's not to like? This longing is part of being human and knowing love." Then you will let ego know that fear is not your choice. Love is your choice. Just imagine how our system might be if people knew they were already complete.

What would you need to purchase? What would you have to own? Who would you have to impress? Who would you need to have on your arm? The answers give you an idea of how much we rely on the fear that we are incomplete and unacceptable as we are, and how unaware we are of our divine connection.

The fear that is a substitute for love is simply a fear of being unacceptable. Virtually all fears can be traced directly back to self-esteem. If you love yourself, you will be able to transform your fears with love rather than allow them to direct your life.

If you have an inner feeling of being complete and whole, knowing the loving presence that is there, then fear becomes a loving invitation to know more or to change something in your life. Fear will no longer threaten you as it did when you were unacquainted with your higher self.

Recently my wife spent a week in silent meditation at a monastery in northern California. She went there for a deeper experience of God; to work on her book about a spiritual approach to childbirth and infant care; and to experience a total week of silence, prayer and meditation. She was deeply affected by the sense of contentment and love within the community of people who had lived there for decades. She described feeling none of the fear that is so often an acceptable part of life.

When you know your higher self intimately, a deeper sense of love is available to you, and fear as you knew it becomes impossible. With this in mind, the answer to the rhetorical question "So what's not to like?" is that there is absolutely nothing not to like. There is nothing to fear when you know you are already divine and complete and do not have to do anything to prove it.

You do not have to join a monastery and live in silence to come to this awareness. You simply have to vow to replace fear with love. When you are able to do this, you are consulting your spirit rather than listening to ego.

THE FOCUS ON FEAR AND THE FOCUS ON LOVE

When you spend time and energy concerned about how others are viewing you, you are in the clutches of your ego. Fear will be your constant companion. A focus on fear is the vehicle that you use for the expression of your humanity. The vehicle is the career you have chosen, the clothes you wear, the possessions you have accumulated, the money you have and all the ways you are expressing yourself.

These vehicles can become the total focus of your life. They are attempts to let the world and yourself know how important you are and to satisfy your ego's insistence on recognition.

A focus on love does not concern itself with needing to impress or with the external status symbols of your life. Love is always expressed in the service of God and in the service of others. It cares not how you dress it up, what you deliver it in or what others think about it. It is concerned only with giving and sharing with others. Love asks nothing in return. Love is secure within itself so it does not fear how it is perceived.

Fear says that what it has to give is never enough because it comes from lack. Love says that it was created by God and is perfect. What it has to give away will always be replenished in a healthy relationship.

When fear is released, the focus of your life shifts from the vehicles of your expression—the approval seeking and avoidance of rejection—to the divine you and what the authentic you is expressing.

Your fear-driven ego will try to convince you that love is not the answer. You will notice thoughts about proving something to others, about shopping and owning grand things or about bills that can't be taken care of with love. These inner dialogues with yourself are your ego telling you to abandon your higher inclinations. It is trying to put you into scarcity consciousness, where fear reigns.

When you are experiencing these kinds of thoughts, you must remind yourself not to accept this false picture. It is an illusion to think that the way of preventing poverty and rejection is having fear instead of love directing your life. When you are on purpose, focused on expressing yourself in a loving way and unconcerned about the manner in which that expression is manifested, the universe begins to handle the details. You are guided, and abundance flows into your life. Your relationships become spiritual partnerships.

When the focus of your life is fear-based, you tend to believe that your value is based upon your performance. If you perform well, you are worthy; if you fail to perform well, you are worthless. Thus, fear will drive you to perform better and better in order to validate yourself.

Childhood ego development occurs in us to provide a feeling of security. In childhood, the fear of not being loved translated to dangerous insecurity. Your ego took on the job of keeping you feeling safe by teaching you how to get love.

So if you were praised and told that you were loved only when you got gold stars or good grades or when you put away your toys, your ego chose performing as the way to be safe or to be loved. Ego still threatens you today with the fear of being unsafe if you are not loved.

What ego does not realize is that fear was valid then because you were without your adult capabilities of survival. That was then and this is now. You are a grown-up in the now-here, and your survival does not depend on the love of an external person. But ego can lead you to believe that your very survival is threatened, as it was in childhood, without the safety of external love.

That fear can cause you to spend your life trying to get the adult equivalent of the childhood gold star, which represents love and security. But this is true only if you continue to allow the fear-driven ego to take care of what was true then but is different now.

When love is the focus of your life, you don't need to fear a poor performance. You know in your heart that you are much more than how you perform. You have grown out of the fear and into love. You know that your worth is never on the line.

This inner knowing allows you to proceed with your higher self at the helm of your life. Your higher self does not require you to perform for love. Fears are taken in stride just as storms are on the sea. They are simply a part of the hero's journey.

When fear is the focus of your life, you will be disappointed and offended if you fail to receive when you give, because you do what you do for positive feedback about yourself. If you are not recognized or acknowledged by others, you live with the possibility that it is because you are inadequate or unloved.

When the focus of your life is on love, you have no expectations about how others should respond to your acts of love. You are about giving and serving, because that is what love is. Your higher self invites you to serve and give without any anticipation of reward. I like what the psychologist Rollo May said about this focus of love. He calls it the essence of life: "But the essence of being human is that, in the brief moment we exist on this spinning planet, we can love some persons and some things."

When you are focused on fear, you concern yourself with the vehicles of your expression, evaluate your worth based on your performance and withdraw your love if it is unreciprocated. These are all ways of the ego, of the false self. Your real self, the loving presence, focuses on radiating love outward from a center of yourself, which cannot be depleted.

In every living thing there are cells, molecules, atoms and subatomic particles. Within each of these life-giving configurations there is empty space between the particles of matter. When these are examined, we realize that something holds them all together. Some invisible force is in the empty spaces where those particles roam. This force was described by Teilhard de Chardin with these words: "Love is the affinity which links and draws together the elements of the world. . . . Love, in fact, is the agent of universal synthesis."

This invisible force, the glue of the universe, is love. When it is absent, fear exists, as do all of the ego-driven behaviors that are associated with fear. When love is present, you have no fear, and ego has the opportunity to acquire a different job description.

SOME TYPICAL FEAR-BASED BEHAVIORS

As you proceed to identify, understand and change your fear-based thoughts and behaviors and replace them with love, think about this quotation from *The Life and Teaching of the Masters of the Far East:* "When the son of man is lifted up to that realm in which he rises above the fallacies of the physical realm, he thinks and acts on the plane of pure intelligence. There he discriminates between those instincts which he shares with every other animal and those divine intuitions which he has in common with God." Those divine intuitions are love-based. Your higher self is pleading with you to listen and know the spirit that resides in you.

The inability to rely on the love that is our very essence shows up in many forms. Listed below are some of the more common behaviors and thought patterns that indicate a dominant fear-based ego.

- *Choosing judgment instead of compassion.* The fear of being, for example, destitute, ill, mentally dysfunctional, homeless or abused causes you to critically judge persons in those situations. The loving presence within you urges you toward love and compassion.

- *An ongoing inner dialogue of self-criticism.* Your ego keeps up a constant critical dialogue to keep you in a state of low-grade fear.

- *An external appearance reflecting your inner critic.* Your ego wants you to believe that you are unacceptable and will gleefully assist you in creating an image to prove that is so. Manifestations like obesity and personal slovenliness often are the fear-based projection of yourself.

- *Avoidance of authentic intimacy.* Ego can influence you to shun all efforts to be loved by others by refusing to allow the risk of an intimate encounter or the development of an intimate relationship.

- *An egocentric lifestyle.* Ego often makes you selfishly pursue your own goals at others' expense. You engage in perpetual conversation about yourself.

- *Excusing your selfish behavior.* We often use economic, social and other types of excuses to defend behavior that does not extend love. For instance, you might excuse unloving or inconsiderate behavior because "it's only my job" or because "everyone does it."

- *Insensitivity and disrespect.* Expressions of disgust or rudeness toward others are based on ego. They are heard in stores, on freeways, in offices, at airports, in restaurants—any place you are in your daily life.

These are some of the common expressions of a fear-based ego struggling to keep you away from the experience of love that is your true essence. Before you begin to change these behaviors and thought patterns, you need to examine the payoffs. What is some part of you receiving as a payoff for listening intently to ego?

THE PREMIUMS YOU RECEIVE FOR USING FEAR INSTEAD OF LOVE

Your ego works for its living. Its payoff is not money but in keeping alive. The following are some examples of the currency that the ego receives for keeping you in a state of fear and avoidance of love.

- *Your ego is not open to making contact with God because it would be immediately put out of business.* Therefore, it is incumbent upon your ego to keep you in a constant state of fear.

    Your ego does not like crisis because crisis will very often get you to look within and open yourself to a higher appreciation of your spiritual self. Thus, your ego promotes a rather smooth-flowing river of misery with fears about your inadequacy and shortcomings.

- *Your ego is in direct conflict with your true purpose for being here.* You are here to give and receive love. Your ego protects you from that vision by keeping you in a belief system that declares you are separate and special. This feeling that you are different than others and at the same time competing with them to validate your specialness means you cannot easily extend your love to them.

- *By hanging onto the fears of your insufficiency, you can avoid taking any risks.* This will prevent you from making the changes that will bring you into contact with your spiritual self. As long as you have self-doubt and all of its attendant fears, you are guaranteed to stay in servitude to your false self.

- *Your ego thrives on guilt.* Your higher self knows that you should forgive yourself, learn from mistakes and release feelings of fear and anxiety.

But ego hands you guilt so that it will thrive. Guilt is the inner fear that you should pay a price for any and all mistakes you have committed in your life. Thus the ego convinces you that you must feel guilty, and it keeps you removed from your true spirit.

- *Your ego doesn't reject love.* It merely provides you with excuses for why you should be skeptical of your divineness. Your ego is exceedingly polite in this matter.

  The polite background ego voice whispers that love is a high ideal—but one that is loaded with danger. There is a good chance you will get hurt, so you should proceed cautiously. It warns you to not give too much love because you may be taken advantage of. Because you are so special, it tells you, others want to take advantage of you.

  All of those ideas keep you in a state of fear—not panic, just fear. A steady stream of anxiety about giving and receiving love is enough to keep you under the influence of ego.

- *Ego promotes inauthentic love.* In your relationships with others, your ego convinces you that your partner is just what you need to fill the emptiness within you. This is a great ruse that will forever keep you from knowing love and peace.

  By definition, if you are incomplete, that is all you will have to give away, because you can't give away what you don't possess. You will give your partner an incomplete person who is afraid of being discovered! There is no way authentic love can flourish in this kind of dishonest atmosphere. You will be unable to know love and to receive it without questioning it.

SOME IDEAS FOR BRINGING LOVE
RATHER THAN FEAR INTO YOUR LIFE

• *Make a copy of this passage from Walt Whitman's* Leaves of Grass. *Tape it to your mirror and read it every morning.* It will help stimulate the inner opening to the love you seek and dissolve fears if you are willing to do what the poet suggests.

I exist as I am, that is enough.
If no other in the world be aware I sit content,
And if each and all be aware I sit content.

One world is aware, and by far the largest to me,
    and that is myself.
And whether I come to my own today or in ten
    thousand or ten million years,
I can cheerfully take it now, or with equal
    cheerfulness,
I can wait.

• *Remind yourself that God created you in perfect love that is changeless and eternal.* Your body is changing, as is your mind, so you are not that body or that mind. You were created as a spirit that is pure love. That is where you want to keep your attention focused.

As you recognize and affirm this aloud each day, you will lose your fear of inadequacy and incompleteness. Constantly recalling the affirmation of being a creation of God beyond the world of the manifest will chase the fears away.

• *Forgive yourself and welcome love back into your life.* When you can do this, a kind of balancing occurs. Rather than atoning for sins with guilt, you are more committed to promoting joy and service. You will begin to do what you originally came here to do.

- *Notice the acts of kindness other people do rather than their wrongdoing.* This is how the loving presence views you. We are all good, decent, loving souls who occasionally get lost. When you can focus on the good in another and hold that in your mind, you are acting from your higher self. This can help dissipate fear and anger.

- *Remind yourself of how much you have to give away and of how precious and valuable your giving is.* You have the same force running through you that allows the planets to move, the earth to orbit, the seeds to sprout and the flowers to open. There is not a separate God for each person. There is one universal intelligence flowing through all of us.

  That is the force of love. Remind yourself of that every time you doubt your own divinity. Affirm to yourself that you are divine and that you love and are loved and will not be pressured by your false-thinking ego to not know this. Remind yourself that the same force flows through you that flowed through Jesus Christ and Buddha. This should help whenever you feel your ego sneaking in attempting to put fears of inadequacy and doubt into your mind.

- *Show others that verbal assaults are meaningless.* Do not give others your energy by arguing against them. Simply pass when others attempt to have you choose guilt.

  Know that you have returned from darkness to the light and that you are allowing your higher self to show you the way. Admit that you had been ruled by ego previously but are no longer ruled. If others continue to insist that you should feel guilty, simply refuse.

- *Accept that you are enough.* When ego begins to try to attract you to taking on fear, say loudly, "I am enough!" You do not need to be anything that you are not. You do not need to prove yourself. You do not need to indulge your ego with fears and to keep your real self at a distance.

  "I am enough" affirms that you choose love and chase doubts and fears away.

- *Acknowledge to yourself the ways you have chosen the false self to guide you and that you are choosing a different guide.* With the higher self as your new guide, you have permission to arrive and relax. You no longer have to prove yourself but can begin in joyful earnestness to travel the path of love.

  This inner atmosphere will erase judgmental thoughts that were planted and nourished previously by ego. Instead of being frightened or offended, as fear-based ego suggested, you use the moment to contemplate love and compassion. Then there is no fertile ground for thinking you are better, more intelligent or luckier.

- *Take the risk of intimacy whenever possible.* Tell someone that you love how you feel, even if fear is present. Do it anyway! By taking action against your fear of intimacy, you invite your higher self, your loving presence, to replace ego's nonloving fear tactics.

  Snuggle up and risk saying how much you love and appreciate someone. Tell that person that you are willing to be vulnerable in order to know him or her better. These open-hearted ways of expressing yourself can defeat fear of intimacy. Use any excuse you can to express your love, and try to ignore the vehicle of expression. It is the substance of what you are and feel that counts, not the vehicle that you use.

- *If those fears ever start to return, stop and ask yourself the question I wrote about earlier: "So what's not to like?"*

You cannot have a better past, so abandon the idea right now. You did what you knew how to do, given the circumstances of your life. Those mistakes of the past were driven by your ego, which wanted to keep you in its grasp. You listened to your false self and recoiled in fear over the idea of anyone knowing your true self.

You moved away from love, but now you are back and making the choice for love. You know deep within you that at your primal level you have been designed for love and happiness. You simply let that false self direct you away from the loving presence that is your essence.

You can choose to return to the brilliant light of love that is always with you. Who you are is that unclouded love. Go there often and all of your fears will be replaced by the love that is always with you.

Let your thoughts remain on love, and let your actions stem from this love. This is the realization of your higher self. It is the realization of your sacred quest. You can truly make the decision to be free from fear and doubt.

There is no greater freedom!

11

FROM OUTWARD APPEARANCE TO INNER SUBSTANCE

Dignity does not consist in possessing
honors, but in deserving them.
—ARISTOTLE

My judgments prevent me from seeing the good that lies beyond appearances.

✳

The most frequently quoted prayer in the Western world includes these words: ". . . thy will be done, on Earth as it is in Heaven." Ego is determined that your conceptions of heaven and earth be separate. For ego, having heaven on earth means being the richest and most famous person in this kingdom. For your sacred self, "heaven on earth" means there are no such distinctions.

Earth, ego insists, is where you should be primarily concerned about appearances and acquisitions. The major focus of your life here, according to ego, has to do with appearances, and your physical appearance takes precedence over inner feelings. The pursuit of your career, the quality and amount of your possessions and the trappings of success are what ego wants you to direct your energy toward. These are absolutely more important to ego than the inner life.

But we all have an awareness of the emptiness and futility of ego's way. You are reading this book partly because you know that in order to have a deeper, richer experience of life you need to know how to make a shift away from ego to the inner self that the loving presence offers.

GOING BEYOND THE WORLD OF APPEARANCES

To understand the way the ego works, you must realize that this false vision of yourself believes that earth is home. If you identify yourself as no more than an earthling, as the ego wants you to, then your happiness and fulfillment will be in the form of the physical things in the manifest world.

But there is an aspect of you that knows that these things do not provide the spiritual fulfillment that is the promise of the sacred quest. Planet earth is not your only home. What it offers you is only partially satisfactory to the invisible you within the form of your body. That inner aspect knows that this life on earth is not its ultimate destiny.

However, most of us have been convinced by the sturdy and determined ego that appearances are what life is about, and that rewards are a result of appearances. The inner self knows that this is all very fleeting because the rewards you receive for youthfulness and physical strength, for example, will diminish as those physical qualities deteriorate.

The nonphysical you is eternally observing the physical transformation of your body. This realm of the higher self is dominated by an inner self that is aware of the realities of earth *and* of heaven. It is immune to the pleas of the ego to focus all of its energy on the earth plane.

Here is how Nisargadatta Maharaj describes it: "The world is the abode of desires and fears. You cannot find peace in it. For peace you must go beyond the world."

And this is what heaven on earth is truly about—an experience of inner peace without the idolatry of possessions and appearances.

The insightful response to the prayer ". . . thy will be done on Earth as it is in Heaven" is found in the awareness that heaven is not of this world. It is in the world of God, the realm where you have destroyed all that you have amassed and where you find the peace that Sri Nisargadatta refers to.

Your higher self is beyond this world of life and death where appearances are touted as all important. Consider the following two ways that those appearances have triumphed over the inner self.

• *Judging others by their outer appearance.* It is a common trait of the ego-driven person to judge others by the external measures of their possessions, appearance and conduct.

Frequently, judgment is polite and without mean-spiritedness when you classify and choose not to encourage friendliness with someone based on their position on your status scale. Nevertheless, it is a technique useful to the ego to keep you from knowing your higher self.

All of the judgment concerning appearances is simply a tool for upgrading oneself by comparison with another. Ego gets you to reconfirm your separateness, and it loves to keep you in a state of separation from others. In that way it manages to prevent you from feeling connected as you are in reality.

When you consult your higher self, you learn that you are a part of the same divine essence that connects all of us to the source of spirit. Your inner self confirms that you are no better than another and that you do not need to judge or to compare yourself against others. There is one God, one source with many different manifestations.

When you have this awareness, you simply cannot

see others in terms of what they possess or how they appear, or even how they conduct themselves. Instead, you relate to them in terms of the divineness that is flowing through them, which is a manifestation of the energy supporting the physical world. On the path of the sacred way, you experience that force flowing through you and others.

You are able to send them love and kindness, without noticing appearances because you sense the sacred energy that flows through both of you. Your higher self leads you to remember the truth about someone, even when they have forgotten it themselves.

Those beings you encounter who are ego-directed are not judged in any way. You are able to simply witness lovingly as your body interacts with theirs, sensing the loving presence within, even when they do not. You and God are partners when your higher self is allowed to lead.

In that partnership you are serenely aware that this home called earth is a temporary stopover. This is the place where inhabitants and their possessions never remain the same. They undergo a continual progression of physical change. Heaven, by contrast, is changeless and eternal—there is an absence of judgment, an absence of possessions and of positions.

"On earth as it is in heaven" ought not to be an expression of empty words but an awareness that your higher self urges you to discard all thoughts of being separate from others and from God. "On earth as it is in heaven" means to begin to live without the false ideas that the ego promotes.

Certainly, many will conduct themselves in ways that show they are not driven by their higher selves. Your task at those moments is to remember the inner self, which they have forgotten they have within themselves. Avoid your inclination to accept ego's invitation to judge them. They, too, are creations of God. They, too, have the source of goodness flowing through them even if they have forgotten it or allowed their egos to dominate their lives. But seeing the conduct of those who are monopolized by their egos is not a reason for you to do the same.

These people will learn from their behaviors. But you need to consult the spirit that is within you for your response. This is the way of taming your ego and experiencing the peace that comes with the refusal to judge others. This is not to say that you should endorse the crass conduct of others or that they should not be held responsible for their behavior. What you want to do is consult your higher self rather than your ego, and refuse to judge or elevate yourself as a result of any comparisons.

- *Judging yourself based on your appearance.* If you've allowed your ego to convince you to judge others by their external appearances, it is likely that you bestow the same spiritual disservice on yourself. When you examine your own life with evaluations based on external appearances and conclude that you haven't measured up to your potential, you can be sure ego is rejoicing.

When you need more of anything to feel positive about yourself, you are always in a race without a finish line, and you cannot achieve spiritual bliss. The way out of this trap of self-repudiation is to recognize that the earth habitat is not your complete home. Edgar Allan Poe reminds us: "All that we see or seem / Is but a dream within a dream." When you know that your lifetime is a dream within a larger dream, you can stop using outer appearances as a meaningful gauge.

Begin to understand that the ego belief system is similar to your nighttime dreams, where you believe the dream is real while you are dreaming and on awakening see the illusion. All life is a projection of your mind—it is a dream within a dream. With this kind of awareness, you can consult your higher self rather than acquiesce to ego demands for bigger, better or more expensive things to validate your existence.

Heaven on earth begins happening when you abandon the false idea that you need to prove to anyone that you have acquired the necessary credentials to be considered a success. I can recall in my own life, years ago, when I first came to this realization.

I was in a counseling session with a man I'll call Richard, who had achieved all that most of us in the Western world would consider necessary to be called successful. He was a multimillionaire, had several homes and traveled all over the world. But he had lived the life of outward appearances exclusively. He knew no other way, so he did not have choices and was instead trapped by his lifestyle.

During the months I worked with Richard, it became clear to me that appearances do not create peace and that peace is truly what the higher self offers. Richard constantly needed to compare himself with others and try to go them one better. His ego was working overtime getting him to verify his superiority.

So he was trapped in a life of striving to prove himself by having affairs with younger women, by buying the most expensive clothing and fragrances and by neurotically obsessing about his hair loss. He was estranged from his grown children, and he constantly worried that his wife would discover his philandering and divorce him, leaving him penniless and feeling worthless. Richard had listened to his ego his whole life, and although his successful facade had grown, he was a wreck.

He lived in terror of being invalidated by loss of the appearance of being a successful man. He longed for a more satisfying experience of life but had no idea that his quest was being forsaken by his own false self. Slowly, he began to discover the inner journey and began paying less attention to the call of his ego.

As we worked in the counseling sessions, I discovered the illusion that ego was perpetrating on both Richard and myself. I too was being directed by ego from my life experience of being taught that success was measured in externals. I watched Richard and knew that I could easily end up having the same fears and shallow values. I felt he had been sent to me so that I could see that. Even to this day, some twenty-five years later, I think of Richard when I am inclined to put appearances over inner substance.

Richard died a few years ago. He, like all of his possessions, is recycled into some other physical form. His spirit is alive and in the place where there are no grades, no possessions, no separations from the source. Heaven on earth means grasping that awareness now and letting your ego retire.

In one of Robert Frost's lighter moments, he penned these words:

Forgive me my nonsense
as I forgive the nonsense of those
who think they talk sense.

The emphasis on measuring one's life based on external acquisitions or accomplishments is nothing more than nonsense. This emphasis on appearance shows up in your life in many ways.

HOW THE PURSUIT OF APPEARANCES SURFACES IN YOUR LIFE

The pursuit of appearances is one of the most common ways that your ego overtakes your daily existence. In order to transcend these inclinations away from inner substance, you must be able to identify these tendencies as they occur. Here are a few of the most frequent examples of this kind of thinking and behavior.

- *Being more concerned with your appearance than with your purpose* (obsession with jewelry, cosmetics and clothing; spending large amounts of your time and money dressing up your body for the sake of appearance).

- *Pursuing grades, awards and external symbols of success instead of the joy of participating and learning* (using your trophy case or collection of merit badges as your source of validation; believing that your children's grades are the most important thing they will receive in school; encouraging your child to please the teachers at the expense of the child's inner peace).

- *A conversation style that reveals how much your ego has control of your life* (spending a lot of your time talking about your accomplishments and victories over others or over the system; discussing other people and their deficiencies and persistently pointing out your superiority—for example, saying that you would never do such a thing and can't understand why anyone would; using your actions as the gauge for how others should conduct themselves).

- *Being preoccupied with spending money* (using the cost of things as an indicator of value; always asking how much something costs or how much someone was paid and judging how much they are worth; using money not only as an indicator of success and status but as the central thought system in your daily life).

- *Believing you are just your body* (being dissatisfied with your appearance and constantly fishing for compliments to validate your sense of physical inadequacy; assessing yourself and your happiness on the basis of physical changes such as sagging, wrinkling, turning gray or slowing down—these are signs that your ego has convinced you that you are exclusively your body and that you are deteriorating rapidly).

- *Allowing the advertising industry to control you.* Advertising in all of its forms is generally used in an effort to convince you that you are incomplete and that you need to purchase something in order to be fulfilled. Consequently, you are bombarded almost every moment that you are exposed to media advertising, which urges you to consume something so you can be a more fulfilled person. Consistent reading, listening to and watching these messages is evidence of ego control.

- *Pointing out the deficiencies in others* (spending time describing what you consider to be physical imperfections, such as a large nose, an unpleasant voice, a snooty personality or an ungraceful aging process).

  The habit of noticing so-called deficiencies is a tool that your ego uses to convince you that you are better than the people you are criticizing. Of course this continues to prevent you from seeing the loving presence that is an invisible resident in those "tattered coats upon a stick," as Yeats described people who are seen independent of their soul.

- *Striving for recognition by pursuing higher positions of authority* (anguishing over not receiving what you think of as your "just due" in the job marketplace; feeling hurt and depressed when your efforts are not rewarded with a better position, title or contract). Often, those rewards serve no other purpose than providing the ground for ego to proclaim your worldly superiority.

The daily stories reporting the astronomical salaries of entertainers and athletes are highly visible evidence of this ego activity. It is irrelevant that the amounts are beyond their ability to spend even after a huge percentage is paid in taxes. The issue is one of ego-oriented status requirements, which leads them to the false belief that they are being insulted if anyone in their field of endeavor is being paid more than they are.

Most of these performers will refuse to play and actually sit out, allowing their egos to convince them of the rightness of their action. They may be unsatisfied, unhappy and miserable, but it has become more important to assuage the ego than to play the sport they love and receive a compensation that is way beyond sufficient, regardless of what anyone else is earning. This inner turmoil over not receiving recognition or compensation delights ego because any inclination to direct attention toward a higher self is distracted when we are coping with turmoil.

• *Eating disorders.* Most eating disorders are, initially, efforts to meet a standard of appearance that someone believes will bring happiness. Ego has convinced people with eating disorders that their true essence is located in the value of their appearance to others.

These people have become preoccupied with appearance to the exclusion of most of the other areas of their lives, and they ultimately destroy their bodies trying to make them perfect in the eyes of others.

THE PAYOFF FOR YOUR EGO

The process of transcending excessive concern with external appearance and shifting to an emphasis on inner substance comes with understanding why your ego controls your life. Below are some of the more common reasons this occurs.

- *The primary function of ego is to keep you from knowing your higher self.* All appearances are masks that you wear to hide from your divine self, which has no concerns with appearances, acquisitions or positions of power.

  If your higher self ruled your life, your ego could no longer function in the manner it does.

- *The state of anxiousness about career ensures that you will not look inward.* Continual preoccupation with career and other roles prevents knowing your inner light. All those thoughts about important decisions to get you to a predetermined level of vocational prowess are really ego thoughts seeding you with anxiety.

- *You attempt to fill the void that ego tells you is within your being.* If you believe that you are what you own, you are superficially centered on things external to yourself. The emphasis on ownership keeps you perpetually in the acquisition mode. The ego wants you to feel incomplete so that you are on an interminable shopping excursion trying to fill the void.

  If you always believe that you need more stuff in order to be valid, you will never look to the nonstuff that is your true validation. Thus, your ego keeps you shopping for more, to ensure its survival.

- *Your ego wants to be the master of everything in your life.* It knows that your wiser higher power has answers for you that are permanent and will provide you free passage to your sacred quest. This need to be in charge of everything is a control center for ego. If ego did not have control, it would fear that you might discover the truth of your authentic self.

- *Ego makes you resistant to taking risks and making changes.* Ego does not want you entertaining any ideas about the benefits of taking risks and allowing change in your life. Those are radical ideas from ego's viewpoint. Ego believes it is much safer for you to concentrate on appearances than to experiment with the value of inner bliss.

    This message has helped to create the culture you live in, which predominantly agrees with the self-absorbing idea of appearance over inner value. The resulting spiritual deficit is at the root of all of our social problems.

SOME IDEAS FOR TRANSCENDING APPEARANCES

- *Take a few moments to become very still.* In silence, start to release your attachment to the importance of outer impressions. You might visualize yourself building a huge bonfire and imagine tossing things into the fire. Throw in your jewelry, clothes, automobiles, trophies, everything, even your job title. With each item that goes into this imaginary fire, feel yourself being freer and freer.

    Again I recommend that you read Marlo Morgan's *Mutant Message Down Under*. She tells about shedding all of her possessions and being taken on a trip by spiritual aborigines where she realizes that the emphasis on appearance keeps us removed from our higher self.

- *Remove the labels attached to your life.* Make an attempt to describe yourself without using any labels. Write a few paragraphs in which you do not mention

your age, sex, position, title, accomplishments, possessions, experiences, heritage or geographic data. Simply
write a statement about who you are, independent of
all appearances.

It is difficult at first to describe your eternal,
changeless and divine self—that part of you which is
not identified with the senses. The observation that we
suffer from the peculiar blindness that sees only the
visible may be the reason for our difficulty. When you
remove the labels, you will see the invisible part of
yourself.

- *Look for the loving presence in others.* Take a day to
  attempt to see the fullness of God in everyone you
  encounter. Rather than seeing only another physical
  being, tell yourself that the Christ in me is meeting the
  Christ in you. Or spend a day silently reciting the word
  "love" whenever you encounter another human being.
  This has such a powerful effect that you may choose to
  use it as a silent background mantra throughout your
  day.

  When we can replace our physical self with the
  spiritual energy that is in all, there is absolutely no
  room for judgment.

- *Defend the absent.* When you are in discussions that
  revolve around taking pot-shots at individuals who are
  not present, practice defending the person in his or her
  absence. Make a habit of being the one person in the
  group who defends the absent persons. You can wonder out loud how that person would explain the ways
  of being that are being criticized, and suggest that
  there may be more than what is seen on the surface.

  These kinds of statements serve to restrain your
  ego's need to compare and feel superior, and they
  serve your higher self, which wants to help others.
  This is a particularly beneficial lesson to teach young
  children, who have a tendency to gang up and "rip"

the absent. Always ask, "Who here is defending the person who isn't here to defend himself?"

- *Remember that you build a muscle by picking up heavier objects.* This applies to your spiritual weight lifting too. You will build yourself up spiritually by attempting tougher and tougher assignments. One of the toughest assignments is to disregard the ego message to evaluate yourself with the criteria of appearance and possessions. But know that each time you are able to be less judgmental toward others or yourself, you are becoming stronger by having taken on the heavier spiritual weights.

- *Exercise compassion and love.* The presence of those who have no possessions can provide an opportunity to practice love and compassion. Use those instances to recognize the fullness of God within these people, even if you choose not to contribute money or other assistance.

  Others' suffering, regardless of whether it is self-imposed or the result of some addiction, represents a spiritual deficit within the community of human beings. You can improve that deficit with kind thoughts of love and compassion in place of ego-induced fear or criticism.

- *Cultivate your calling.* Make an attempt to shift your career objectives from self-absorption to a *calling.* That's right, a calling. Remind yourself that this is an intelligent system and that you are here to be love and have love by serving. Use your talents and special interests to fulfill your service with your calling.

  Your life work will take on a dramatic shift toward abundance, and you will feel on purpose and on the path of the sacred quest.

- *Affirm.* Make affirmations a daily practice. Create your

own or begin with these: *Feed before you are fed.* In a restaurant, ask everyone else to order and assist them before placing your own order. At the dinner table, assist each person with their helpings before loading up your own plate. *Give before you get.* Make an effort to be more giving and less oriented toward receiving.

Send anonymous contributions or gifts. Bring unexpected gifts to friends, family or strangers. Give a book you've enjoyed, flowers from your garden or any small token to others for no reason than the giving. Pay the toll of the car behind you to practice giving without receiving.

- *Reduce the importance of grades.* Take the pressure off your children by removing the emphasis on grades. Teach them to pursue their own interests and talents for the purpose of knowing themselves and serving others. This will aid them in finding their higher selves and discovering that they have the source of all knowledge within. They need to learn early that their worth is not found in SAT scores or college entrance exams.

- *Practice generosity.* Remember, if you are not generous when it is difficult, you will not be generous when it is easy. Many people who give willingly of their possessions and their money are not doing it because they "have it to give." They are coming from a special heart space that is attracted to serving and sharing.

    In some way, all of us have it to give. Perhaps not in the same amount, but all of us can give something in the service of each other and in service of our higher selves.

- *Have many moments of mindfulness.* Perceive how miraculous you are in any given moment and attempt to bring your awareness to the moment. Everything in your life is an opportunity to practice mindfulness.

By being mindful of your surroundings, paying attention to all that you encounter with an attitude of awe and awareness, you transcend the ego's need to gather, accumulate and consume. Instead you put your focus on the individual moments of life and experience them through your spiritual self. Your life unfolds in moments. Paying attention to present moments teaches you about your spirit in a profound and ego-restraining manner.

To know what is truly meant by the words "earth as it is in heaven," you must go beyond the realm of this world. C. S. Lewis wrote these profound words, which I find useful in the contemplation of the nonphysical realm: "If I find in myself a desire which no experience in this world can satisfy, the most probable explanation is that I was made for another world."

Nothing in the manifest world will satisfy the desire to know the way of your sacred self. The way to that world where judgment is impossible, possessions are not even a consideration and bliss is perpetual is not along the path of ego. That path leads away from the experience of earth as it is in heaven.

12

FROM STRIVING TO ARRIVING

To go with the drift of things,
To yield with a grace to reason,
To bow and accept the end
Of a love or of a season.

—ROBERT FROST

I know that I am already whole and
I need not chase after anything
in order to be complete.

The message of this chapter can be summed up in two
words: Lighten up! Your higher self demands nothing of
you. You do not have to prove yourself to God. You were
created as an extension of the highest spiritual force, the
very essence of the universe. You did not arrive in now-
here incomplete in any way. You do not have to strive to
prove anything. Unless, of course, you choose to listen to
the omnipresent false self, which stipulates that if you
don't stay busy pursuing something you are a failure.

It can be difficult to finally just lighten up and understand that life is what happens while you are making
other plans. This is it! Each and every instant of your life
takes place in the present moment.

Using your present moments to chase after future
moments is an ego-based activity. Your ego wants you to
feel incomplete so that it can control your life. When you
are finally able to say that you have arrived, you will
know what it feels like to be free. You will have gotten
free of your false self, which would keep you in perpetual

motion chasing after more and more until your final breath.

Your higher self does not want you to be lazy or without purpose but to realize the power in knowing that you have arrived. When you know that this moment is your entire life, you are not focused on past or future moments, and you release the stress and tension that accompanied the striving lifestyle. With that release, you become more productive and peaceful than you were when you looked behind or ahead of yourself and did not allow your mind to rest in the still center of the present moment.

Contrary to what your ego attempts to convince you, you will not simply vegetate, become homeless or an irresponsible drifter when you stop striving. What will happen is that you will lighten up and become so engrossed in your mission that you are more vibrant. With this power, you discover that you are free to serve whatever you are intuitively drawn to.

When you stop striving and start knowing that you are on a divine mission, and that you are not alone, you will be guided to the experience of arriving. That experience will introduce you to the bliss of being in the realm of spirit, where there is no worry or guilt. Being fully in the now means that you will experience heaven on earth because you are completely absorbed in the soul of the holy instant.

By exploring some new concepts from the perspective of your soul, you will learn about the things you want to change in order to move closer to arriving and away from striving.

THE COMPONENTS OF SHIFTING TO ARRIVING

To experience the bliss of knowing that you are here now in this moment—and that it is all there needs to be, all that there ever was and all that you ever will know—you must learn to trust your higher self and let go of those ingrained teachings from all the egos that have influenced your life up until now. You will begin to realize that you are not on trial in the now-here. You will soon realize that your mission is to serve and extend the love that is your basic essence. Period.

You don't have to do more, even though you may choose to do a great deal. Your overriding objective is to stay focused on sending and receiving *agape,* the love of God. If you incorporate the following ideas into the practice of your daily mission, you will succeed in your objective.

- *Nothingness.* Your ego tries to convince you that the state of nothingness is an impoverished and undesirable place. If you experience nothingness, ego wants you to believe it is because you are unfulfilled. Ego further insists that feeling unfulfilled or empty is intolerable.

  You must create a new relationship with this concept of nothingness or emptiness if you are to make a shift from a striving to an arriving way of living your life in the now-here.

  Nothingness has a very positive value in your life. It is out of nothing that all is created. If you sit in silence and listen to the first sound that you make, you are forced to admit that it came from the nothingness, the silence. Out of nothing you created a wave that we call a sound. Without the nothingness you could not have sound.

  Space is considered to be nothing—no particles, no form. So we describe it as nothing. To fear this empty space or to deny its value as a part of us means doubting our own existence. We came from nothingness— the no-where I've described throughout this book—to the world of form, the now-here. We have an intimate connection with both the nothingness and the world of form. We are both. Both are part of us. We need both space and form to exist.

It is important that you get to the place of being able to love nothingness with at least the equal enthusiasm you feel for the somethingness of your life. Both are essential aspects of your existence. In that unified field you will find the secret that sits in the center of your being, the no-thing-ness. Here you will get acquainted with the peace of arriving and surrender the anxiety of using up your precious moments striving.

- *Surrender.* To understand the concept of surrendering, you will not be able to rely on your ego. Ego never wants you to even consider surrendering. It would much rather you hang on to the belief that you must strive and cling to the familiar way.

  The more you stay with what you are accustomed to, the more you will hang on to the worries and stress that are of the physical world. This constant frenetic behavior keeps you occupied and unable to make the connection to the world of spirit and your sacred quest.

  The notion of being attached to what happened to you in the past can be very deeply ingrained in you by your false self. You must learn to recognize ego's attachment to the past when it uses this to keep you stuck in striving. Surrender the belief that your past is what is driving your present.

  Surrendering also means learning to recognize the signals from your higher self that something within you needs to be witnessed. This means surrendering to whatever is, in the present moments of your life. For many people it can be confusing to discern whether it is ego or spirit that is at the helm.

  I find that using the image of a boat moving along the surface of a lake is helpful in making the distinction between ego and higher self. I visualize the wake of the boat as a symbol of the past. The wake is not driving the boat. It is merely the trail that is being left behind by the present moment movement of my boat image. What drives the boat is the energy generated in the now. I do not credit or blame the past for the boat's present state of arriving in this spot on the lake.

I then breathe slowly and deeply into the image and ask my higher self to complete the inner picture. If the boat is faltering in any way, I witness it lovingly, without blame, just surrendering to whatever is. This is quite different than ego's directions to go forever or faster, or to get a bigger or snazzier boat.

If ego chatter erupts, it is because ego is feeling threatened by this observation. It fears my quiet acceptance of arriving without striving. It wants me to stop this nonsense and get on with striving.

If ego is not threatened and the image of the boat is not faltering, then I know I am afloat. I interpret the boat's progress as a symbol that I am proceeding in life without ego's influence forcing me to look to the past and that I am not ignoring signals from my higher self to care for any accidental damage from the past.

If you try this and hear a critical voice almost nagging you to get on with it, know that it is ego chatter. Surrendering means surrendering to what is, not to what ego wants it to be right now or what ego thinks it should have been in the past.

Surrendering means letting go and being here *now* and nowhere else. It means knowing within you that you are here in this moment and that everything that has ever happened to you is like the wake behind the boat. As you watch the wake of the boat, you see that it stays for a few moments and then it slowly fades from your awareness. So too is your life precisely like that. Your past slowly fades away and all that is left is now.

That past cannot drive you in this now, and that

past needn't be held responsible for the boat's problems. That means that you do not blame the past *and* that you do not deny the existence of a problem if that is what is happening *now*. What you do is surrender to what is happening in this moment.

Practice surrendering by creating a new agreement with now. Agree to know that your past is a trail of present moments that are all left behind, and at the same time know that if you are having difficulty in this present moment you will surrender to that reality.

Don't let ego convince you to blame the present on the past, and don't let ego convince you to strive to fix the problem without the input of your higher self. Ego will try to get you to fix the present pain or difficulty with ego solutions for fear that you will get too cozy with your loving presence.

Ego fears most of all that your surrender to what is in the now will lead you to the ultimate surrender—the acceptance of death, that most embarrassing of events for the ego.

Several years ago I received the following piece from a reader in Milwaukee. It is titled *There Is No Death*, author unknown.

> I am standing upon the seashore. A ship at my side spreads her white sails to the morning breeze and starts for the blue ocean. She is an object of beauty and strength and I stand and watch her until at length she hangs like a speck of white cloud just where the sea and the sky come to mingle with each other.
>
> Then someone at my side says, "There! She's gone!" Gone from my sight, that is all. She is just as large in mast and hull and spar as she was when she left my side, and she is just as able to bear her load of living weight to her destined port.
>
> Her diminished size is in me, not in her. And

just at the moment when someone at my side says, "There! She's gone!" there are other eyes watching her coming, and other voices ready to take up the glad shout. "There she comes!" And that is dying.

Surrendering invites your loving presence to be available in every now moment. What a pleasure each moment can then be. Even the last moment.

- *Acceptance.* Once when I was asked to define enlightenment, the best I could come up with was "the quiet acceptance of what is." I believe that truly enlightened beings are those who refuse to allow themselves to be distressed over things that simply are the way they are.

  To arrive rather than to strive means applying the wisdom of Reinhold Niebuhr's so-called Serenity Prayer: "God, grant me the serenity to accept the things I cannot change, the courage to change the things I can, and the wisdom to know the difference." Knowing the difference can be the most difficult part!

  The ego tries to prevent you from having the wisdom of your higher self by keeping you in a fighting or a striving mood. Ego wants you to believe that you must be upset and anguished to prove you are a worthy person who cares about world problems. This ego-agitated approach to problems prevents you from ever becoming part of the solution for things that can be changed.

  Acceptance does not imply endorsement. It merely refers to a state of mind that allows you to be peaceful and know the difference between things you can help to eradicate and things that simply just are the way they are. If you are in a state of acceptance, you are free of internal stress and can actually be more open to listening and helping.

  You do not learn when you are talking to others or

being judgmental and angry to yourself. Quiet listening and inviting your higher self to participate is the way to the wisdom of knowing the difference between what you can change and what you accept as presently unchangeable. Nonacceptance can be your ego insisting that its way is the right way rather than accepting what might be God's divine design, which you are unable to perceive in its entirety.

There is a spiritual solution to every so-called problem that we encounter. All of our social ills derive from a spiritual deficit that I address in the final chapter of this book. Your desire to fix those deficits is just as much a part of divine design as are the deficits. By shifting from nonacceptance and judgment to acceptance, you actually become part of the solution.

Acceptance means arriving at a place of peace. It is the place that William Blake referred to when he wrote the following: "If the doors of perception were cleansed, everything would appear as it is . . . infinite."

Cleanse those doors of judgment and see your higher self telling you that this is a divine universe and an intelligent system that you are a part of. Even if you don't understand how and why so many things are transpiring the way they are, that is not a reason to be upset about them. Acceptance leads to solutions. Judgment and nonacceptance feed the ego's hunger for more problems and more striving.

There is an ancient Zen teaching that says: "If you understand, things are just as they are. If you do not understand, things are just as they are." This is the essence of acceptance and the way of arriving rather than striving.

- *Bewilderment.* When you are busy striving for something, you have very little time or energy for being in awe of your immediate surroundings or immersing yourself with wonder in the present moment. A state of bewilderment occurs when you take time to appreciate all that you are, all that you have and all that you can become.

Your physical being is an enormous miracle—its thousands of working parts function with a divine organizing intelligence. Consider your blood circulation, air inhalation and oxygenation, your eyes, muscles and bones all responding to a brain and nervous system that is beyond comprehension. There are miles of arteries and veins, intestines with infinitely tiny microbes, all working in unison with that divine intelligence that creates the body you occupy.

To be in a state of bewilderment, stop and behold the wonder of you. Allow yourself to enjoy the bewilderment and awe of who and what you are. There is the miraculous machine that houses you, and there is the incomprehensible mystery of the ghost in the machine that is your mind and soul, observing all.

Your higher self becomes readily accessible when you contemplate the mystery of who you are. The stress that ego thrives on is gone, so your authentic self is available. Your ego will try to bring you back to its reality, threatening that you will become indolent and nonproductive. But you can override ego if you see the mystery revealed as the presence of God everywhere. Then you will "sell your cleverness and buy bewilderment," as Rumi instructed.

- *Patience.* As you make the transition to arriving in place of striving, your higher self reveals the presence of spirit, which is the organizing intelligence of the manifest world. Your faith will shift to a knowing, and you will begin to patiently rely on the gentle counsel that spirit provides.

   The need to strive for answers will disappear. It will be replaced by a patient knowing that divine design will reveal what the next step along the path of your sacred quest will be.

   I have found this kind of patience to be an enormous

virtue and guide in my life. When I feel inclined to listen to my ego, I am able to call up the attitude of patience and say simply, "I am leaving it in your hands. My ego is pushing but it just doesn't feel right, so I will silently wait to see in what direction I am to go. Use me as you see fit."

This is not an abdication of self-responsibility, as the ego would like me to believe. Ego is impatient. It wants to keep the action going. Ego's use of impatience is an extremely effective way to keep us from our sacred self.

Our loving presence offers us the infinite patience that originates with God. It has taken me over fifty years to know many of the concepts I write about in these pages. God has been patient. I have done things in my life that today make me shudder in contempt, yet God somehow stuck it out with me, patiently seeing the potential for something grander. I have stolen and shoplifted in my earlier days, lied all too frequently, been promiscuous and unfaithful, used substances—and through all this and much more, God showed me her infinite patience.

The stories of the lives of Saint Paul and Saint Francis of Assisi describe the same kind of patience. This infinite patience is available to you at all moments. Regardless of where you have been, how you have lived or how much you have relied upon your false self, God's infinite patience is ever present.

Because of the existence of divine patience, you too can develop this kind of patience. Great things have absolutely no fear of time—they are patient, largely because your higher spiritual self knows that time does not exist except in our minds. Infinity and eternity are concepts that deny the existence of time. Your higher self is a part of infinity and eternity and offers you patience.

These then are the five categories of arriving. By cultivating a new attitude toward nothingness, surrender, acceptance, bewilderment and patience, you will feel a dramatic shift take place—a shift away from constant striving for something more than the now. You will arrive in the precious present with the serenity that accompanies your higher self.

SOME TYPICAL STRIVING BEHAVIORS

The inclination to avoid an arriving attitude can appear in too many ways to describe here. Here are only a few examples. By noting them when they appear, you will begin to understand why you have opted for striving. Then you can begin to make decisions to leave them behind as you embark on your sacred quest.

- *Putting stress in your body.* High blood pressure, internal chaos, ulcers, nail biting, smoking, excessive drinking and eating are all evidence of a perpetual state of striving and anxiety.

- *Measuring your happiness quotient based on your position either on the job or in the community.* You constantly pursue higher positions of power and prestige to demonstrate your competence or value.

- *Seeking external success symbols.* You put your attention on grades, trophies, ratings or any other symbolic merit badges that you need to feel good about yourself.

- *Living with a constant inner dialogue of worry and anxiety.* You have conversations with yourself that revolve around such things as shortages in your life, the need to get the promotion, fear that your security is at risk unless you have more money, and anxiousness about your family's lack of motivation. These thoughts remove you from the present moment and squander it in worry or fear.

- *Putting a price tag on everything that you do.* You have an ongoing inner thought process centered on money and financial matters. Your tendency is to use a monetary gauge as your exclusive means of evaluation of yourself and others.

- *Making "trying" and "effort" the cornerstones of your life philosophy.* You feel that you must always be busy in order to be valid. You judge others as lazy or incomplete if they enjoy being instead of doing.

- *Finding fault with what is.* You are unable to accept the unpredictability of nature's ways. You are preoccupied with fear of death and attracted to conversations bemoaning the disasters that occur.

- *Being unable to spend quiet time alone.* You fill every moment with talking on the telephone, watching television or planning for future events. You are constantly concerned over upcoming deadlines. You reject the idea of meditation or contemplation as a waste of time.

- *Not being able to allow silence to be a natural part of your interaction with others.* You feel compelled to fill any silent gaps with activity or conversation.

- *Tending to do everything quickly.* You are impatient with those who do not talk, move, eat or drive fast enough to suit your standards. You rush through life and judge those who move at a slower pace.

These are a few of the potentially endless types of striving behaviors. When we rely on our false self rather than our spiritual consciousness, these behaviors become a habitual part of our lives. It is possible to transform these ego-dominated patterns when you explore why your ego pushes so hard in this direction.

THE SUPPORT SYSTEM YOUR EGO HAS ERECTED FOR STRIVING

Here are some of the primary reasons ego pursues the path of striving. I've listed some ideas for making the transition from striving to arriving.

- *Ego wants you to believe its misrepresentations.* The biggest misrepresentation is that you are your body and your accomplishments. If it can keep you convinced that that is true, then you will continue working hard proving yourself with striving behavior. By staying focused on striving, you will not see your higher self.

- *Ego promotes the false idea that the feelings of emptiness or nothingness are intolerable.* To ensure ego's dominance, it encourages you to avoid contemplative or meditative activities and to strive to fill every feeling of nothingness with activity, noise, conversation or substances. There is never a time for arriving.

- *Ego persistently directs your attention toward the past or the future.* Using your thoughts up on the past or the future obliterates the present moment. If you shift your attention to the present moment, you automatically let go of stress about the past or future. In that present moment you meet God, which ego is sure is a bad idea.

- *When you believe that your past drives your present, you accept the false belief that the wake is moving the boat.* The reality is that the wake is nothing more than the trail left behind, as is your past behavior. As long as you believe that you can't escape the past and that it is driving your life today, you are in the clutches of your ego and are unable to take the risks and responsibilities that go with becoming a spiritual being.

- *Ego uses the fear of death as a motivator to keep you pursuing hedonism, acquisitions and additional power.* The idea of death as a natural act of shedding the worn-out body is terrifying to the ego. It knows that you will be unable to invite your higher self into your awareness if it can keep you striving for more and believing that that is what your life is meant to be.

- *Ego insists that you must be impatient or you will lose your place along with your credibility.* In this way it is reinforcing its program of teaching you that you are separate from everyone, so you need to always try to get ahead of them. Because it is you versus them, it is impermissible for you to be patient. This keeps you constantly striving.

Some Ideas for Transcending the Striving Trap

- *You can stop the inner push of ego when it is campaigning for you to strive for more.* Use the simple and pleasing realization that you need do nothing. "I need do nothing" is a helpful affirmation to read each day. This simple reminder will invite your higher self to become more active in your life.

- *When you encounter a personal dilemma about what you want to go after in your life, turn the decision over to your sacred self.* Create a sentence that you repeat silently and aloud each time you begin trying to figure out what to do—something like, "Decide for me, I leave it in your hands." Then let go and listen.

    Your answers will come as you develop the internal willingness to allow your higher self to guide you. This may sound like a cop-out, but I have found this technique helpful in many problem areas of my life. When I say, "I am asking you to decide for me," I find that answers appear readily.

    Miraculously, the right person will show up and say to me precisely what I needed to hear, or a book will arrive in the mail with underlined passages that are just what I was looking for, or the phone will ring and I will be guided to the right source. In order to do this, you must be able to let go and just allow your higher awareness to exercise itself.

- *Practice stepping back and witnessing your ego in action.* Don't attempt to do something about your striving ego. Don't fight it, subdue it, control it or destroy it. That would just make the ego real.

    You must remember that your ego is not real. Ego is a false belief that you have about yourself being separate from your higher self and from other living things. By witnessing your ego, you are choosing love and being connected to the loving presence.

- *Be still and know.* These four words will help you to get past striving and to know the bliss of being here now. When you allow yourself to be still, you will understand the futility of constant striving and chasing after more.

Think of how amusing it is to watch a puppy or a kitten chasing its tail. The animal doesn't realize that arriving is impossible when the tail itself is propelled by the desire to catch it. The desire keeps the tail just out of reach.

Your false belief keeps you striving for happiness in the form of something more. When you feel yourself caught in the incessant striving, recall the four words "Be still and know."

- *Make an effort to wake between three and six o'clock in the morning and spend twenty minutes meditating.* I have found this to be the most creative time of the day for accessing my higher self.

  Commit yourself to this meditation time no matter how difficult it is to get out of bed. Fight the temptation to go back to sleep, and get up and go to a place you've chosen where you can be undisturbed and quiet. Meditate for twenty minutes. Then go back to sleep if you want to.

- *In the midst of a tumultuous meeting or a frantic encounter with your children, get up and excuse yourself for a moment.* When you've removed yourself physically from the tumult, give yourself five minutes to get centered and ask God this question: What is my purpose here and how may I serve you in the midst of this confusion?

  After a few moments of silence, return to the meeting. You will discover that the calmness and acknowledgment of the presence of God help you to see your role more clearly. You will know that you are already whole and recognize the test for what it is. You may also recall the two rules for being peaceful: Don't sweat the small stuff, and It's *all* small stuff.

- *Make it a practice to go for a walk alone as often as possible.* This is one of the simplest and quickest ways to get in touch with your sacred self. You can enhance this experience by creating your personal mantra to repeat in time to your footsteps—a sentence like "Divine design shines through me" or a single word such as love, beauty or peace.

  Ralph Waldo Emerson was an avid solitary walker. On the wall of his personal library was this quotation: "I think it is the best of humanity that goes out to walk. In happy hours, I think all affairs may be wisely postponed for walking."

- *Keep in mind the advice offered in* A Course in Miracles: *"Only infinite patience produces immediate results."* Learn to be patient with yourself and those around you.

  As you get into your car, visualize how you want the drive to be and practice being patient with everything that shows up along your route. Being patient can take place within your mind by simply having an inner dialogue of respect for the natural unfolding of events. A simple background silent mantra also fosters patience.

  Impatience is a learned response that is a killer in many ways. You can remove this ego-driven tendency by witnessing yourself in frantic motion and allowing your higher awareness to replace the impatience with love and acceptance.

- *Spend special moments in awe of the miracle that life truly is.* Awe is the loving appreciation for God's work and the presence of the divine intelligence.

  By giving yourself uninterrupted moments for appreciation, you allow yourself the freedom to arrive rather than strive. Being in a state of awe or bewilderment, you choose to be free of ego demands and allow the loving presence to be felt. When you celebrate the present moment this way, you are truly arriving and being in that moment.

One of the great teachers in my life was Paramahansa Yogananda, a man who came out of India to teach the ways of the higher self to the people of the West. I have read many of his speeches and have found great comfort in his writings as well as reading about his life. One of my favorite sayings applies to the contents of this chapter. I offer it to you to ponder as you move toward an awareness of arriving rather than striving.

Seek spiritual riches within. What you are is much greater than anyone or anything else you have ever yearned for.

That is the voice of your higher self reminding you to quietly accept yourself and turn off the yearning. You are never going to get it all, you *are* it all already.

13

FROM DOMINANCE TO TOLERANCE

To accuse others for one's misfortunes
   is a sign of want of education.
To accuse oneself shows that one's
   education has begun.
To accuse neither oneself nor others
   shows one's education is complete.
                                    —EPICTETUS

I am aware that I do not need to dominate anyone in order to be spiritually awake.

✳

Your higher self wants you to be at peace. Your ego wants to keep you in a state of turmoil in order to maintain its mastery and control over your life. You've probably listened to your ego most of your life.

The result of listening to ego is that most of us allow ego to talk us into choosing dominance rather than tolerance as our style of interacting with life. Making the change from dominance to tolerance requires disciplining ego and listening to your sacred self.

I am writing from my personal experience in this matter, and it is one of the toughest assignments my higher self has presented me with. I have spent many years being dominated by my ego, and I have unwittingly made dominance and judgment, rather than tolerance, a cornerstone of my relating.

The suggestions in this chapter are all from my personal experience of transcending my ego-driven instincts. Making the transition from dominance to tolerance is especially difficult because the desire for ego satisfaction is so strong. Ego is extremely persuasive after a lifetime of enjoying the benefits of its dominance. It does not want to relinquish control.

Your higher self will gently take over when you no longer control others. You will begin experiencing unconditional love, and in the process you will finally find the peace that you crave.

To move toward the tolerance that your higher self encourages and away from your ego-driven need to control and judge, you will want to examine the qualities that sustain a tolerant approach to life.

REPLACING DOMINANCE WITH TOLERANCE

Listed below are the major characteristics of tolerance. With tolerance, notice that you become more in tune with your higher self as you forsake the stubborn demands of ego. Realize that what ego has done to you, you have done to others.

Learning about these vital ingredients for creating a tolerant attitude is a way of educating ego and yourself. In the process you can let go of the habitual ego responses that lead you away from true fulfillment.

- *Letting things be.* To become more tolerant and less controlled by your false self, start practicing being satisfied with what is. Your ego is never quite content. If you choose one thing, your ego will persuade you to consider something else.

    If someone you love acts meekly toward you, your ego wants that person to be more assertive; if that person is assertive, your ego decides to dislike assertiveness. If you eat too much, you start thinking about how nice it would be to be thinner; go on a diet, and all of your thoughts will be about food. If you stay at home for a long period, your ego starts telling you how nice it is to travel; go on the road, and you start thinking about how nice it would be to stay home. You're in a relationship and begin to imagine it would be nicer to be uninvolved; you're not in a relationship, and you start wanting to be in one. Your children are running around the house and you start thinking about escaping; you aren't at home and think of nothing but your children.

If you identify with this kind of inner dialogue, rest assured that ego has temporarily separated you from your sacred self. In its ongoing program to convince you of your separateness, it needs to separate you from oneness with the center of your being. Then it can keep you in that state of trying to dominate and control others as a way of trying to achieve your balance and bliss. Trouble is, you cannot get there if you are separated from the awareness of your higher self.

As you begin listening to your higher self in quiet and contemplative moments, you begin relaxing and taking the pressure off. You stop the false thinking that everyone in your life needs to be dominated or controlled by you or that others must live up to your expectations for you to be happy.

People are the way they are, and your need to dominate or change them in any way is the edict of your false self. Your ego is, as usual, trying to convince you of your separateness. It also doesn't want you to catch on to how it is controlling your life, so it convinces you that if you don't dominate others, they will get the best of you.

Ego projects its controlling attitude on others to keep you from seeing it at work within you. At the same time, it causes you to view tolerant people as controllable. Clever ego gets you coming and going. It gets you into dominant behavior to hide its way of controlling you and at the same time it makes you dislike the tolerant, controllable persons. Why would you ever want to choose tolerance with this model?

You won't choose tolerance if you are unable to get free of those false ego beliefs. But when you gain the awareness that all of us are connected in this universe—with the same divine intelligence running through each and every one of us—and that the higher self is knowable and real, then all the surface satisfactions of dominating, controlling and judging others become unappealing.

Your higher self has absolutely no need to dominate anyone or anything. This is the ticket to freedom. Right now, though, in this very moment, your ego is working to convince you that higher self and tolerance are ridiculous ideas. Ego will argue that tolerance means permitting criminal behavior and health and social problems. Its favorite example is that it would mean permitting the Hitlers of the world to commit atrocities while we tolerantly look on. Your higher self can see beyond this logic, so of course you can too. If you are willing.

Your higher self knows that letting go of intolerance does not imply endorsement of evil. The evils that exist in the world are independent of your opinion about them. We will eradicate evil and bring peace to the world, not by judging others but by radiating love. If you let go of judgment and the inclination to dominate and control others, you are able to replace hate and intolerance with love and harmony.

When Mother Teresa was asked if she would march against the war in Vietnam, she replied, "No, but if you have a march for peace, I'll be there." When you become peaceful within, that is what you will have to give away. When you are dominated by your ego, you dominate others. If there is no inner harmony, there is no outer harmony. Ego needs the illusion of enemies in order to control you. When you are controlling others, it is because you have permitted ego to be in control.

The paradox here is that you will affect the world in the ways that you wish when you cease trying to improve conditions with intolerance and judgment. It is only when you are not controlled by ego that you can choose to not control others. What you believed was power when you dominated others was actually the external activity of ego controlling you.

Your impact on the world at large begins with the smaller world of yourself. You will foster freedom and peace when you are free of ego's control and know the peace of your higher self traveling the path of the sacred quest. One of the first steps along your path is learning tolerance by practicing seeing the world as it is rather than as you demand it to be.

- *Listening.* Your ego wants you talking. Your higher self wants you listening. Ego is intolerant. Your higher self is highly tolerant. Therein lies a major difference in attaining your sacred quest.

When you meditate and get very quiet, you learn the art of listening. It is as if God is talking to you rather than you talking to God. Then you begin to know what it feels like to trust your inner guidance. You are even able to listen with compassion to ego's talk. You hear ego's chatter as the expression of fear and as its desire to protect you by keeping you safely separate from others. You are introducing tolerance into your life.

Ego wants to keep you talking in the false belief that it is safer and better to show others how you are different and separate from them. The more you talk and use yourself as a reference point, the more inclined you are to boast and display intolerance, which satisfies ego's agenda.

But protecting ego this way is an exercise that prevents you from the true freedom of knowing your higher self, which begins happening when you begin listening. So ego intensifies its chatter whenever you attempt to meditate or listen to your inner self. It is through listening, even to your intolerant ego, that you will learn tolerance.

It is also through listening that you abandon your self-absorption and your need to dominate or be ego-dominated. When you gently draw out others by really hearing their stories, you are showing love and respect. This goes for ego too. Refusing to listen or showing contempt are intolerant attitudes of the highest order.

Ego's need to chatter and display its superiority is convincingly demonstrated in the following story from *The Heart of the Enlightened*, edited by Anthony de Mello. What the story reinforces is the success that comes our way when we listen tolerantly.

Once upon a time there was an inn called the Silver Star. The innkeeper was unable to make ends meet even though he did his very best to draw customers by making the inn comfortable, the service cordial, and the prices reasonable. So in despair he consulted a sage.

After listening to his tale of woe, the sage said, "It's very simple. You must change the name of your inn."

"Impossible!" said the innkeeper. "It has been the Silver Star for generations and is well known all over the country."

"No," said the sage firmly. "You must now call it the Five Bells and have a row of six bells hanging at the entrance."

"Six bells? But that's absurd! What good would that do?"

"Give it a try and see," said the sage with a smile.

Well, the innkeeper gave it a try. And this is what he saw. Every traveler who passed by the inn walked in to point out the mistake, each one believing that no one else had noticed it. Once inside, they were impressed by the cordiality of the service and stayed on to refresh themselves, thereby providing the innkeeper with the fortune that he had been seeking in vain for so long.

There are few things the ego delights in more than correcting other people's mistakes.

As you cultivate the influence of the higher self in your life, you will find it easier to gently let go of ego's demands that you dominate conversation or impose your views on others. You will find pleasure in stultifying your own self-aggrandizing impulses and in listening to others for a change. You will begin to enjoy your conscious efforts to be tolerant through the spiritual practice of active listening.

- *Giving.* You can neutralize the impact of your ego quite readily through the act of giving. The process of giving involves more than handing over a few presents. Real giving involves being aware of the needs and wants of others.

  Think back to the moment when you were most in love. That experience of strong, passionate love made you automatically aware of the needs of your partner. That awareness is also found in the love a parent has for a child.

  With this kind of love in your heart, you are willing to give whatever is necessary. Your thoughts are not about wanting to dominate or control the other person. There is only the loving pleading of your higher self wanting to give all that you can to the loved one. Marriages often fail because one of the partners stops giving. If both were willing to give 100 percent to the relationship, there would be more than enough to provide for a successful and happy marriage.

  When only one partner gives 100 percent, it is a sacrifice. It is important to distinguish between giving and sacrificing. A sacrifice is generally *for* something.

The sacrifice is only made to achieve something. When you are sacrificing, you are giving to get, and you are in ego's mode, which programs you to believe you are so important and special that you deserve something for your giving. Ego wants you pumped up and believing that giving indicates your superiority—as if your generosity sets you apart from others who are not as munificent as you.

If you give because you feel that you have to, you are not authentically motivated by your higher self. It is the ego at work here too, telling you that you are so much better than the recipients of your giving. Ego even considers giving grudgingly, which is evidence of superiority.

But giving as a means of fostering tolerance and love through your sacred self is different. This kind of giving occurs when you contribute to the needs or wants of others with no expectation of return or acknowledgment. It is the same kind of giving that the mother extends to her baby. This is the kind of giving that tolerance nourishes. It is the kind of giving that happens as you learn tolerance for yourself and for others.

As you cultivate a sense of giving, you will experience that *giving is receiving* and *receiving is giving* in all its tautological splendor. One of my favorite passages in the New Testament describes this kind of giving. In Luke 6:35, Jesus says: "But love ye your enemies, and do good, and lend hoping for nothing again; and your reward shall be great, and ye shall be the children of the highest: for he is kind unto the unthankful and to the evil."

Mindfulness of others' needs is one of the most blissful experiences that we can know. Recall how exciting it was to give presents to parents, grandparents and siblings. It equaled and may even have surpassed your excitement about receiving gifts. You were receiving when you gave.

It is your sacred self that encourages you to give

unconditionally. It is your ego that wants a reward. But that is only because this is what ego knows as long as you continue to reward it for keeping you separate from your loving presence. Give your ego the experience of knowing the love and tolerance of your higher self and you will automatically begin functioning the same way in your outer life.

- *Intimacy.* When you respond to the encouragement of your ego, you find that it is constantly necessary to exercise some degree of authority over others. This is what ego demands because it believes that is how it gets the power it requires. When this occurs, all possibility of intimacy evaporates.

   Intimacy is the way of the higher self. This does not mean merely engaging in close sexual encounters. Showing intimacy is a way of communicating and being with another person, which sends a clear message of unconditional loving and caring.

   Ego fears all such encounters and is extremely active when opportunities for intimacy present themselves. The ego is so overwhelming in this area that the mere thought of committing to another in unconditional love can be more frightening than open-heart surgery without anesthesia!

   "Watch out, they'll try to own you if you become too intimate. You'll lose your freedom!" are the kinds of statements ego bombards your thoughts with. The ego knows all about ownership and dominance because it is doing this to you all the time. Ego dominates you and fears being dominated, and it equates intimacy with domination.

   To be intimate is to be tolerant and to accept another unconditionally. It means showing kindness and respecting the needs and wants of the other person. If you fear this kind of human contact, ego is threatening you with the danger of intimacy.

   When you learn to travel the sacred path, you discover that love is the least threatening experience there is. Love asks nothing and demands nothing. It calls for giving, sharing and being vulnerable, with God as your inner guide communicating infinite love.

Showing intimacy is a way of communicating in which you are able to extend love to the other person without needing to be right or to make the other person wrong. When a person you speak with feels accepted, loved and listened to, after a conversation you both have enjoyed intimacy. If you had to make them wrong to prove your point, or if you judged them in any way, you succumbed to the demands of your ego.

If you are in a partnership with someone and you find yourself shunning intimacy, you can be sure your ego is actively discouraging your sacred self. The fear of your knowing your higher self means that ego will do whatever it has to in order to keep you from intimacy. Convincing you that you are superior is a way to prevent you from the vulnerability that intimacy requires. Thus you will go from one dominant/submissive relationship to another, avoiding intimacy.

These are the fundamentals of becoming more tolerant and allowing your higher self to transcend the authoritarian and dominant impulses of the ego. These ego-directed behaviors crop up in a myriad of ways, some of which you will recognize in this next section.

YOUR AUTHORITARIAN DOMINANT EGO AT WORK

- *Excessively using self-references and always bringing the conversation back to yourself.* Rather than drawing someone else out and exploring their feelings, you use every excuse to have the attention focused on you.

- *Taking a hurry-up approach to life, which leaves no time for contemplation or quiet time.* Always needing to be ahead of the driver in front of you, racing through caution lights rather than slowing to a stop, constantly using telephones and pagers, even at theaters and restaurants—these and many others are behaviors that keep you in control and leave no time for gently being in the lives of others in meaningful ways.

- *Giving orders and demanding perfection from family members and coworkers.* You refuse to listen to any contrary points of view. You do things like bark out demands in restaurants as a way of insinuating others are inferior to you.

- *Being preoccupied with your own concerns, career goals, accomplishments and daily experiences.* You insist that others always hear your stories and seldom are interested in theirs.

- *Publicly correcting the mistakes of others and flaunting your superior knowledge.* You correct such things as grammatical errors, improper use of words, factual errors, etiquette blunders, memory lapses and fashion faux pas (and you do it in front of others to impress them).

- *Withholding intimacy and closeness and blaming the other person for lack of intimacy.* You refuse to be intimate and loving if someone does not live up to your expectations. You use any mistake on their part as your reason to withhold intimacy, which really scares the hell out of you.

- *Needing to win in conversations rather than to communicate and share.* You use the time while someone else is talking to prepare your own self-centered reactions rather than listening to what they are saying and responding to their feelings and concerns.

- *Building yourself up at the expense of others.* You use boasting, bragging and self-centeredness as your primary conversational tools.

- *The inability to give without getting.* You keep track of who responds to your greeting cards and refuse to send to those who are not reciprocating. You give to a charity or help another and then are upset when a thank-you does not arrive on your time schedule. You give to get rather than give unconditionally.

- *Using your standards as an example of how others ought to be.* You treat others as less important who have not performed according to your standards of excellence, or who have failed to win the trophies you consider important. You dismiss those who do not dress or speak the way that you do. You judge the worthiness of others based on things like their jewelry or cars.

- *Dictating to those who are smaller, younger or less educated.* You subject others to your control by threatening reprisal, by bullying or by withholding financial support. You use your superior financial position as an indicator of your specialness.

These, along with a potentially infinite list of others, are some of the more common examples of how the need to be dominant and superior shows up in your life. These tools of the ego are used by virtually everyone at one time or another.

In order to go beyond these ego-driven thoughts and behaviors, it is helpful to know the reward system that your ego has erected. When you know what it is that you are getting out of these behaviors, it makes changing them a much more likely proposition.

HOW YOUR EGO IS REMUNERATED FOR THIS DOMINANCE AND WHY IT FEARS TOLERANCE OF YOUR HIGHER SELF

- *Your ego is your long-time companion and it doesn't want you to abandon it.* Your false self knows that you will not need it to play a dominant role in your life if you become tolerant and shift your emphasis to serving others. Consequently, your ego tells you over and over, "You are separate and better than those around you. In order to prove this, you must exercise some control over their behavior. Be dominant and you will gain the respect of others. Respect from others is how you get validated."

  Your ego needs you to be puffed up so that you will listen to it and believe its false message.

- *Your ego thrives on your feelings of incompleteness and your fear that you are inadequate.* Hence, you will be persuaded to avoid too much intimacy for fear of being revealed. You protect yourself from such revelations by listening to your ego and avoiding true intimacy.

- *By looking outward at all of the things and people that you need to control, you fill your life with the task at hand.* So you fill up your time dominating and controlling the external world, and you have no time left for looking inward. The ego wins when you need to dominate, and winning is very important to your ego.

- *By being reluctant to give of yourself and be aware of the needs and wants of others, you can keep your attention on yourself.* Your ego is threatened when you detach from self-centeredness or look outward to see how you can serve others. Consequently, your ego encourages you to remain self-centered.

  If you do give, your ego gets the focus back on you by demanding to be acknowledged and appreciated for being humanitarian. Either way, the ego—not your higher self—wins again, and your sacred quest is pushed to the background.

- *When you are dominating others, you are guaranteeing that conflict will exist.* Conflict is the workplace of the ego.

  No one, and I mean no one, wants to be told how to live, what to be, how to think. In short, no one wants to be dominated. When you assume this role, you create conflict immediately. Your false self then goes to work convincing you of your need to win the conflict and demonstrate your superiority.

  Your higher self eschews conflict and encourages tolerance and love. Your ego loves the conflict and will encourage it.

- *There are few things the ego delights in more than correcting the mistakes of others.* Ego seizes this double opportunity to point out mistakes and simultaneously feel more important than others.

This is the payoff system for the ego. Now that you understand why you have listened to your ego's requirements for control and domination, you can start shifting some of those attitudes toward tolerance.

Being an authoritarian person may provide you with those ego-gratified appearances, but they do not lead to a more satisfying, deeper experience in your daily life. Your relationships will always suffer and you will feel a sense of emptiness and of being off purpose as long as you adhere to those ego demands.

By shifting your attention to your higher self, you will discover a more satisfying path.

SOME SUGGESTIONS FOR ALLOWING YOUR HIGHER SELF TO GUIDE YOU TOWARD MORE TOLERANCE

- *Curb your need to be right.* You can accomplish this by catching yourself just as you are about to speak, and asking yourself if you want to be guided by your ego or your higher self. If you truly want to work on this area of restraining your ego, then simply respond to what the person has just said without offering an argument or advice. As you practice this technique, your ego will fade and your relationships will improve.

- *Practice active listening.* Try to hear the emotions within the content of a person's conversation. Remove your defensiveness or need to fix or explain. Just listen with your heart and paraphrase what the person has said to you. Hear what the other person is *feeling* and respond to that. You will automatically begin to eliminate your intolerance.

- *Demonstrate tolerance and love by ignoring what may have transpired in the past.* Avoid the inclination to make someone wrong by pointing out the fallacies of their point of view with examples from their past. Let go of the desire to win, and cultivate the desire to communicate.

- *Give yourself some quiet time to talk with God and to seek the help of your spiritual guides.* Doing this daily will introduce you to a more peaceful and quiet way of being. You will find that the energy you previously used overpowering people will be slowly put to use in serving rather than swaying others.

- *Halt yourself just as you are about to intervene in a family or business dispute.* Count to twenty-five and listen. The pause will usually allow the dispute to get resolved without your interference. If it is difficult to restrain yourself, then move out of hearing range.

  Learn to allow others to work out their difficulties without feeling that you are the only one who can fix things. Your ego is pushing you to intervene and show how powerful you are, while your higher self wants you to experience peace and harmony. Choose the latter.

- *Stifle any and all public tendencies to correct others.* Make a rule that you will never correct someone in front of others. No one appreciates being publicly corrected.

  If you feel the need to teach someone the errors of their ways, get quiet and ask yourself how God would handle the situation. If the person is an adult, gently and privately ask if he or she wants to be corrected. You may be surprised to discover how unimportant it is for many people to know the proper or correct way of saying or doing things. It is usually the person doing the correcting who places so much importance on the correct way.

- *Try giving anonymously to the needy.* If you insist on being recognized for your gift, then you are not giving from your higher self. Give up giving to get!

    Be generous and find joy in knowing that your contributions are helping others. Celebrate yourself for giving that is not ego-based.

- *When tempted to judge others, remind yourself that they are part of the same divine creation as you are.* Let go of some of those ego-based judgments of assessing others based on appearances or acquisitions.

    See the fullness of God in everyone that you meet and remember that the world of the manifest is not all that there is. There is the Christ in you meeting the Christ in that person also. If you can see it in this way, you will be less tempted to judge them by their possessions of appearance.

- *If you have difficulty with intimacy, feel the fear and do it anyway.* Know that you are having a tough time offering your love, but resist the ego's demand to withdraw. Instead, reach out to the person you love and tell them how much they mean to you. Do it even if you feel that they don't deserve it or they won't respond properly. Take the risk and fight the impulse to withhold. You will feel more loving and fulfilled for having taken that risk.

    Your higher self pleads with you to extend your love and be unafraid of being vulnerable. Loving is about giving. If you get back, fine; but if not, you are still lovable.

- *Remember that no one on this planet wants to share in your conflicts.* People want the peace that is the way of their higher selves. Ego loves turmoil and conflict, which is why there are so many conflicts in the world. Ego fighting ego.

    If you know in your heart that you are being guided

by your false self when you promote conflict, then perhaps you can get a bit quiet and go within just before you are about to embroil someone in a conflict. I have found that when I meditate for even thirty seconds before I am about to engage in conflict, I somehow manage to get in touch with my higher self—and the need to be right just disappears.

In *Man's Eternal Quest*, Paramahansa Yogananda wrote: "God is the repository of all happiness; and you can contact Him in everyday life. Yet man mostly occupies himself in pursuits that lead to unhappiness."

The activity that leads mostly to that unhappiness is the need to make others wrong and the tendency to dominate and control. Consult God and know that this loving presence is available to you. Abandon your reliance on your ego and all of its false logic, and experience the tolerance, love and peace of your sacred self.

14

FROM TOXICITY TO PURITY

Blessed are the pure in heart: for they
shall see God.

—MATTHEW 5:3

I will work this day at my purest intentions
for the highest good of all.

✳

In Confucianism there is a principle called Jen. This principle refers to the belief that there is goodness, pure
goodness, at the center of our being where the self or the
spirit can be found. Each person is perceived to be good
when they are their true self. The principle of Jen implies
that one cannot help but be pure when they are themselves. Lives take on a toxic quality when we ignore our
authentic selves and listen to the false self.

To allow your highest self to triumph in this conflict
between purity and toxicity, you must let go of any idea
that at your core you are evil or a sinner. You need to
realize that the central facet of your being is pure, good
and beautiful. As Saint Matthew put it so perfectly, this
purity of heart will allow you to know God.

Of course, the opposite is true as well. If you practice
a toxic life, in thought or behavior, you will be unable to
know the divine spirit within you, and your ego will continue to dominate your inner and outer life.

The pure in heart are distinguishable from the toxic in
heart by their thoughts and behaviors. Your sacred self

desires you to have both pure thoughts and pure behavior. Your ego strongly resists purity and campaigns for toxicity in a multitude of ways. In order to engage this conflict, you must understand how you can identify and challenge yourself in these two areas.

PURIFYING YOUR THINKING

What you think about expands into action. The more conscious you become of the ways you use your mind, the more you will be able to leave behind toxic ways of thinking. When you know that your thoughts expand into action, you become very careful about what you think because you know that your thoughts literally poison your life.

Purifying your thoughts is a variation on the theme of higher awareness. So you might want to start with a review of the keys to higher awareness found in Part II. The first three—banishing doubt, cultivating the witness and shutting down inner dialogue—are essential to taming the ego and beginning to recognize and change toxicity to purity.

Toxic thinking is a habit of using your mind as an interpreter. Let go of that habit of constant interpretation and begin to live your life free of ego's comments. Your willingness to confront the ways that you have been thinking is your opening to the purification process. The ability to suspend judgment will allow you to reach the higher ground (where you know the presence of the divine force) and experience the richer awareness that goes with the triumph of the higher self over the ego.

Just knowing that you can choose less toxic thoughts is an important insight. Many people have never had this insight. Consequently, they spend their entire lives defending the position that their thoughts are unchangeable.

You, on your sacred path, know better. You know that who you are is something grander than the thoughts you think and more divine than the body where the thoughts occur.

Your thoughts and behaviors are habits. The ways that you have allowed your inner world to work are habits resulting from your experience of your life, including the beliefs that you've received from all the well-meaning people who taught you about life. To purify your thinking and make your mind work exactly as you want it to, be willing to examine these habits of thought. Then you will begin the purifying process and see the opening to your sacred self.

FREEING YOURSELF OF PREJUDICE

The word "prejudice" means to prejudge. We engage in toxic thinking whenever we allow ourselves to be in a judgmental mode. And when we judge in advance, our thoughts are even more toxic.

When I was doing research for my book *What Do You Really Want for Your Children?* I was intrigued by data indicating that children who were taught to believe, without question, what authorities said were children with the highest rate of prejudice. That conclusion is understandable when you realize that prejudging, based only on what others have said, prevents developing a mind of one's own.

Prejudiced thinking comes from treating your mind like a rental space for the thoughts and beliefs of others. Learning to furnish your mind with your personal interpretation, even for a moment, frees you to know yourself and others through your higher self. When your mind is occupied by prejudice, ego is the landlord.

Prejudging is a way of interpreting the motives and behaviors of others according to your ego-influenced standards. It is not restricted to the racial or religious antagonisms that we've come to associate with the word "prejudice." Whenever you define members of a different generation as inferior or outlandish or outmoded, you are engaging in prejudice.

To free yourself of prejudgment habits, which come with the territory of the ego, take an inventory of your thoughts and keep track of how much of your inner energy is devoted to prejudging others. Ask yourself if you are willing to continue renting out your mind for others' thoughts to occupy.

The antidote for having toxic prejudging thoughts is to suspend your ego and listen to your higher self. You will begin knowing that no one on this planet is superior or special in the eyes of God, just as no one is nonspecial.

Purifying your thinking is really nothing more than practicing seeing the fullness of God in everyone. The moment that you sense a prejudgment entering your mind, suspend it and replace it with the thought that you do not want to poison your mind. Shift the thought to a witnessing position of accepting and seeing the loving presence within all. The sacred Sanskrit greeting "Namaste" is a reminder of this kind of pure thinking. It translates loosely to "I celebrate the place in you where we are both one."

Purifying your thoughts in this area of prejudgment happens when you are willing to acknowledge the presence of uncounted beliefs that you have received from others and when you want to be in relationship with the pure thoughts emanating from your sacred self. You are then willing to begin breaking the habits of prejudgment and replacing them with the idea in the Namaste greeting.

FREEING YOURSELF OF YOUR LIBIDO

Your higher self urges you to view a person of the opposite sex as a soul who has a body. Your ego, however, is determined that you see that person as a physical body.

Your libido represents your basic biological urges and sexual desires. They are vital and are not to be viewed with contempt or scorn. However, when the libido becomes the controlling influence in how you use your mind, your thinking can become toxic and drift far from the bliss and harmony that your sacred self offers. To purify your thinking in this area, you will have to carefully examine all that you have learned about your sexual nature, beginning with childhood.

When I examine the beliefs about male sexuality that I grew up with, I realize that I was exposed to toxic thinking that couldn't help but interfere with my spiritual development. Movies, magazines, songs, advertising and adult males all sent messages teaching me to relate to a female as a physical body. The goal was the conquest of her body. Sex and sexual innuendo were considered the penultimate objective of my human quest.

This is the kind of learning that I've referred to throughout this book—it affects the thinking process and function. Our thoughts are trained to focus on sexual conquest. Every time we encounter an attractive member of the opposite sex, our thoughts begin to swirl around the messages of our libido.

The reason that this kind of thinking becomes toxic is that it uses up all of our mental energy in the activity of processing people as bodies rather than spiritual beings. Our minds become warped with the false idea that our own worth and value as human beings is somehow connected to the successful conquests that we collect and display to get approval from other members of our ego-based gender.

Relationships with the opposite sex become focused exclusively on appearance and external beauty. For men, breast size often becomes more important than making a spiritual connection. Having sex becomes a substitute for exchanging love and being spiritual partners. Women, too, make value judgments about the appearance of other men and women. All potential for knowing the bliss offered by our highest spiritual self is removed from awareness in favor of using our mind to see appearance rather than substance in other humans.

This has been a significant realization for me as I've become aware of my capacity for allowing my higher self to be the force that I respond to. I've found that my early training as an ego-dominated male was extremely powerful and was not easy to change.

When you are motivated by your libido, your thoughts are overwhelmed almost all the time. Your inner world is almost exclusively oriented around sexual thoughts and evaluations based upon appearances. To change your thinking in this area does not mean that you will become a prude or asexual.

What you will do is free yourself to see the inner beauty that is in each and every one of us. You will also realize that all physical appearance is temporary and constantly undergoing change. If you gain your sense of power and value through the physical appearance of yourself and others, where will your power be when those physical traits begin to shift, as they are all destined to do?

There is no inner reward in a conquest, even though you may have been trained to believe that. There is no inner reward in a conquest even though you feel like there is when you talk at length about it with your friends who have been through the same training course. When the conquest is completed, there is a sense of emptiness and a strong desire to change the scene as soon as possible.

Sexual union that is free of the idea of conquest and is focused on the sacred self that is a part of both of you does not leave you with an empty feeling or the desire to change the scene. You want to be close to each other after the physical act is completed. There is no empty feeling when you are a spiritual partner making love to the person you adore because you touched their soul first.

Becoming free from the libido in this way occurs as

you purify your thoughts of others as well as of yourself. Make a deliberate and conscious effort to change the toxic, libido-based thinking of a lifetime. Do it one thought at a time. You will find yourself creating the inner peace that comes from knowing your highest self.

Remember, God does not play favorites. In reality, no one is any better looking or more gorgeous than anyone else. The only difference between a flower and a weed is a judgment. Ego-based judgments convince you that physical appearances and sexual conquests of those who are judged most attractive are of primary importance. Keep in mind that every thought or judgment concerning others as sexual objects is a thought that keeps you away from your higher self and close to ego's domination.

If you are a woman reading these words, be careful not to allow your ego to convince you that you are beyond such thinking. I have only used male examples here because of my lifetime of masculine sexual education. I have observed women making value judgments about the appearance of other men and women, using similar innuendo and lewd conversational style.

To purify our thoughts in the area of the libido, we must commit to tackling all of the judgmental thoughts that occur regardless of our sex, marital status or physical age. I give some suggestions for how to go about this in the final section of this chapter.

FREEING YOURSELF OF ADDICTIVE THINKING

The succinct definition of addictive thinking is believing that you must have something external to yourself in order to avoid suffering. When your thoughts are focused on the absolute need to have something, they are being subjected to ego's training system. Remember, the ego wants you to feel that you are incomplete so that it can keep you striving for something instead of looking within and knowing the peace and harmony of your sacred self.

As long as your thoughts are centered on your incompleteness you will need to strive for something else in order to keep your ego satisfied. The something else might be our typical addictions such as alcohol, drugs, sugars, caffeines and so on. Or we might be addicted to approval, danger, money or other success symbols. The key here is to understand that striving for things is your ego at work.

When you become acquainted with your higher self, you discover that all the pleasures that your addictions provide are both counterfeit and fleeting. The pleasures that any substance offers—from nicotine and caffeine to cocaine and heroin—are all experienced in the body as sensations that disappear almost immediately. When the demand for more of the substance becomes an addiction, you are on the path of ultimately poisoning both your body and your mind.

In all instances, you need to examine your addictive thinking. Virtually every spiritual tradition teaches that your higher self is the presence of God within you. When you know this power within yourself, you no longer think in terms of anything that you *must* have or do with reference to external needs. In Christianity, this inner knowing is referred to in the commandment that says ". . . for behold, the kingdom of God is within you." In Confucianism we are told, "What the undeveloped man seeks is outside. What the advanced man seeks is within himself." In Buddhism we are reminded, "If you think the Law is outside yourself you are embracing not the absolute Law but some inferior teaching." In Shintoism we are implored, "Do not search in distant skies for God. In man's own heart is He found." And finally, in Hinduism we are told, "God bides hidden in the hearts of all."

If you examine each of these spiritual traditions and many others, you will see that addictive thinking is that which violates the very basic principles of your highest self. Within each and every one of us is a divine power that needs no substance or anything external to itself to know bliss (unless one seeks out counterfeit, fleeting bliss that demands more and more of the substance to remain satiated).

The advanced man that Confucius referred to is the person who has looked within himself, discovered that he is more than a body that craves things and then is able to witness the body. When you become detached from the belief that your body is who you are, you also detach yourself from the demands that your false self places on you.

To become free of any and all addictive thinking, you will find it necessary to let go of ego's demands. Get quiet and become the observer of your body and its cravings rather than be the craving or the poison. You will then be able to see the celestial light of God giving you the strength to leave the addictive thoughts.

As you witness the craving, you can see it come and go. You know that the false self is weakening at the same time that it continues intermittently to whisper warnings about falling for the "spiritual stuff" and suggest that you deserve the bliss now, in this moment, just one more time. This is all part of ego's conditioned thinking telling you that without that external something you will be denied bliss and pleasure.

To get free of this thinking, you need to abandon your ego for the moment and take solace in your newfound bliss in your strength of resistance. Call upon your higher self and engage in a conversation with God in which you surrender this problem.

When you begin resisting ego's domination and demands for addictive behavior, you will know a far superior and longer-lasting bliss than any external substance or dose of approval can ever provide. You will know pure rather than toxic thinking for perhaps the first time in your life.

FREEING YOURSELF OF CONTRARY THINKING

Toxic thinking is that which sees the bad rather than the good in the world. Here again, the ego is at work encouraging you to avoid anything that tells you that this is a divine place. Once you begin to see the good in all and to know that even the things that none of us can understand are in some mysterious way a part of God's plan, your ego will wither away and lose its influence over you.

When your thinking is pure you begin processing the world in a new way. World events are not what bring you down; rather it is the way they are interpreted. Practice releasing your need to interpret.

Toxic thinking tells you that you must make an issue out of something because your ego is invested in being right. If things are not going the way your ego thinks they should, you have a reason for being upset. This creates internal dissonance, which is the goal of the ego. If you are internally disrupted, you are unlikely to adopt a peaceful or tranquil viewpoint.

Minor irritation can and will keep you from experiencing the peace of God, just as surely as anger and hatred will. Any time that you value something more than you value peace, you know that your ego is exerting its influence over you.

If you want to know supreme happiness, you must work at removing contrary thinking from your life. You must surrender the interpretation of people and events and leave behind negativity and pessimism. Victor Hugo once wrote, "The supreme happiness of life is the conviction that we are loved; loved for ourselves, or rather in spite of ourselves."

When you are negative and contrary, you send out a message that you are uninterested in receiving love. Negativity will bring more of the same back to you. When you make the shift to your higher self, when you are experiencing bliss within, the ego moves aside, albeit reluctantly, and makes way for positive, loving ways of experiencing life. You know that your higher self will bring you the supreme happiness that Victor Hugo mentioned.

I sometimes think of myself as a sort of reverse paranoid. People who are paranoid believe that the world and everyone in it is out to harm them in some way. I think of reverse paranoids as people who believe that the world and everyone in it is out to provide for them, to protect them and to do them some good.

This is simply a shift in attitude that reassures us about the divine intelligence. Our higher self reminds us to keep our thoughts on serving and in that way to realize the fulfillment of our desires. Everyone you meet—in some unproven but known manner—is a part of the conspiracy to make your life divine and blissful.

Try thinking of yourself as a reverse paranoid. You will see your contrary thinking and all of ego's tricks disappearing only to be replaced with your sacred self bringing to you the love that is the supreme experience of happiness.

FREEING YOURSELF OF COMPARISON THINKING

It is common to hear people talking about the uniqueness of each and every person. Our egos would have us believe that each and every one of us is special and a one-of-a-kind creation deserving individualized attention from everyone, including God. I cannot argue with this position other than describe it as a surface interpretation of ourselves. On the surface—that is, when we judge by physical appearances, talents, behavioral quirks and personalities—each person is unique and indeed quite special. But the focus of this book is the spiritual dimension beyond surfaces.

The ego-driven person judges by appearances in the physical plane and consequently uses comparisons. The person who is grounded in his or her higher identity knows that all of these differences are merely surface observations, and at our core all of us share the same universal essence. The force that flows through you sitting here reading these pages is also flowing through me. There is not a separate God for each of us. It is our egos that convince us of our separateness from each other.

When you begin to view people in terms of their divine essence, and literally see the fullness of God in each and every person that you encounter, you stop comparing. The idea that other people should be judged based upon how they compare with you is tantamount to the idea that you are a favorite in the eyes of God. It is as if you believe that God's creations that are unlike you in appearance, personality, interest or talents are errors.

But how could there possibly be an error of creation when this is an intelligent system? How could a divine, all-knowing God make an error?

As your thinking becomes more pure, you begin seeing the connections that link all of us together in something far more significant than surface appearances. To think of yourself as superior to another, or more talented, or more beautiful means that ego is getting you to deny your inner spirit, which is connected to those whom you are judging.

There is no room for feeling superior or comparing yourself with others when you are operating from your sacred self. Every being, including yourself, is an individualized expression of God.

Comparison thinking is popular in our culture. Beauty contests, athletic contests, advertising skits, body-building competitions and academic competitions are just some of the many ways of comparison thinking that you are exposed to constantly. Clearly, the message is that some are more beautiful or more gifted than others, and they are judged to be superior.

I am not suggesting that these external factors are nonexistent. Indeed, some people run faster, compute quicker and have more body mass than others. But to use these distribution factors, which are passed out genetically, as indicators of how we must think is to give in to the ego, which puts all of its emphasis on appearance.

Notice the differences and enjoy the competitions, but know in your heart that you needn't judge others based on physical differences.

When you have purified your thinking, you will look past those obvious differences that are measurable on the physical plane. You will note them, enjoy them, compete against them if you choose. But you will never use your thinking to judge anyone as superior to anyone else based on physical characteristics and performances. Your thoughts will always stay with the higher self, which tells you that we are all of the same essence.

The following words are attributed to Buddha: "Be a lamp unto yourself. Hold to the truth within yourself." Remind yourself of this truth and your thinking will stay pure. When you listen to this advice, comparison thinking no longer toxifies your life. *A Course in Miracles* offers another way of remembering this: "See no one as a body. Greet him as the Son of God he is, acknowledging that he is one with you in holiness."

PURIFYING YOUR EMOTIONS

Your emotions are physiological reactions to your thoughts. These feelings show up in your body and they flow directly from the ways that you choose to use your mind. Your emotions do not just happen to you, they are choices that you make.

If your body is racked with toxic emotional responses such as guilt, anger, worry, fear, shyness or anxiety, you must examine the thinking process that supports those feelings. The physiological reactions to these emotions include higher blood pressure, flushed skin, deepened respiration, increased heart rate, knotted feelings in the stomach, ulcers, rashes and nail biting, among others.

Your emotions can be identified in the physical body that you are learning to observe. But you must also know that the support system for these emotional reactions is your choice of thoughts. If you are engaging in the toxic thought process mentioned above, you will be producing toxic emotional responses that put your body in a state of anxiousness and imbalance.

The truth is that you are totally responsible for what you think. By putting into practice the four keys to higher awareness presented in Part II of this book, you will start seeing your thoughts as choices. The world does not rule your mind, nor does your body rule your thoughts. It is the reverse. The invisible commander in the command center, called your brain, is pure and peaceful.

Thoughts that are toxic—such as prejudicial, libidinous, contrary, addictive and comparative thoughts—can be observed and allowed to leave. Simply watch them come and then choose to no longer place your invisible commander's scope on them.

This simple formula is the secret to creating the emotional reactions in your body that flow from love, acceptance, peace, tolerance, compassion, kindness and forgiveness. These thoughts of purity, directed by your higher self, will bring about the emotional reactions of bliss, homeostasis, balance, contentment, joy and calmness. Therefore, to purify your emotions, you must purify your thoughts and then observe as you shift around those ancient toxic emotional reactions that you have become accustomed to calling your heritage, or your genetic destiny.

There was a time when I expected to receive an acknowledgment when I gave a gift. If I did not receive the thanks that I expected, I would be upset and inwardly accuse the recipient of ingratitude. I could notice the physical changes in my body brought on by my thoughts.

Today, I listen to my higher self rather than my ego,

and I am able to give anonymously. My higher self guides me to give for no other reason than the wish to help. I no longer give to get. My thoughts in this one area are purified, and therefore all of the angry, frustrating emotional responses are replaced by a feeling of balance and well-being.

Similarly, I have removed the painful emotional response of jealousy from my body, by changing the way that I process the world. Rather than allowing my ego to be in charge, I turn to my higher self for guidance. I let go of telling myself that I should feel slighted when someone achieves more than I have. I consult my higher self and silently witness my thoughts. From this vantage, I see that love is what I can send to all those who are on this planet with me, regardless of external appearances or differences.

Keep in mind that your ego is that very small part of your mind which has adopted the role of boss in its attempts to protect you with its false idea that your physical being is all that you are. From this incomplete picture of your totality, ego breeds toxic emotional reactions as well as toxic behavior.

As you proceed on the path to your sacred self, keep in mind the words of my teacher Nisargadatta Maharaj:

> When you know beyond all doubting that the same life flows through all that is and you are that life, you will love all naturally and spontaneously. When you realize the depth and fullness of your love of yourself, you know that every living being and the entire universe are included in your affection. But when you look at anything as separate from you, you cannot love it for you are afraid of it. Alienation causes fear and fear deepens alienation.

This alienation that Maharaj refers to shows up as the stress and physical reactions that we call toxic emotions. Memorizing this passage from *I Am That* will help you shift to emotional purity. New and undiluted behaviors will result.

PURIFYING YOUR BEHAVIOR

Your behavior on the physical plane flows directly from your thoughts and emotions. As Emerson reminded us, "The ancestor to every action is a thought." Poisonous thinking obviously leads to toxic behavior. To purify your behavior, you must tackle toxic thinking.

Long-term toxicity assists the development of addictive behaviors. Regardless of how many treatment programs you enter or cure-alls that you attempt, if you are going to rid yourself of addictive behavior, you will have to do it on your own. No one else can do it for you. No program can do it for you. No magic elixir will do it. Only you, with your personal thought process, can change addictive behaviors that you have chosen at the urging of your counterfeit pleasure-seeking ego.

The most effective way to rid yourself of toxic addictive behavior is to go directly to your higher self and turn the problem over to God. That's right. Just turn it over. Surrender, knowing that the highest force in the universe is within you.

I absolutely love this passage from *A Course in Miracles:* "I am content to be wherever He wishes, knowing He goes there with me. I will be healed as I let Him teach me to heal." When you surrender to that higher force and enter the silence of your self, you will experience all that I have written about in this book. You will sense that you no longer have to rely on your false self for any temporary high. You will feel the presence of your higher self with you at all times. Temptations to return to addictive habits will be dissipated with your new ability to surrender and your willingness to help heal others.

Even a relapse will be part of the divine order because you know that the moment will arrive when you are totally free of the addiction, as long as you stay focused on purified thinking. Your thoughts are the most important thing you have in the battle to discontinue addictive behavior. Your thoughts are in the invisible realm where your higher self is found.

Your false self will continue to urge you to take the fleeting pleasure. But as you use your thoughts to trust in the spirit within you, your ego's impact will diminish.

You will be guided by your higher self to purify your addictive behavior, and you will be given direct help as you continue to remain committed to this process. The people who supply you with your poisons will be unable to get through to you. Your telephone call to a supplier will be unanswered. Your supplier will be unavailable. You will be called out of town, or you'll get sidetracked, or other activities will suddenly crop up just as you were about to weaken. The universe will conspire to help you with your commitment to purity when you willingly and authentically turn this problem over to your higher self to resolve.

Ultimately, you will look back at your addictive behaviors with incredulity, wondering how you could have been so stupid. However, your higher self will remind you that it was all part of the divine design. You had to go through those experiences in order to know how to transcend them. You will eventually be grateful for your toxic past, giving thanks daily for the emergence of your higher self. You will have tamed your ego through a program of purifying thoughts, emotions and behaviors.

As you begin noticing how everything is working together helping you purify your life, you will see every area of your life improving. Automatically you will begin engaging in a healthier way of being with exercise and food choices. When your thoughts have shifted to the spiritual realm, the physical realm spontaneously responds to a higher call.

This shift to new and purer behaviors is not a difficult transition. An audience participant recently explained to me that he longed to become a more spiritual person with a pure heart but that it was very difficult for him. I told him that he needed to recognize that this was his false self at work, attempting to convince him that it was difficult so that he would not make the necessary effort.

When you listen to ego and become convinced that it is too difficult to let go of your toxic habits, you are under the control of that false self. The fact is that when you turn those habits over to God and surrender and listen, and then shift to the four keys to higher awareness, everything begins to synchronize to purify your life. If you are convinced that it is difficult, you are listening to your ego. If you *know* that you are not alone and that you are infinitely capable of anything you can conceive of, then you are listening to your higher self.

The habit of pursuing destructive behavior goes well beyond consuming substances. Toxic behavior that interferes with creating a spiritual partnership can also be purified by turning this habit over to your higher self.

Your higher self wants you to have peace and love in your life, not the turmoil of chase and conquest. Your higher self knows that you crave a spiritual partnership, a place where you feel serenity rather than tumult.

Any behavior that is toxic to your life will be purified through the reliance on the holy spirit within you. As you shift your thoughts away from ego's influence, your emotional responses and your conduct will shift as well.

You have seen what toxic thoughts, feelings and behaviors are like and how they show up in your life. As you remove these obstacles to your heightened awareness, you will want to be mindful of the reasons why you've permitted your ego to poison your life with its demands.

As you examine the payoffs in the following section, keep in mind that you have the choice to remove these obstacles at will by consulting your higher self. As you realize now, when your ego is forced to face the bright light of your celestial higher self, it fades from its role of dominance.

YOUR EGO'S COMPENSATION FOR PROMOTING TOXICITY RATHER THAN PURITY

- *Your ego always wants to promote the false idea that you are separate from everyone, including God.* If you are perpetually in a state of seeking your pleasures from external sources, you are convinced that your happiness comes from those external sources. As you pursue this external-oriented pleasure, you are kept from the experience of quieting and knowing the bliss of a pure heart. Consequently, the ego guarantees its survival by getting you to destroy yourself little by little.

- *When you engage in prejudicial thinking, you are literally making a judgment about yourself as a being who is superior to those being judged.* The goal of your ego is to convince you that those others are inferior to you. This kind of thinking allows the ego to maintain its role of controller.

- *The ego benefits enormously when you view others as sexual objects.* It convinces you that your own worth is found in your conquests. It allows you to boast of your sex appeal and see yourself as stronger than your conquest. As long as you listen to ego, you will have to prove yourself on this physical plane. For ego there is no better way to prove your superiority as a physical being than to conquer another's physical body.

Ego is frightened of the idea that you are a soul with a body. If you begin seeing others as spiritual beings having a human experience, ego fears it will not be able to convince you to continue to prove yourself through your libido. Thus, your ego encourages you to listen to your biological urges and to act on them.

- *Your addictions are the supreme joy of your ego.* The more you rely on the need for external approval or substances of any kind, the less likely you are to turn within and receive your bliss from your spiritual self. As long as you can be persuaded that you are primarily a physical being whose sexual satisfaction has top priority, your ego is assured of its position of prominence. If you abandon your need for these external fixes, it is like telling your ego to take a hike. Thus, your false self will promote the idea of gaining your pleasures from anything but the celestial light of your spirit within.

- *The idea of you being in a state of inner turmoil and disruption is fine with the ego.* Your ego maintains just enough discontent to keep you in turmoil and not enough to send you looking for the peace that is within you. Having this constant background discontent makes you believe that you cannot escape it. Your ego pushes you into a steady river of discontent, not dumping you completely on the rocks.

You are encouraged by your ego to find fault, be pessimistic and generally see the negative side of life. The more you do this, the more your false self maintains its power over you. It is trying to keep you from feeling so desperate that you are driven to seek your spiritual nature. If you begin seeking purity and peace through your higher self, ego knows that you will begin experiencing more optimism and contentment. Ego is doing what it needs to do to prevent that.

- *As long as you feel the need to compare yourself with others, you are doing the handiwork of the ego.* Once you see that others are on their sacred quest, you cannot help but send love rather than judgment, and ego is too insecure to allow that. Consequently, your false self encourages you to compare yourself with others and to be upset when others defeat you or have more things and appear to find happiness.

  When you discard this false idea that comparing is something that is appropriate for human beings to do, you will no longer have to consult your ego.

These are some of the major payoffs for the ego in promoting toxic thinking, feeling and behavior. Now it is time to shift your attention to some ways of being that will attract purity into your life.

NEW WAYS OF BEING PURE IN BODY, MIND AND SPIRIT

- *When you feel yourself being persuaded by the demands of your body, take a few moments to become silent and listen for direction from your higher self.* Just listen and make an effort to postpone the immediate fleeting pleasure of the senses for a few moments.

  It is in these precious few moments that you will find the strength to forsake the demands of the ego. Even if you postpone your reliance on the body pressure for a moment or two, you will have made progress. What you think about will eventually come to be your habit. Giving yourself permission to think about shifting to a higher spiritual base will get the wheels in gear to override the ego.

- *Begin keeping track of the judgmental thoughts that you allow yourself to have each day.* Increasing your awareness of this judging habit will help you to consult your loving presence as these judgmental attitudes surface.

  If your first inclination is to have a judgment thought about the physical appearance of someone, notice that you are doing that and redirect your thought to consider the fullness of God within that person. This perspective will awaken in you an awareness of how you habitually think in terms of judging others. It will also provide you with a more peaceful countenance, since judgment leads to more hostile internal and external reactions.

  As you catch yourself in judgmental attitudes, you will begin to break the habit. You will eventually replace that habit with pure thoughts of connectedness toward everyone that you meet.

- *When you find yourself relapsing and indulging in toxic thinking or behavior, ask your sacred self to intervene.* Turn the thought or behavior over with an affirmation of surrender and trust that you will be guided. This kind of affirmation puts you in touch with energy far removed from the debilitating demands of your ego.

  While it is true that you may take some time to purify yourself entirely, it is also true that relapses will gradually occur less frequently. Each time that you do slip, you will be aware of the influence of your ego. The awareness will heighten your determination until eventually you will listen only to your higher self.

- *Forgive yourself for any and all toxic behavior that you have practiced up until now.* All of your poisonous thinking, feeling and behavior was also a way of teaching you to transcend ego identity. You apparently needed those excursions into toxic hell in order to know what you no longer want for your life.

Rather than cursing the past, bless it and forgive yourself entirely. When you know that all of those experiences were a part of the divine design of your life, you can afford to forgive. The time will then arrive when you look back with amazement that you ever could have carried on in such destructive ways.

But for now, just forgive yourself. Bless the past and listen to your soul speak of love and forgiveness.

- *Rather than continually making an issue of things with your immediate family and friends, try letting go of your ego investment in favor of a more peaceful point of view.* When you realize that you are about to be contentious, ask yourself if you want to make an issue of this and experience the painful results or if you would rather create a peaceful atmosphere.

  A few moments consulting with the invisible force that wants you to be at peace will shift you away from toxic confrontation. You only need a few seconds to pause and know how preferable peace is. Your ego will intensify and you will have to consciously make the option of peace available to you.

- *Work to eliminate the minor irritations you carry around.* Remind yourself that your ego prefers you to experience a steady flow of misery with these minor irritants.

  For example, give the waiter a little slack by sending him love rather than irritability when your order has taken too long to arrive. Remind yourself that your children are tiny and that they will make repetitious demands as their way of getting what they want. Ignore the weather changes that you judge ruinous to your plans; instead, be thankful for any weather.

In other words, be aware of the minor irritations and see them as opportunities to learn more about the higher part of yourself that is peaceful. The minor nuisances are designed by your ego to provide you with a daily level of toxicity. Turn in the direction of your sacred self and a daily intake of purity.

- *Keep the word* Namaste *in your awareness.* Use it as a greeting and to remind yourself of your connection to everyone. When you honor the place in others that they share with you, you move past the toxic reaction of feeling competitive while removing any possibility of enmity existing within yourself. I think of *Namaste* all the time, particularly when my old ego keeps trying to convince me that I do not share the invisible force with another.

- *Work at being able to experience bliss without the need for anything external.* As you learn to meditate and quiet your inner dialogue, something wonderful will happen. You will get high without the external substance. You will feel giddy, euphoric and lightheaded in a purer way than you ever felt before. You will know this feeling without the toxic ingredient of something that will ultimately destroy your body tissue and alter your brain chemistry.

  Your body's natural pharmacy produces euphoria with the cooperation of a mind you have trained with meditation. As you slip into the state of bliss of the unified field, you will experience your chemistry changing. When you realize that you can have this experience, you will not be attracted to external poisons for their euphoric effect.

- *If you are tempted to slip under the influence of your toxic ego, remember that there are two ways to have the tallest building in town.* One way is to tear down all the other buildings. This method will certainly require violent effort and battle with the owners of the buildings you are destroying. You will probably also lose your building in the process.

The second way to have the tallest building in town is to work on your own building, ignoring the height of the other buildings. Apply this analogy to building your personal happiness.

If you opt for the toxic activity of putting everyone else down in order to build yourself up, you will be in a constant state of turmoil. However, if you select the second option and work on yourself, sending love to those around you, you will assure yourself of a pure heart and a loving existence.

- *Entertain the thought that you remove habits from your life by coaxing them one step at a time.* Try to catch individual toxic thoughts in the moment they are occurring. One moment at a time, one day at a time—and you will be able to achieve the transition from toxic to pure.

  If you attempt to change it all at once, your ego will celebrate because you will give up and give in to habits. But today, in this moment, make one internal determination that you no longer will live the toxic life—and you are on your spiritual path.

  For example, if you are overweight and make a decision to spend time walking around the block rather than sitting and eating something, you are purifying your thinking. The thought will produce the behavior. You are still overweight, but you have transcended your ego for a moment. This is your building step toward the next pure thought, and the next, until you are trusting your loving presence to lead you.

This is a beginning prescription for becoming aware of the power that you have given to your ego to promote toxicity. Glance at the quotation at the beginning of this chapter and remind yourself that as you develop a pure heart you will come to know God. Practice some of these strategies to develop a pure heart and say good-bye to the toxic influence of your ego.

This concludes Part III of *Your Sacred Self*. These chapters represent the major conflicts between ego (your false self) and your sacred self. They have played a major role in your life. Their resolution will affect your life.

As you begin to transcend your ego identities in every area of your life, you will heighten your awareness of the divine self within you. As you work to resolve the conflicts between your higher self and your false self, you will know the freedom and bliss that are your destiny.

Rabindranath Tagore is a divine spirit from India whose words always cut right to the heart of the matter. In a conversation with God, he says:

> I came out alone on my way to my tryst. But who is this me in the dark?
> I move aside to avoid his presence but I escape him not.
> He makes the dust rise from the earth with his swagger; he adds his loud voice to every word I utter.
> He is my own little self, my lord, he knows no shame; but I am ashamed to come to thy door in his company.

I believe that we can transform the world through this kind of change of consciousness. That change is taking place in you at this very minute. You will radiate it outward as you continue to walk the way of your sacred self. The last chapter of this book concludes with my vision of what our world would be like if we all knew that we were here on a sacred quest.

Part IV

TOWARD AN EGOLESS WORLD

Determine that the thing can and shall
be done, and then we shall find the way.
—ABRAHAM LINCOLN

15

CREATING A COLLECTIVE SPIRIT OF SACRED SELVES

※

But if on the contrary Man sees a new
door opening above him, a new stage
for his development; if each of us can
believe that he is working so that the
Universe may be raised, in him and
through him, to a higher level—then a
new spring of energy will well forth in
the heart of Earth's workers. The whole
great human organism, overcoming a
momentary hesitation, will draw its
breath and press on with strength
renewed.

—PIERRE TEILHARD DE CHARDIN

I will radiate my sacred self outward
for the collective good of all.

This final chapter will not be an odyssey into all the evils of our society. I do not intend to end this book cataloging all the problems that we have created as a result of allowing our egos to be the dominant force in our world.

This is not to say that I fail to recognize that we have plenty of problems that have grown out of our preoccupation with satisfying our egos. Nor am I blind to the fact that our individual egos have interacted in ways that have produced war, crime, addiction, poverty, social inequities and government tyrannies.

We have created a world ego that reflects, on the global level, the same lack of depth and richness that exists in our individual lives. Throughout this book I have presented reasons for taming the personal ego and suggestions for how to do that. The very same can be said for doing this on a global level. I hope it is as obvious to you as it is to me that the collective ego will benefit when we transcend our individual egos.

You as a single individual have a sacred quest. That quest involves coming to *know* your higher spiritual nature and inviting it to show you the way of the sacred self in your daily life. This means denying the demands of your ego if those demands contradict the guidance of your higher self.

Our world is a collection of individuals urged on by the loving presence within all of us to achieve the sacred quest personally and collectively. The world will become a peaceful, fulfilled, cooperative, loving, truthful, tolerant and pure environment as the individual parts that make up the collective consciousness restrain their egos. As is the microcosm, so is the macrocosm. The whole behaves precisely as does its individual parts.

Many people I speak to tell me that they feel powerless to affect the global community. They believe that, given the scope of the world's problems, their efforts are so infinitesimal as to be insignificant.

They simply are not seeing that it is precisely through a change in individual consciousness that the world will be transformed. All of the problems that we face as a group reflect those we have individually.

The world is encountering a spiritual deficit that reflects our need to consciously get on the path of our sacred quest. The solution to individual and global problems is to overcome the spiritual deficit. When you make the shift in consciousness allowing yourself to be an agent of heightened awareness, you are contributing to the transformation of our world.

You are not separate from the other souls on this planet. You share the identical energy that embodies the souls of Rwanda and Pakistan, for example. You are the lamp and God is the electricity. It flows through you as surely as it flows through all living things. When you make the decision to choose the guidance of your higher self over your false self, you have plugged in to the divine inner energy. When you run your life based on the principles of the higher self, you are contributing to the transformation of the entire world.

The physical changes that will take place in the world

will happen automatically, just as they will in your body when you shift to your sacred self. This is inevitable. The ego fades in the brilliance of the divine light. You find you are behaving in more peaceful and loving ways. So too will this take place on a global level.

You must strengthen your will to choose the sacred path when your ego calls you a fool for believing there could ever be a world without war. If your ego can convince you, you will become part of the collective ego's falseness. Individuals who choose ego propaganda are individuals who will build more bombs and manufacture more weapons.

Currently there are some six billion people on the planet. About three million are at war or in conflicts and skirmishes that cause them to kill and torture each other. But that means that there are five billion, nine hundred ninety-seven million who are not at war! That is a hopeful statistic which our egos do not want us to consider.

By contrast, the collective ego strives to keep the populace nervously on the edge with reminders to view the world in terms of us versus them. This ego viewpoint not only reinforces the insane escalation of ways to kill each other but is also responsible for most of our social problems.

I am not suggesting that we ignore problems of homelessness, hunger, disease and the like. I *am* suggesting that our collective ego has convinced us that these problems are out of control. The truth is that we have made remarkable strides in spite of the pessimistic ego, through the care and love of those who are motivated by their sacred self to serve.

Of all the people in the world, 99.9 percent have some place to go each night. All may not have luxurious homes, but on the whole we have figured out a way to house all but a small percentage of the people on our planet. Many of us are working each day to fill the gap and make it 100 percent. Yet the pictures that our ego presents are of rampant homelessness, hopelessness and a fear-based collective consciousness. This is true of hunger as well.

We are making gigantic strides helping those who live on the edge of starvation. This is happening through the efforts of people inspired by their higher selves, not by ego's pessimism. Obviously, one person dying of malnutrition is too many, and we can and will do something to ensure that we live in a world where such a thing no longer exists. But that will not be accomplished by the pessimistic view of the ego, which insists that we are separate from or better than those living in poverty. Were the entire world to suddenly shift away from the separateness of the ego and listen to the truth of our sacred selves, there would be no possibility of anyone starving.

To say that such a world is an impossibility is to listen to the ego, which is working collectively as well as individually to keep us convinced of our separateness.

UNDERSTANDING THE WORLD EGO

The world ego is an extension of our personal ego. It will lead us as a group into the same morass that our individual egos have, only on a much larger and more observable scale. The world ego does not exist in the physical sense because it is an idea. It is not who we are as a people but what we believe we are as a collection of people. Go back to the characteristics of the ego that I presented in Chapter 7, and simply extend those qualities to the entire world.

The world ego is our false self, and this is the primary characteristic that we need to recognize. We want to believe that we are our physical bodies and that the territories we occupy are so important that we are willing to kill each other in order to maintain those boundary lines.

We have become convinced that our true identities are located in tribal ancestries, traditions, histories, genealogies and the color and shape of our bodies. We have lost sight of our authentic identities because of the labels that our egos have assigned to us.

Our egos have coalesced into a worldwide false perception of ourselves based on an unwillingness to know our true spiritual nature. Although all of our spiritual leaders have reminded us of our divinity and implored and even commanded us to *love one another,* the world ego has won this battle and produced ancient enmities and uncountable horrors in the long history of humanity.

As a result of listening to the false self and ignoring our connection to the holy spirit, terrestrial humankind has lived in a theater of war that has created societies governed by primitive consciousness. As a people, we are capable of creating societies governed by the divine consciousness that we all share. We are all extensions of the same God, manifested in a physical form with specific identifiable attributes.

We can work individually on our personal egos and find the truth of our highest selves. Then we will extend that sacred self outward and humankind will no longer be ruled by lower instincts and primitive intelligence—instead we will be ruled by the holy spirit that is in all of us. If that sounds like an impossible task to you, then you are once again caught in ego's trap. Your ego does not want you to believe in such a possibility because it will mean the demise of your false self.

The spiritual solution to the major problems that face the world is to bring into positions of power those who are not motivated and driven by their egos but see the collective good as their primary objective. We need leaders who do not manifest primitive tendencies of consciousness such as hate, envy, greed, blood thirstiness and intolerance but are grounded in love, tolerance, truth and purity. These leaders are emerging and will continue to emerge as we take responsibility for transcending our own individual egos and knowing the true spirit of God. The world ego will be driven into obsolescence as we become truly aware of our sacred selves.

Your sacred self is waiting to share with you and the rest of the world the knowing that we are all of the same eternal essence, an extension of God. In that knowing is the absence of the belief that we are tribal members willing to kill for the physical distinctions that are such a minor part of our existence.

That notion of separateness is what the world ego feeds on. It is an extension of all the individual egos in conflict with each other, fighting their battles to prove just how separate they are from each other. In truth, none of us are separate from God. None of us are separate from each other. Living on a round planet symbolizes the impossibility of choosing up sides.

We all share the same oxygen, drink from the same water, walk and reside on the same soil. And whether we like to admit it or not, we are all intimately sharing each other's continually changing atoms and molecules. The only constant in the physical world is change. Everything that is manifested in a material form is changing at all moments. This continuous shift of atoms means that there is no separateness in the quantum scientific sense or in any other sense. Your sacred self is waiting for you to make the choice to let your ego know this truth.

Your ego wants separateness, and so too does the world ego. As long as the world ego believes so strongly in being separate, there will be conflicts to assuage that ego pressure. The presence of nation-states and artificial boundaries will continue under the domination of the world ego. Nationalism represents the selfishness or egoism of a nation and will prevail as long as the ego is honored as truth.

As we move toward unity we will create a world ordered by the higher self, which sees everyone as an inhabitant of the same kingdom. Then there will be no special interests being served; no forts being built on borders; no more nuclear weapons created; and no passports, customs or even exchange of currency. What will be is the knowing that we are one people. We will know that we are not the separate boundaries that we hang onto to coddle that world ego and promote the ideas that billions of people have needlessly died for.

As we substitute love for fear and allow our sacred selves to appear, the need for separateness will gradually disappear. It is happening right now, despite the efforts of many people driven by their egos to maintain the symbols of separateness, which are gradually melting away. The work of the spirit is subtle and patient.

There is nothing more powerful than an idea whose time has come, and the death of the world ego is long overdue. No more young people being sent off to die to preserve ancient borders. No more killing of our brothers and sisters whose customs are different in our physical world but who are connected to us in the world of our sacred self. The movement toward the sacred self will make the seductive voice of the world ego less appealing.

We can no longer afford this veil of separateness that the world ego begs us to embrace. The weapons that exist today, if used, will kill even those who use them. We all share the same environment, breathe the same air. To pollute it with radioactivity is the same as firing weapons at ourselves, which is precisely what we do whenever we fire any weapon at anyone. When Jesus said, "Father forgive them, for they know not what they do," he was begging us to realize that we are one. Your higher self knows this—so too does the highest part of the world collective.

The false part, the ego, insists that we are not only separate but special. In this creed of specialness, ego tries to convince us that we are more favored than others and that the special status is nurtured by following a spiritual master who is our ticket to heaven. This god of specialness hates certain people and loves others depending on their belief systems. The ego uses this kind of thinking to control us.

When you center yourself and find your quiet inner sacred space, you know the loving presence that does not discriminate. You know that specialness is not something bestowed on some and not on others. You know that it is absurd to believe that a Muslim baby will burn in hell because of not having Buddhist or Christian beliefs. You know that Australian aborigines are equal in importance to royalty. Your sacred self tells you this, and so does all of our spiritual literature.

Your personal ego's message of specialness is echoed and intensified in the collective world. The world ego wants it to be easy to ignore those who have less. Then less industrialized societies that are not as literate can be viewed as "them," which ego interprets as less favored. They can be considered as not chosen by God. That makes it possible to overlook them or use our superior weapons to eliminate them. This is how it becomes possible for people to watch real bombing and destruction on television and tell themselves that the victims are getting what they deserve.

But the sacred self knows that "Thou shalt not kill" does not have an asterisk. When we kill peasants in the process of overthrowing a dictator, our sacred self knows that we are violating our highest commandments by making some people disposable.

In truth, no one is special. We are all equal and we all share the same spirit. If you believe anyone is special, it means that someone else is not. The world ego will work very hard to keep this idea of specialness alive because it allows the kinds of actions that perpetuate the existence of the ego.

We will move away from that position as we pursue our individual sacred quest. When the loving presence is known, we will be unable to view others as less special or ourselves as more so. This will represent a victory of unselfishness over selfishness in all forms throughout the world.

Tom Brown, Jr., describes this attitude in a wonderful quote taken from his challenging book, *The Quest:*

Man living in the island of self is living but a small part of what life is all about. Man must transcend the barriers, the prisons of ego and thought, and reach the Creator. All Islands, all circles, must be bridged. Each world must be understood, then finally fused into an absolute and pure "oneness." Then there can be no inner or outer dimension, no separation of self, just a pure oneness where man is at once all things. It is in this fusion of worlds that man will know all things and live the deeper meanings of life. . . . Then and only then can man ever hope to touch God.

As you travel the path of your sacred quest you will help to dispel the absurdity of specialness that the ego so assiduously promotes. You will see an end to this kind of thinking in your life and on a world scale as well.

On the world scene at this point in history we see huge conflicts being played out merely to assuage the part of the ego that was offended. When you are easily offended, it is the self-absorbed ego that gets hurt and insists on proving how special and important you are. The same thing happens collectively. This collective ego is at work on the global scale and in our local cities as well.

The world ego is easily offended. When ego is offended, it needs revenge. It needs to retaliate to demonstrate its importance and specialness against whatever is perceived to be the cause of the offense. So, when an ego-dominated nation is offended by the words of a petty tyrant, it redresses the grievance by aggression and killing.

So too are our cities filled with young people who rely so strongly on their egos that they are willing to arbitrarily kill those who do not meet their self-imposed standards. They are convinced that they are special and entitled to everything that proves their specialness. If they do not get it, they are offended and create riots and mayhem, killing and looting.

This represents a gigantic lack of spiritual awareness.

We need to put God back into the consciousness of these young people, replacing the deficit with higher awareness. Then these problems will begin to dissipate. When people discover their sacred self, they are no longer offended by what they do not have. Instead, they are willing to give of themselves and are free of needing more or comparing themselves with others. This change in emphasis from ego self to sacred self will eventually eliminate the problems of welfare and war.

When the collective ego is offended, the world becomes embroiled in destruction. When the higher self is consulted, there is nothing to be offended about! One only sees what has to be done and begins to live out of the love that the inner silence proclaims. Consider this statement by the Danish theologian Søren Kierkegaard:

> The present state of the world and the whole of life is diseased. If I were a doctor and were asked my advice I should reply Create Silence.

Indeed, by going within and teaching all of those who are so eager to redress their grievances to do likewise, we would see a major shift in consciousness and much more compassion and tolerance. Ultimately, we'd see the peace that all of us on this planet want so desperately.

The higher part of ourselves that I have written about throughout this book reflects a vision that is infinite. This is assuredly not the vision of the ego. The ego is just as cowardly on a collective scale as it is on an individual basis. The world ego is frightened of a mass appeal to overcome our spiritual deficit.

When people face inward and embrace a more loving perspective, the power of the sacred self will create change not only in the community but in the entire world as well. The world ego will do all that it can to prevent this kind of inner approach. It will ridicule those who promote meditation, peaceful demonstrations and the love of God as a way out of the morass of social evils. The ego wants conflict.

Ego's vision is ensconced in the material world, and it endorses a kind of taking up arms against those who propose improving life by opposing ego. Ego is cowardly in that it fears the celestial light of God. This system is sustained exclusively by habit and fear of the higher self. Let anyone suggest that there is a spiritual deficit that needs love, peace, kindness and compassion to be incorporated in the curriculum of life, and they are scoffed at as unrealistic or childish. What the ego-based system encourages is more spending and more separateness.

A shift in consciousness will surely melt the old system in which an unholy alliance exists between a few powerful, well-entrenched bureaucrats and the powerlessness of the masses. In the old system, bureaucrats provide themselves with benefits that are denied to those who pay the bills for the bureaucrats, then hide under the guise of special privilege when confronted with their cowardice. This is where the cowardice of the world ego shows its shameless face over and over.

The collective ego insists that we cannot afford to make too many changes; that we cannot afford to provide everyone with the same privileges as those who are in power; that those who buck the system are troublemakers and need to be silenced.

The higher collective spiritual awareness knows better. It knows we have nothing to fear as long as we are operating from love rather than a desire to serve ego. Sacred self knows that genuine power is within the self, not in the institutions that we have created which distance the masses from those who have amassed power. The collective ego is cowardly, yet it will fight to maintain the influence that it has over so many who are victims of the entrenched system.

As you begin to consult your higher self, you will affect the collective consciousness and force those who are hanging onto the ego-based system to relax their hold. The ego always fears the light and therefore operates in secrecy and dark rooms. When the motivation for all of those in charge is based exclusively upon the principles of higher awareness, then the collective ego dries up and withers away.

The primary emphasis of the collective ego is power. This power is measured usually in monetary terms. The more money you have, the higher degree of specialness you are awarded, and the longer you get to stay in charge.

Thus the world ego loves to spend money, particularly your money. You will be told how important it is for us to spend billions of your earnings on an unworkable system that will protect us from outer space missiles, and sure enough the money will be appropriated. You are told by the ego system that we need more sophisticated weapons so that we can conduct warfare from inside air-conditioned fortresses where we can press a button and wipe out thousands of people and all of their possessions, without ever even having to witness the suffering we are creating.

The fact that a commandment has been violated and that we have participated in the mass murder of our brothers and sisters is not a notion that the ego entertains. Those are enemies, ego reminds us. They are bad, and we need more and more money to be able to kill them with more sophisticated means of destruction.

The collective ego convinces itself that money makes it special, and thus it will throw dollars at any problem and pride itself on the undertaking. Consume, consume, consume. More is better. The more you accumulate, the fancier your toys, the bigger your shopping malls, the more petrol that you use in your automobiles—the more successful you are. It is a push away from peace toward a style of consumerism and capitalism that is defended as the way of civilization.

Yet your higher self knows that there is no peace in more-is-better. It is just as true on the collective level as it is on the individual plane. The higher self urges you to simplify and to avoid contributing to anything that hurts others or increases the separation from your spiritual source.

As you listen more closely to your sacred self and

transcend your ego, so too will the world ego be shifted away from power, control and money back to the basic virtues of higher awareness—back to peace, beauty, love, purity, tolerance, patience and compassion. This does not mean that the benefits of technology cannot be enjoyed. It means that the ego will not be the motivating force in our lives. What we truly are as a people is a force that craves peace and simplicity.

We want that deeper awareness that comes with the sanity of the higher self. It is insane to continue believing that we are a collection of tribes, each with a separate identity and a special mission. It is insane to believe that anyone who does not fit into our particular tribal mentality is a potential enemy.

We know that there is not a separate God for each of us, or even for each of our tribes. We know that there is a universal divine intelligence that flows through all of us, and in that sacred space within us we are all one and the same. We know that we are spiritual beings trying to learn how to be human. We know that the best within us is love, kindness and compassion.

Yet our egos, both individually and collectively, have campaigned long and hard to promote a false idea. How sane is it for people to be killing each other over disputes that ancient egos created long before we arrived? How sane is it for us to believe that some of us deserve to eat the food that God provides and that others do not deserve it by virtue of their geographic location? How sane is it for us to pump up our youth with the philosophy of the free ride by leading them to believe that if they want something they deserve it? How sane is it to show our children pictures of violence as entertainment and allow them to adopt the ego belief that it is human nature to hurt others as a way to defend a right to be special and separate?

As our higher selves begin to triumph over ego in the daily decision making of our lives, we will truly be making progress on the path of the sacred quest for all of humanity. You must banish all doubt about your ability to facilitate such a quest and begin to know that you are both the microcosm and the macrocosm.

There is a universe within you—a unified field of all possibilities that you can reach as you become the compassionate witness. Be silent and shut down the inner dialogue. Most important, transcend the false self that we call the ego. That is when the healing will occur.

The world ego is destined to be restrained as more individuals look within and consult the highest part of themselves. The doubts are vanishing and the spiritual revolution is well under way. Moving toward an egoless world is not some far-fetched idea, any more than the disintegration of the Iron Curtain was a far-fetched idea. To those who heard such talk a few years before it happened, it did indeed seem absurd. But ideas, thoughts and inner knowing are powerful instruments for the disintegration of the false self.

One of the simplest and most powerful ways of doing this is taught by Eknath Easwaran; writing in his book *Meditation,* he advises us to spend thirty minutes every morning in meditation repeating the Prayer of St. Francis. In saying this prayer we both transcend the ego and invite the sacred self to guide us throughout the day. I invite you to join me in this daily prayer as we share the path of the sacred quest.

The Prayer of St. Francis

Lord, make me an instrument of thy peace.
Where there is hatred, let me sow love;
Where there is injury, pardon;
Where there is doubt, faith;
Where there is despair, hope;
Where there is darkness, light;
Where there is sadness, joy.

O divine Master, grant that I may not so much seek
To be consoled as to console,

To be understood as to understand,
To be loved as to love.
For it is in giving that we receive;
It is in pardoning that we are pardoned;
It is in dying to self that we are born to eternal life.

If you have the same knowing about your world, dramatic changes will take place as we collectively put to use the greatest force in the universe—the force of love.

It seems only fitting to quote my spiritual teacher Nisargadatta Maharaj as I close this book. He reminds us of the simplicity of creating a society that is based on spiritual principles:

> My stand is clear; produce to distribute, feed before you eat, give before you take, think of others before you think of yourself. Only a selfless society based on sharing can be stable and happy. This is the only practical solution. If you do not want it, then— fight.

I want it. I encourage you to do the same. God bless you!

INDEX